Photo by Hugh K. Robertson, Vancouver

George Bojadziev obtained his PhD in Mathematics at the Technical University of Sofia, Bulgaria. He was Professor at the same university until 1970. Since 1971 he has been with Simon Fraser University, British Columbia, Canada. His research activities in nonlinear phenomena, perturbation methods, stability, population dynamics, neural networks, intelligent control of robot manipulators, and fuzzy logic have resulted in more than 160 research publications (some of which he coauthored) and 5 books. Currently he is Professor Emeritus.

Maria Bojadziev obtained her Professional Degree in Mechanical Engineering at the Technical University of Sofia. She was Assistant Professor at the University for Chemical Engineering, Sofia. Since 1975 she has been with British Columbia Institute of Technology, British Columbia, Canada, as Mathematics Instructor. Her major research interests are nonlinear vibrations, dynamics and control of robot manipulators, and fuzzy logic control. She has authored or coauthored 30 papers and one book and organized 3 workshops on fuzzy logic and intelligent control.

ADVANCES IN FUZZY SYSTEMS — APPLICATIONS AND THEORY

Honorary Editor: Lotfi A. Zadeh (*Univ. of California, Berkeley*)
Series Editors: Kaoru Hirota (*Tokyo Inst. of Tech.*),
George J. Klir (*Binghamton Univ.–SUNY*),
Elie Sanchez (*Neurinfo*),
Pei-Zhuang Wang (*West Texas A&M Univ.*),
Ronald R. Yager (*Iona College*)

Published

Advances in Fuzzy Systems — Applications and Theory – Vol. 23

Fuzzy Logic
for Business,
Finance, and
Management

2nd Edition

George Bojadziev
Simon Fraser University, Canada

Maria Bojadziev
British Columbia Institute of Technology, Canada

World Scientific

NEW JERSEY · LONDON · SINGAPORE · BEIJING · SHANGHAI · HONG KONG · TAIPEI · CHENNAI

Published by

World Scientific Publishing Co. Pte. Ltd.

5 Toh Tuck Link, Singapore 596224

USA office: 27 Warren Street, Suite 401-402, Hackensack, NJ 07601

UK office: 57 Shelton Street, Covent Garden, London WC2H 9HE

British Library Cataloguing-in-Publication Data
A catalogue record for this book is available from the British Library.

Advances in Fuzzy Systems: Applications and Theory — Vol. 23
FUZZY LOGIC FOR BUSINESS, FINANCE, AND MANAGEMENT
(2nd Edition)

ISBN-13 978-981-270-649-2
ISBN-10 981-270-649-6

Printed in Singapore by World Scientific Printers (S) Pte Ltd

To our dear children
Luba and Nick
and
to our beloved grandchildren
Lara-Maria and Nicole-Ann.

Contents

Foreword

Following on the heels of their successful text *Fuzzy Sets, Fuzzy Logic, Applications*, George and Maria Bojadziev have authored a book that reflects a significant shift in the applications of fuzzy logic—a shift which has become discernible during the past few years.

To see this shift in a proper perspective, a bit of history is in order. The initial development of the theory of fuzzy sets was motivated by the perception that traditional techniques of systems analysis are not effective in dealing with problems in which the dependencies between variables are too complex or too ill-defined to admit of characterization by differential or difference equations. Such problems are the norm in biology, economics, psychology, linguistics, and many other fields.

A common thread that runs through problems of this type is the unsharpness of class boundaries and the concomitant imprecision, uncertainty, and partiality of truth. The concept of a fuzzy set is a reflection of this reality—a reflection which serves as a point of departure for the development of theories which have the capability to model the pervasive imprecision and uncertainty of the real world.

Most of the initial applications of the theory of fuzzy sets—or fuzzy logic, as it is commonly referred to today—dealt with languages, automata theory, and learning systems. In the early seventies, however, introduction of the concepts of a linguistic variable and fuzzy if-then rules opened the door to many other applications and especially applications to control. Today, control is the dominant application area of fuzzy logic, with close to 1,500 papers on fuzzy logic control published annually. More recently, however, the arrival of the information revolution has made the world of business, finance, and management a magnet for methodologies which can exploit the ability of modern information systems to process huge volumes of data at high speed and with high reliability. Among such methodologies are neurocomputing, genetic computing, and fuzzy logic. These methodologies fall under the rubric of soft computing and, for the most part, are complementary and synergistic rather than competitive.

Within soft computing, the main contribution of fuzzy logic is a machinery for computing with words—a machinery in which a major role is played by the calculus of fuzzy rules, linguistic variables, and fuzzy information granulation. In this context, *Fuzzy Logic for Business, Finance, and Management* provides a reader-friendly and up-to-date exposition of the basic concepts and techniques which underlie fuzzy logic and its applications to both control and business, finance, and management. With high skill and sharp insight, the authors illustrate the use of fuzzy logic techniques by numerous examples and case studies. Clearly, the writing of *Fuzzy Logic for Business, Finance, and Management* required a great deal of time, effort, and expertise. George and Maria Bojadziev deserve our thanks and congratulations for producing a text that is so informative, so well-written, and so attuned to the needs of our information-based society.

Lotfi A. Zadeh
January 20, 1997

Preface to the Second Edition

In the present edition we made corrections in Case Studies 17 (Chapter 5) and 20 (Chapter 6). Also several minor misprints were corrected.

We think that the aim of the book outlined in the preface to the first edition does not require an expansion for the time being.

We must offer our thanks to Bill McGreer for the use of his excellent software skills to make corrections to the old manuscript.

We thank World Scientific for giving us the opportunity to have a second edition of the book. Special thanks also to Senior Editor Steven Patt for his courtesy at all stages.

Vancouver, Canada
November 2006

George Bojadziev
Maria Bojadziev

Preface to the
First Edition

The aim of our first book, *Fuzzy Sets, Fuzzy Logic, Applications* (World Scientific, 1995), was both to bring fuzzy sets and fuzzy logic into the university and college curriculum, and to introduce engineers and scientists to the theory and applications of this field.

This book, our second on fuzzy logic, is an interdisciplinary text written for knowledge workers in business, finance, management, economics, and sociology. The objective is to provide guides and techniques for forecasting, decision making, and control (meaning suggestion for action) based on "if ... then" rules in environments characterized by uncertainty, vagueness, and imprecision.

Traditional or classical modeling techniques often do not capture the nature of complex systems, especially when humans are involved. In contrast, fuzzy sets and fuzzy logic are effective tools for modeling, in the absence of complete and precise information, complex business, finance, and management systems. The subjective judgement of experts who have used fuzzy logic techniques produces better results than the objective manipulation of inexact data.

Fuzzy logic stems from the inability of classical logic to capture the vague language, common-sense reasoning, and problem-solving heuristic used by people every day. Fuzzy logic deals with objects that are a matter of degree, with all the possible grades of truth between "yes" and "no." It can be viewed as a broad conceptual framework encompassing the classical logic which divides the world on the basis of "yes" and "no."

This book shows the reader in a systematic way how to use fuzzy logic techniques to solve a wide range of problems and arrive at conclusions in business, finance, and management. Using these techniques does not require a level of mathematics higher than that of high school. Real-life situations are emphasized. Although the core of the book is based on previously known material, the authors also, as in a monograph, present original results and innovative treatment of classical problems using fuzzy logic. The book can also be used as a text for university and college students in business, finance, management, economics, and sociology.

Following this preface are seven chapters, each divided into sections. Each chapter ends with bibliographic references and additional information that may interest the reader. A superscript number after a word or sentence refers the reader to the relevant note at the end of the chapter. The authors have provided a wealth of examples to illustrate their points. The reader will find applications in 27 case studies listed on page xvii. The book ends with a list of references and a subject index.

Chapter 1 begins with a brief review of classical sets. It then provides a basic knowledge of fuzzy sets and fuzzy relations. Fuzzy numbers are introduced as a particular case of fuzzy sets.

Chapter 2 deals with fuzzy logic. It starts with classical and many-valued logic since both provide the basis for fuzzy logic. The important concepts of linguistic variables and linguistic modifiers are introduced. These concepts are used later to model complex systems in words and sentences.

Chapter 3 is devoted to forecasting. It is based on the use of the method of fuzzy averaging as a tool for aggregating the opinions of individual experts. Applications explained include the Delphi technique for forecasting technological advances and for time forecasting in project management.

Chapter 4 covers decision making: a process of problem solving pursuing goals under constraints. Two methods are discussed: (1) Decision making as the intersection of goals and constraints; (2) Decision making based on fuzzy averaging. Various case studies are presented, including pricing models for new products. Multi-expert decision making is applied to investment models.

Chapter 5 presents fuzzy logic control architecture adjusted for the needs of business, finance, and management. It shows how decisions, evaluations, and conclusions can be made by using and aggregating "if ... then" rules. As an illustration, a client financial risk tolerance model is designed.

In chapter 6 the fuzzy logic control methodology is applied to a variety of real-life problems: a client asset allocation model, pest management, inventory control models, problem analysis, and potential problem analysis.

Chapter 7 briefly reviews standard relational databases containing crisp data; these are the foundation for the fuzzy databases. The emphasis is on formulating queries of a fuzzy nature to databases in order to retrieve information that can be used to aid decision making. Applications are shown for small companies databases, and stocks and mutual fund databases.

Acknowledgments

First we wish to thank Prof. Lotfi Zadeh, the founder of fuzzy sets and fuzzy logic. His ideas inspired our interest in the subject, an interest which led us to write two books. We also thank him for his willingness to write the foreword.

We also express our gratitude to the authors whose books and articles are listed in the references. Their contributions are reflected in this book.

We thank Chris Tidd, financial advisor with Odlum & Brown, for permission to use material published in his mutual fund advisory letter.

We deeply appreciate the discussion with and advice from our daughter Luba Ebert, son Nick Bojadziev, and son-in-law Tyrone Ebert concerning the topics on decision making in management.

We thank Q. Joy Wang and H. Yang for the skillful and careful typing of the manuscript, including the figures and tables.

We are grateful to World Scientific Publishing Company for bringing out this book and permitting us to use material from our first book *Fuzzy Sets, Fuzzy Logic, Applications*, published by the same company.

Our final thanks go to the editor, Yew Kee Chiang, for his superbly professional work.

Vancouver, Canada   *George Bojadziev*
November 1996   *Maria Bojadziev*

List of Case Studies

Chapter 1

Fuzzy Sets

This chapter begins with a brief review of classical sets in order to facilitate the introduction of fuzzy sets. Next the concept of membership function is explained. It defines the degree to which an element under consideration belongs to a fuzzy set. Fuzzy numbers are described as a particular case of fuzzy sets. Fuzzy sets and fuzzy numbers will be used in fuzzy logic to model words such as profit, investment, cost, income, age, etc. Fuzzy relations together with some operations on fuzzy relations are introduced as a generalization of fuzzy sets and ordinary relations. They have application in database models. Fuzzy sets and fuzzy relations play an important role in fuzzy logic.

1.1   Classical Sets: Relations and Functions

Classical sets

This section reviews briefly the terminology, notations, and basic properties of *classical sets*, usually called *sets*.

The concept of a *set* or *collection* of objects is common in our everyday experience. For instance, all persons listed in a certain telephone directory, all employees in a company, etc. There is a defining property that allows us to consider the objects as a whole. The objects in a set are called *elements* or *members* of the set. We will denote elements by small letters $a, b, c, \ldots, x, y, z$ and the sets by capital letters

1

$A, B, C, \ldots, X, Y, Z$. Sets are also called ordinary or crisp in order to be distinguished from fuzzy sets.

The fundamental notion in set theory is that of *belonging* or *membership*. If an object x belongs to the set A we write $x \in A$; if x is not a member of A, we write $x \notin A$. In other words for each object x there are only two possibilities: either x belongs to A or it does not.[1]

A set containing finite number of members is called *finite* set; otherwise it is called *infinite* set. We present two methods of describing sets.

Listing method

The set is described by *listing* its elements placed in braces; for example $A = \{1, 3, 6, 7, 8\}$, $B = \{\text{business, finance, management}\}$. The order in which elements are listed is of no importance. An element should be listed only once.

Membership rule

The set is described by one or more properties to be satisfied only by objects in the set:

$$A = \{x \mid x \text{ satisfies some property or properties}\}.$$

This reads: "A is the set of all x such that x satisfies some property or properties." For example $R = \{x \mid x \text{ is real number}\}$ reads: "R is the set of all x such that x is a real number"; $R_+ = \{x | x \geq 0, x \in R\}$ reads "R_+ is the set of all x which are nonnegative real numbers."

Universal set

The set of all objects under consideration in a particular situation is called *universal set or universe*; it will be denoted by U.

Empty set

A set without elements is called empty; it is denoted by ϕ.

Interval

The set of all real numbers x such that $a_1 \leq x \leq a_2$, where a_1 and a_2 are real numbers, form a closed interval $[a_1, a_2] = \{x \mid a_1 \leq x \leq a_2, x \in R\}$ with boundaries a_1 and a_2. It is also called *interval number*.

Equal sets

Sets A and B are *equal* , denoted by $A = B$, if they have the same elements.

Subset

The set A is a *subset* of the set B (A is *included* in B), denoted by $A \subseteq B$, if every element of A is also an element of B. Every set is subset of itself, $A \subseteq A$. The empty set ϕ is a subset of any set. It is assumed that each set we are dealing with is a subset of a universal set U.

Proper subset

A is a *proper subset* of B, denoted $A \subset B$, if $A \subseteq B$ and there is at least one element in B which does not belong to A. For instance $\{a, b\} \subset \{a, b, c\}$. If $A \subseteq B$ and $B \subseteq C$, then $A \subseteq C$.

Intersection

The intersection of the sets A and B, denoted by $A \cap B$, is defined by

$$A \cap B = \{x \mid x \in A \text{ and } x \in B\}; \tag{1.1}$$

$A \cap B$ is a set whose elements are common to A and B.

Union

The union of A and B , denoted by $A \cup B$, is defined by

$$A \cup B = \{x \mid x \in A \text{ or } x \in B\}; \tag{1.2}$$

$A \cup B$ is a set whose elements are in A or B, including any element that belongs to both A and B.

Disjoint sets

If the sets A and B have no elements in common, they are called *disjoint*.

Complement

The *complement* of $A \subset U$, denoted by $\overline{A}$, is the set

$$\overline{A} = \{x \in U \mid x \notin A\}. \tag{1.3}$$

The complement of a set consists of all elements in the universal set that are not in the given set.

Example 1.1

Given the sets

$$A = \{1, 2, 3, 4\}, \quad B = \{1, 3, 5, 6\}, \quad U = \{1, 2, 3, 4, 5, 6, 7\},$$

then using (1.1)–(1.3) we find

$$A \cap B = \{1, 3\}, \quad A \cup B = \{1, 2, 3, 4, 5, 6\}, \quad \overline{A} = \{5, 6, 7\}, \quad \overline{B} = \{2, 4, 7\}.$$

$\square$

Convex sets

Consider the universe U to be the set of real numbers R.

A subset S of R is said to be *convex* if and only if, for all $x_1, x_2 \in S$ and for every real number λ satisfying $0 \leq \lambda \leq 1$, we have

$$\lambda x_1 + (1 - \lambda)x_2 \in S.$$

For example, any interval $S = [a_1, a_2]$ is a convex set since the above condition is satisfied; $[0, 1]$ and $[3, 4]$ are convex, but $[0, 1] \cup [3, 4]$ is not.

Venn diagrams

Sets are geometrically represented by circles inside a rectangle (the universal set U). In Fig. 1.1 are shown the sets $A \cap B$ and $A \cup B$.

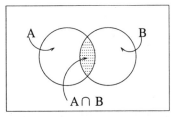 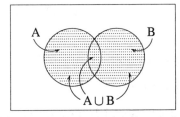

Fig. 1.1. Venn diagrams for $A \cap B$(intersection), $A \cup B$(union).

Ordered pairs

It was noted that the order of the elements of a set is not important. However there are cases when the order is important. To indicate that a set or pair of two elements a and b is *ordered*, we write (a, b), i.e. use parentheses instead of braces; a is called *first element* of the pair and b is called *second element*.

Cartesian product

Cartesian product (or *cross product*) of the sets A and B denoted $A \times B$ is the set of ordered pairs

$$A \times B = \{(a, b) \mid a \in A, b \in B\}. \tag{1.4}$$

Example 1.2

(a) Given
$$A = \{1, 2, 3\}, \qquad B = \{1, 2\},$$
then according to (1.4) we find

$$A \times B = \{(1, 1), (1, 2), (2, 1), (2, 2), (3, 1), (3, 2)\};$$

geometrically it is presented on Fig. 1.2 (a).
(b) If $X, Y = R$, the set of all real numbers, then

$$X \times Y = \{(x, y) \mid x \in X, y \in Y\} = R \times R$$

is the set of all ordered pairs which form the cartesian plane xy (see Fig. 1.2(b)).

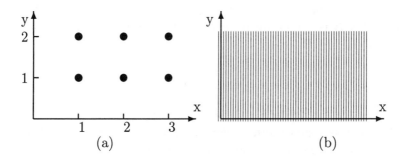

(a)   (b)

Fig. 1.2. (a) Cartesian product $\{1, 2, 3\} \times \{1, 2\}$; (b) Cartesian plane.

□

Relations

The concept of *relation* is very general. It is based on the concepts of ordered pair (a, b), $a \in A$, $b \in B$, and cartesian product of the sets A and B.

A *relation* from A to B (or between A and B) is any subset $\Re$ of the cartesian product $A \times B$. We say that $a \in A$ and $b \in B$ are related by $\Re$; the elements a and b form the *domain* and *range* of the relation, correspondingly. Since a relation is a set, it may be described by either the listing method or the membership rule. The relation $\Re$ is called *binary relation* since two sets, A and B, are related.

Example 1.3

Let $A = \{x_1, x_2, x_3\}$ and $B = \{1, 2, 3, 4\}$.
We list some binary relations generated by A and B:

$$\Re_1 = \{(x_1, 1), (x_2, 1), (x_3, 4)\},$$
$$\Re_2 = \{(x_1, 2), (x_1, 3)\}, \quad \Re_3 = \{(x_2, 2), (x_3, 1)\},$$
$$\Re_4 = \{(x_1, 1), (x_1, 2), (x_1, 3), (x_1, 4), (x_2, 1), (x_4, 1)\}$$

are relations from A to B;

$$\Re_5 = \{(1, x_2), (2, x_3), (3, x_1)\}, \quad \Re_6 = \{(1, x_1), (2, x_1)\},$$
$$\Re_7 = \{(1, x_1), (1, x_2), (1, x_4)\}, \quad \Re_8 = \{(2, x_1), (3, x_3)\}$$

are relations from B to A; the empty set ϕ is a relation; the cross product $A \times B$ is a relation from A to B and the cross product $B \times A$ is a relation from B to A.

□

Functions

A *function* f is a relation $\Re$ such that for every element x in the domain of f there corresponds a unique element y in the range of f. For instance the relations in Example 1.2 are not functions.

We often say that f *maps* x onto y; y is the *image* of x under f. Then we can write $f : x \to y$. However, it is customary to use the notation $y = f(x)$.

Generalization

The notions of ordered pair, Cartesian product, relation, and function can be generalized for higher dimensions than two. For instance when $n = 3$ we have:

Ordered triple (a, b, c);
Cartesian product

$$A \times B \times C = \{(a, b, c) | a \in A, b \in B, c \in C\};$$

Relation from $A \times B$ to C is any subset $\Re$ of $A \times B \times C$.

Function $z = f(x, y)$ is a relation such that for every pair (x, y) in the domain of f there corresponds a unique element z in its range.

Characteristic Function

The membership rule that characterizes the elements (members) of a set $A \subset U$ can be established by the concept of *characteristic function* (or *membership function*) $\mu_A(x)$ taking only two values, 1 and 0, indicating whether or not $x \in U$ is a member of A:

$$\mu_A(x) = \begin{cases} 1 & \text{for} & x \in A, \\ 0 & \text{for} & x \notin A. \end{cases} \tag{1.5}$$

Hence $\mu_A(x) \in \{0, 1\}$. Inversely, if a function $\mu_A(x)$ is defined by (1.5), then it is the characteristic function for a set $A \subset U$ in the sense that A consists of the values of $x \in U$ for which $\mu_A(x)$ is equal to 1. In other words every set is uniquely determined by its characteristic function.

The universal set U has for membership function $\mu_U(x)$ which is identically equal to 1, i.e. $\mu_U(x) = 1$. The empty set ϕ has for membership function $\mu_\phi(x) = 0$.

Example 1.4

Consider the universe $U = \{x_1, x_2, x_3, x_4, x_5, x_6\}$ and its subset A,

$$A = \{x_2, x_3, x_5\}.$$

Only three of the six elements in U belong A. Using the notation (1.5) gives

$$\mu_A(x_1) = 0, \quad \mu_A(x_2) = 1, \quad \mu_A(x_3) = 1,$$
$$\mu_A(x_4) = 0, \quad \mu_A(x_5) = 1, \quad \mu_A(x_6) = 0.$$

Hence the characteristic function of the set A is

$$\mu_A(x) = \begin{cases} 1 & \text{for} & x = x_2, x_3, x_5, \\ 0 & \text{for} & x = x_1, x_4, x_6; \end{cases}$$

The set A can be represented as

$$A = \{(x_1, 0), (x_2, 1), (x_3, 1), (x_4, 0), (x_5, 1), (x_6, 0)\}.$$

$\square$

Example 1.5

Let us try to use crisp sets to describe *tall men*. Consider for instance a man as tall if his height is 180 cm or greater; otherwise the man is not tall. The characteristic function of the set $A = \{\text{tall men}\}$ then is

$$\mu_A(x) = \begin{cases} 1 & \text{for} & 180 \leq x, \\ 0 & \text{for} & 160 \leq x < 180. \end{cases}$$

It is shown in Fig. 1.3, where the universe is $U = \{x \mid 160 \leq x \leq 200\}$.

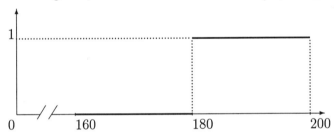

Fig. 1.3. Membership function of the set *tall men*.

Clearly this description of the set of *tall men* is not satisfactory since it does not allow gradation. The word *tall* is vague. For instance, a person whose height is 179 cm is not tall as well as a person whose height is 160 cm. Yet a person whose height is 180 is tall and so is a person with height 200 cm. Also the above definition introduces a drastic difference between heights of 179 cm and 180 cm, thus fails to describe realistically borderline cases.[2]

$\square$

The concept of characteristic function introduced here will facilitate the understanding of the concept *fuzzy set*, the subject of the next section.

1.2 Definition of Fuzzy Sets

We have seen that belonging or membership of an object to a set is a precise concept; the object is either a member to a set or it is not, hence the membership function can take only two values, 1 or 0. The set *tall men* in Example 1.5 illustrates the need to increase the describing capabilities of classical sets while dealing with words.

To describe gradual transitions Zadeh (1965), the founder of fuzzy sets, introduced grades between 0 and 1 and the concept of graded membership.

Let us refer to Example 1.4. Each of the six elements of the universal set $U = \{x_1, x_2, x_3, x_4, x_5, x_6\}$ either belongs to or does not belong to the set $A = \{x_2, x_3, x_5\}$. According to this, the characteristic function $\mu_A(x)$ takes only the values 1 or 0. Assume now that a characteristic function may take values in the interval $[0, 1]$. In this way the concept of membership is not any more *crisp* (either 1 or 0), but becomes *fuzzy* in the sense of representing partial belonging or *degree of membership*.

Consider a classical set A of the universe U. A *fuzzy set* $\mathcal{A}$ is defined by a set or ordered pairs, a binary relation,

$$\mathcal{A} = \{(x, \mu_\mathcal{A}(x)) \mid x \in A, \mu_\mathcal{A}(x) \in [0, 1]\}, \qquad (1.6)$$

where $\mu_\mathcal{A}(x)$ is a function called *membership function*; $\mu_\mathcal{A}(x)$ specifies the *grade* or *degree* to which any element x in A belongs to the fuzzy set $\mathcal{A}$. Definition (1.6) associates with each element x in A a real number $\mu_\mathcal{A}(x)$ in the interval $[0, 1]$ which is assigned to x. Larger values of $\mu_\mathcal{A}(x)$ indicate higher degrees of membership.[3]

Let us express the meaning of (1.6) in a slightly modified way. The first elements x in the pair $(x, \mu_\mathcal{A}(x))$ are given numbers or objects of the classical set A; they satisfy some property (P) under consideration partly (to various degrees). The second elements $\mu_\mathcal{A}(x)$ belong to the interval (classical set) $[0, 1]$; they indicate to what extent (degree) the elements x satisfy the property P.

It is assumed here that the membership function $\mu_\mathcal{A}(x)$ is either piecewise continuous or discrete.

The fuzzy set $\mathcal{A}$ according to definition (1.6) is formally *equal* to its membership function $\mu_\mathcal{A}(x)$. We will *identify* any fuzzy set with its membership function and use these two concepts as *interchangeable*. Also we may look at a fuzzy set over a domain A as a function mapping A into $[0, 1]$.

Fuzzy sets are denoted by italic letters $\mathcal{A}, \mathcal{B}, \mathcal{C}, \ldots$ and the corresponding membership functions by $\mu_{\mathcal{A}}(x), \mu_{\mathcal{B}}(x), \mu_{\mathcal{C}}(x), \ldots$.

Elements with zero degree of membership in a fuzzy set are usually not listed.

Classical sets can be considered as a special case of fuzzy sets with all membership grades equal to 1.

A fuzzy set is called *normalized* when at least one $x \in A$ attains the maximum membership grade 1; otherwise the set is called *nonnormalized*. Assume the set $\mathcal{A}$ is nonnormalized; then $\max \mu_{\mathcal{A}}(x) < 1$. To normalize the set $\mathcal{A}$ means to normalize its membership function $\mu_{\mathcal{A}}(x)$, i.e. to divide it by $\max \mu_{\mathcal{A}}(x)$, which gives $\frac{\mu_{\mathcal{A}}(x)}{\max \mu_{\mathcal{A}}(x)}$.

$\mathcal{A}$ is called empty set labeled ϕ if $\mu_{\mathcal{A}}(x) = 0$ for each $x \in A$.

The fuzzy set $\mathcal{A} = \{(x_1, \mu_{\mathcal{A}}(x_1))\}$, where x_1 is the only value in $A \subset U$ and $\mu_{\mathcal{A}}(x_1) \in [0, 1]$, is called *fuzzy singleton*.

While the set A is a subset of the universal set U which is crisp, the fuzzy set $\mathcal{A}$ is not.

Instead of (1.6), some authors use the notation

$$\mathcal{A} = \{\mu_{\mathcal{A}}(x)/x, x \in A, \mu_{\mathcal{A}}(x) \in [0, 1]\},$$

where the symbol / is not a division sign but indicates that the top number $\mu_{\mathcal{A}}(x)$ is the membership value of the element x in the bottom.

Example 1.6

Consider the fuzzy set

$$\mathcal{A} = \{(x_1, 0.1), (x_2, 0.5), (x_3, 0.3), (x_4, 0.8), (x_5, 1), (x_6, 0.2)\}$$

which also can be represented as

$$\mathcal{A} = 0.1/x_1 + 0.5/x_2 + 0.3/x_3 + 0.8/x_4 + 1/x_5 + 0.2/x_6;$$

it is a discrete fuzzy set consisting of six ordered pairs. The elements $x_i, i = 1, \ldots, 6$, are not necessary numbers; they belong to the classical set $A = \{x_1, x_2, x_3, x_4, x_5, x_6\}$ which is a subset of a certain universal set U. The membership function $\mu_{\mathcal{A}}(x)$ of $\mathcal{A}$ takes the following values on $[0, 1]$:

$$\mu_{\mathcal{A}}(x_1) = 0.1, \quad \mu_{\mathcal{A}}(x_2) = 0.5, \quad \mu_{\mathcal{A}}(x_3) = 0.3,$$
$$\mu_{\mathcal{A}}(x_4) = 0.8, \quad \mu_{\mathcal{A}}(x_5) = 1, \quad \mu_{\mathcal{A}}(x_6) = 0.2.$$

The following interpretation could be given to $\mu_{\mathcal{A}}(x_i), i = 1, \cdots, 6$. The element x_5 is a *full* member of the fuzzy set $\mathcal{A}$, while the element x_1 is a member of $\mathcal{A}$ a *little* ($\mu_{\mathcal{A}}(x_1) = 0.1$ is near 0); x_6 and x_3 are a *little more* members of $\mathcal{A}$; the element x_4 is *almost* a full member of $\mathcal{A}$, while x_2 is *more or less* a member of $\mathcal{A}$.

The fuzzy set $\mathcal{A}$ can be given also by the table

$$\mathcal{A} \triangleq \begin{array}{c|cccccc} & x_1 & x_2 & x_3 & x_4 & x_5 & x_6 \\ \hline & 0.1 & 0.5 & 0.3 & 0.8 & 1 & 0.2 \end{array}$$

where the symbol $\triangleq$ means "is defined by."

Now we specify in two different ways the elements x_i in A:

(a) Assume that $x_i, i = 1, \cdots, 6$, are integers, namely, $x_1 = 1, x_2 = 2, x_3 = 3, x_4 = 4, x_5 = 5, x_6 = 6$; they belong to the set $A = \{1, 2, 3, 4, 5, 6\}$, a subset of the universe $U = N$, the set of all integers. The fuzzy set $\mathcal{A}$ becomes

$$\mathcal{A} = \{(1, 0.1), (2, 0.5), (3, 0.3), (4, 0.8), (5, 1), (6, 0.2)\};$$

its membership function $\mu_{\mathcal{A}}(x)$ shown in Fig. 1.4 by dots is a discrete one.

(b) Assume now that $x_i, i = 1, \ldots, 6$, are friends of George whose names are as follows: x_1 is Ron, x_2 is Ted, x_3 is John, x_4 is Joe, x_5 is Tom, and x_6 is Sam. They form a set of friends of George,

$$A = \{\text{Ron, Ted, John, Joe, Tom, Sam}\},$$

a subset of the universe U (all friends of George). The fuzzy set $\mathcal{A}$ here expresses *closeness of friends* of George on $A \subseteq U$:

$$\mathcal{A} = \{(\text{Ron}, 0.1), (\text{Ted}, 0.5), (\text{John}, 0.3), (\text{Joe}, 0.8), (\text{Tom}, 1), (\text{Sam}, 0.2)\}.$$

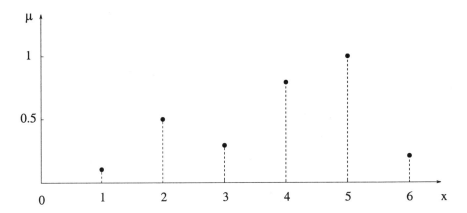

Fig. 1.4. Fuzzy set $\mathcal{A} = \{(1, 0.1), (2, 0.5), (3, 0.3), (4, 0.8), (5, 1), (6, 0.2)\}$.

□

Example 1.7

Let us describe numbers *close* to 10.

(a) First consider the fuzzy set

$$\mathcal{A}_1 = \{(x, \mu_{\mathcal{A}_1}(x)) \mid x \in [5, 15], \mu_{\mathcal{A}_1}(x) = \frac{1}{1 + (x - 10)^2}\},$$

where $\mu_{\mathcal{A}_1}(x)$ shown in Fig. 1.5 is a continuous function.

The fuzzy set $\mathcal{A}_1$ represents real numbers *close* to 10.

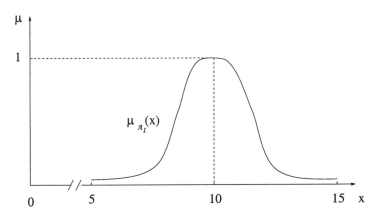

Fig. 1.5. Real numbers *close* to 10.

(b) Integers *close* to 10 can be expressed by the finite fuzzy set consisting of seven ordered pairs

$$\mathcal{A}_2 = \{(7, 0.1), (8, 0.3), (9, 0.8), (10, 1), (11, 0.8), (12, 0.3), (13, 0.1)\}.$$

The membership function of $\mathcal{A}_2$ is shown on Fig 1.6 by dots; it is a discrete function.

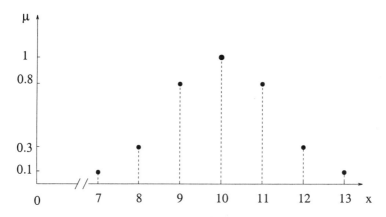

Fig. 1.6. Integers *close* to 10.

□

Example 1.8

We have seen in Example 1.5 that the description of *tall men* by classical sets is not adequate. Now we employ for the same purpose the fuzzy set $\mathcal{T} = \{(x, \mu_T(x))\}$, where x measured in cm belongs to the interval [160, 200] and $\mu_T(x)$ is defined by (see Fig 1.7)

$$\mu_T(x) = \begin{cases} \frac{1}{2(30)^2}(x - 140)^2 & \text{for} \quad 160 \le x \le 170, \\ -\frac{1}{2(30)^2}(x - 200)^2 + 1 & \text{for} \quad 170 \le x \le 200. \end{cases}$$

The membership function $\mu_T(x)$ is a continuous piecewise-quadratic function. The numbers on the horizontal axis x give height in cm and the vertical axis μ shows the degree to which a man can be labeled *tall*. According to the graph in Fig. 1.7, if a person's height is 160 cm, the person is a little tall (degree 0.22), 180 cm stands for almost tall (degree

0.78), 200 cm for tall (degree 1). The segment $[0.22, 1]$ of the vertical axis μ expresses the *quantification* of the degree of vagueness of the word *tall*.[4]

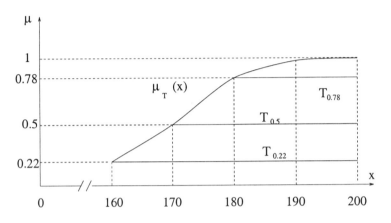

Fig. 1.7. Description of *tall men* by fuzzy set.

□

Further we define α-*level interval* or α-*cut*, denoted by A_α, as the crisp set of elements x which belong to $\mathcal{A}$ at least to the degree α:

$$A_\alpha = \{x \mid x \in R, \mu_\mathcal{A}(x) \geq \alpha\}, \quad \alpha \in [0, 1]. \tag{1.7}$$

It gives a *threshold* which provides a *level of confidence* α in a decision or concept modeled by a fuzzy set. We may use the threshold to discard from consideration those element x in A with grades of membership $\mu_\mathcal{A}(x) < \alpha$.

Example 1.9

Consider Example 1.8, the set $\mathcal{T}$, *tall men*. It has an infinite number of α-*level* intervals (α-*cuts*) denoted by $\mathcal{T}_\alpha$ where α varies between 0.22 and 1. Some α-cuts shown in Fig. 1.7 are given below:

$$\mathcal{T}_{0.22} = \{x \mid x \in R, 160 \leq x \leq 200\}, \mu_\mathcal{T}(x) \geq 0.22,$$
$$\mathcal{T}_{0.5} = \{x \mid x \in R, 170 \leq x \leq 200\}, \mu_\mathcal{T}(x) \geq 0.5,$$
$$\mathcal{T}_{0.78} = \{x \mid x \in R, 180 \leq x \leq 200\}, \mu_\mathcal{T}(x) \geq 0.78$$

For instance we may choose as a threshold the α-*cut* $\mathcal{T}_{0.5}$ thus discarding from consideration men whose height is below 170 cm.

$\square$

A fuzzy set $\mathcal{A}$, where the universe $U = R$, is *convex* if and only if the α-level intervals $\mathcal{A}_\alpha$ (see (1.7)) are convex for all α in the interval (0, 1]. In such a case all α-*level* intervals $\mathcal{A}_\alpha$ consist of one segment (see Fig. 1.8(a)). Otherwise the set is nonconvex (see Fig. 1.8(b)).

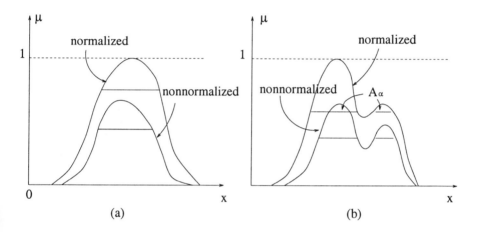

Fig. 1.8. (a) Convex fuzzy sets; (b) Nonconvex fuzzy sets.

1.3 Basic Operations on Fuzzy Sets

Consider the fuzzy sets $\mathcal{A}$ and $\mathcal{B}$ in the universe U,

$$\mathcal{A} = \{(x, \mu_A(x))\}, \quad \mu_A(x) \in [0, 1],$$
$$\mathcal{B} = \{(x, \mu_B(x))\}, \quad \mu_B(x) \in [0, 1].$$

The operations with $\mathcal{A}$ and $\mathcal{B}$ are introduced via operations on their membership functions $\mu_A(x)$ and $\mu_B(x)$.

Equality

The fuzzy sets $\mathcal{A}$ and $\mathcal{B}$ are *equal* denoted by $\mathcal{A} = \mathcal{B}$ if and only if for every $x \in U$,

$$\mu_A(x) = \mu_B(x).$$

Inclusion

The fuzzy set $\mathcal{A}$ is *included* in the fuzzy set $\mathcal{B}$ denoted by $\mathcal{A} \subseteq \mathcal{B}$ if for every $x \in U$,

$$\mu_A(x) \leq \mu_B(x).$$

Then $\mathcal{A}$ is called a *subset* of $\mathcal{B}$.

Proper subset

The fuzzy set $\mathcal{A}$ is called a proper subset of the fuzzy set $\mathcal{B}$ denoted $\mathcal{A} \subset \mathcal{B}$ when $\mathcal{A}$ is a subset of $\mathcal{B}$ and $\mathcal{A} \neq \mathcal{B}$, that is

$$\left. \begin{array}{ll} \mu_A(x) \leq \mu_B(x) & \text{for every } x \in U, \\ \mu_A(x) < \mu_B(x) & \text{for at least one } x \in U. \end{array} \right\}$$

For instance the nonnormalized sets in Fig. 1.8 (a) and (b) are proper.

Complementation

The fuzzy sets $\mathcal{A}$ and $\overline{\mathcal{A}}$ are complementary if

$$\mu_{\overline{A}}(x) = 1 - \mu_A(x) \quad \text{or} \quad \mu_A(x) + \mu_{\overline{A}}(x) = 1. \tag{1.8}$$

The membership function $\mu_{\overline{A}}(x)$ is symmetrical to $\mu_A(x)$ with respect to the line $\mu = 0.5$.

Intersection

The operation *intersection* of $\mathcal{A}$ and $\mathcal{B}$ denoted as $\mathcal{A} \cap \mathcal{B}$ is defined by

$$\mu_{A \cap B}(x) = \min(\mu_A(x), \mu_B(x)), \quad x \in U. \tag{1.9}$$

If $a_1 < a_2$, $\min(a_1, a_2) = a_1$. For instance $\min(0.5, 0.7) = 0.5$.

Union

The operation *union* of $\mathcal{A}$ and $\mathcal{B}$ denoted as $\mathcal{A} \cup \mathcal{B}$ is defined by

$$\mu_{A \cup B}(x) = \max(\mu_A(x), \mu_B(x)), \quad x \in U. \tag{1.10}$$

If $a_1 < a_2$, $\max(a_1, a_2) = a_2$. For instance $\max(0.5, 0.7) = 0.7$.

Example 1.10

Consider the universe $U = \{x_1, x_2, x_3, x_4\}$ and the fuzzy sets $\mathcal{A}$ and $\mathcal{B}$ defined by the table

x	x_1	x_2	x_3	x_4
$\mu_A(x)$	0.2	0.7	1	0
$\mu_B(x)$	0.5	0.3	1	0.1

Using (1.9) and (1.10) gives

x	x_1	x_2	x_3	x_4
$\mu_{A \cap B}(x)$	0.2	0.3	1	0
$\mu_{A \cup B}(x)$	0.5	0.7	1	0.1

□

Schematic representation of operations on fuzzy sets

Fuzzy sets are schematically represented by their membership functions (assumed continuous) inside of rectangles. In Fig. 1.9 are shown $\mu_A(x)$ and $\mu_B(x)$, in Fig. 1.10 the complements $\mu_{\overline{A}}(x)$ and $\mu_{\overline{B}}(x)$, and in Fig. 1.11 the union $\mu_{A \cap B}(x)$ and the intersection $\mu_{A \cap B}(x)$.

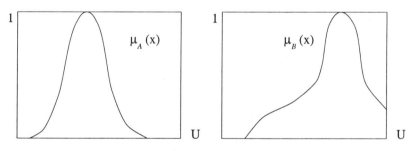

Fig. 1.9. Membership function $\mu_A(x), \mu_B(x)$.

Figure 1.11 shows that $\mathcal{A} \cap \mathcal{B} \in \mathcal{A} \cup \mathcal{B}$.

Law of excluded middle and fuzzy sets

The classical sets possess an important property, the *law of excluded middle*,[2] expressed by $\mathcal{A} \cap \overline{\mathcal{A}} = \phi$ and $\mathcal{A} \cup \overline{\mathcal{A}} = U$. It is illustrated in Fig. 1.12 by the means of Venn diagrams.

The law of excluded middle is not valid for the fuzzy sets since $\mathcal{A} \cap \overline{\mathcal{A}} \neq \phi$ and $\mathcal{A} \cup \overline{\mathcal{A}} \neq U$. This is illustrated in Fig. 1.13.

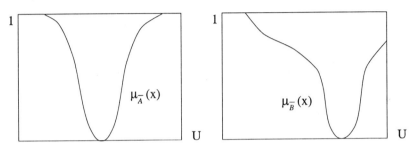

Fig. 1.10. Membership function $\mu_{\overline{A}}(x), \mu_{\overline{B}}(x)$.

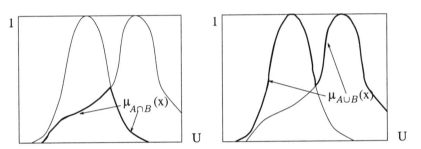

Fig. 1.11. Membership function of intersection and union.

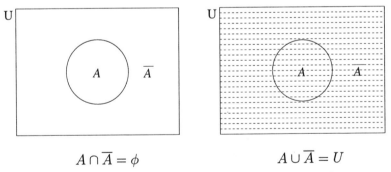

$$A \cap \overline{A} = \phi \qquad\qquad A \cup \overline{A} = U$$

Fig. 1.12. The law of excluded middle for classical sets.

It is natural that the law of the excluded middle is not valid for fuzzy sets. In classical sets every object does or does not have a certain property, expressed by 1 or 0. Fuzzy sets were introduced to reflect the existence of objects in reality that have a property to a degree between 0 and 1. There are many shades of *gray* color between *black* and *white*.

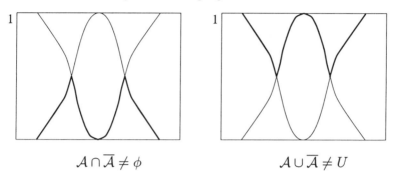

$$\mathcal{A} \cap \overline{\mathcal{A}} \neq \phi \qquad\qquad \mathcal{A} \cup \overline{\mathcal{A}} \neq U$$

Fig. 1.13. The law of excluded middle is not valid for fuzzy sets.

The lack of the law of excluded middle in fuzzy set theory makes it less specific than that of classical set theory. However, at the same time, this lack makes fuzzy sets more general and flexible than classical sets and very suitable for describing vagueness and processes with incomplete and imprecise[3] information.

1.4 Fuzzy Numbers

A *fuzzy number*[5] is defined on the universe R as a *convex* and *normalized* fuzzy set. In Figs. 1.14(a),(b) are shown two fuzzy numbers, with a maximum and with a flat.

For instance, the normalized fuzzy set in Fig. 1.8(a) is a fuzzy number while the sets in Fig. 1.8(b) are not. The fuzzy set in Fig. 1.7 is also a fuzzy number.

The fuzzy set in Fig. 1.6 is a fuzzy number in the set of integers while the fuzzy set in Fig. 1.4 is not. Also we may consider a fuzzy number with a flat in the set of integers.

The interval $[a_1, a_2]$ is called *supporting interval* for the fuzzy number. For $x = a_M$ the fuzzy number in Fig. 1.14 (a) has a maximum. The flat segment (Fig. 1.14(b)) has maximum height 1; actually it is the α-*cut* at the highest confidence level 1.

Fuzzy numbers will be denoted by bold capital letters $\mathbf{A}, \mathbf{B}, \mathbf{C}, \ldots$, and their membership functions by $\mu_{\mathbf{A}}(x), \mu_{\mathbf{B}}(x), \mu_{\mathbf{C}}(x), \ldots$.

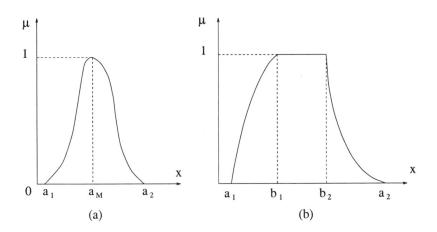

Fig. 1.14. Fuzzy numbers: (a) with a maximum; (b) with a flat.

Piecewise-quadratic fuzzy number

The membership function $\mu_A(x)$ of a piecewise-quadratic fuzzy number shown in Fig. 1.15 is bell-shaped, symmetric about the line $x = p$, has a supporting interval $A = [a_1, a_2]$, and is characterized by two parameters, $p = \frac{1}{2}(a_1 + a_2)$ and $\beta \in (0, a_2 - p)$. The *peak-point* (the maximum point) is $(p, 1)$; 2β called *bandwidth* is defined as the segment (α-cut) at level $\alpha = \frac{1}{2}$ between the points $(p - \beta, \frac{1}{2})$ and $(p + \beta, \frac{1}{2})$, called *crossover points*.

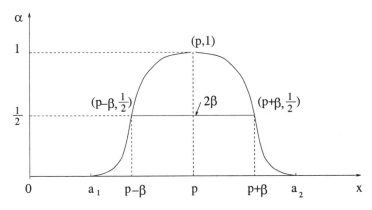

Fig. 1.15. Piecewise-quadratic fuzzy number.

The curve on Fig. 1.15 is described by the equations

$$
\mu_{\mathbf{A}}(x) = \begin{cases}
\frac{1}{2(p-\beta-a_1)^2}(x-a_1)^2 & \text{for } a_1 \leq x \leq p-\beta, \\
-\frac{1}{2\beta^2}(x-p)^2 + 1 & \text{for } p-\beta \leq x \leq p+\beta, \\
\frac{1}{2(p+\beta-a_2)^2}(x-a_2)^2 & \text{for } p+\beta \leq x \leq a_2, \\
0 & \text{otherwise.}
\end{cases}
\tag{1.11}
$$

The interpretation for the fuzzy number (1.11) is real numbers *close* to the number p. Since the word *close* is *vague* and in that sense *fuzzy*, it cannot be defined uniquely. That depends on the selection of the supporting interval and the bandwidth which are supposed to reflect a particular situation. For instance the fuzzy set *tall men* (Example 1.8) is a particular case of (1.11) (left branch) on the interval [160, 200] with $a_1 = 140, p = 200$, and $\beta = 30$.

Example 1.11

The manufacturing price of a product is *close* to 28. It can be described by the fuzzy number **A** in Fig. 1.16 where $a_1 = 23, a_2 = 33, p = 28, \beta = 3$.

The membership function $\mu_A(x)$ can be obtained from (1.11) by substituting the specific values of a_1, a_2, p and β given above.

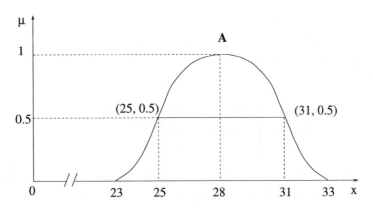

Fig. 1.16. Product price *close* to 28.

□

1.5   Triangular Fuzzy Numbers

A *triangular fuzzy number* **A** or simply triangular number with membership function $\mu_A(x)$ is defined on R by

$$\mathbf{A} \triangleq \mu_{\mathbf{A}}(x) = \begin{cases} \frac{x-a_1}{a_M-a_1} & \text{for } a_1 \leq x \leq a_M, \\ \frac{x-a_2}{a_M-a_2} & \text{for } a_M \leq x \leq a_2, \\ 0 & \text{otherwise,} \end{cases} \quad (1.12)$$

where $[a_1, a_2]$ is the supporting interval and the point $(a_M, 1)$ is the peak (see Fig. 1.17). The third line in (1.12) can be dropped.

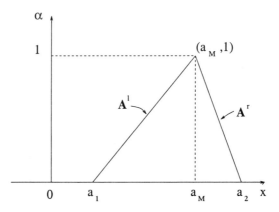

Fig. 1.17. Triangular fuzzy number.

Often in applications the point $a_M \in (a_1, a_2)$ is located at the middle of the supporting interval, i.e. $a_M = \frac{a_1+a_2}{2}$. Then substituting this value into (1.12) gives

$$\mathbf{A} \triangleq \mu_{\mathbf{A}}(x) = \begin{cases} 2\frac{x-a_1}{a_2-a_1} & \text{for } a_1 \leq x \leq \frac{a_1+a_2}{2}, \\ 2\frac{x-a_2}{a_1-a_2} & \text{for } \frac{a_1+a_2}{2} \leq x \leq a_2, \\ 0 & \text{otherwise.} \end{cases} \quad (1.13)$$

We say that (1.13) represents a *central triangular fuzzy number* (see Fig. 1.18(a)). Similarly to the piecewise-quadratic fuzzy number, it is very suitable to describe the word *close* (*close* to a_M).

Triangular numbers are very often used in the applications (fuzzy controllers, managerial decision making, business and finance, social sciences, etc.). They have a membership function consisting of two linear segments A^l (left) and A^r (right) joined at the peak $(a_M, 1)$ (see Fig. 1.17) which makes graphical representations and operations with triangular numbers very simple. Also it is important that they can be constructed easily on the basis of little information.

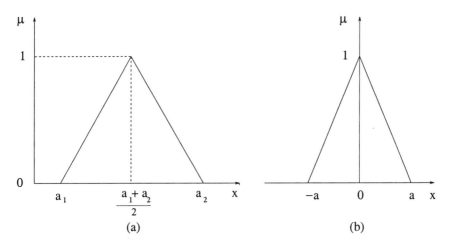

Fig. 1.18. (a) Central triangular number; (b) Central triangular number symmetrical about μ.

Assume while dealing with an uncertain value we are able to specify the smallest and largest possible values, i.e. the supporting interval $A = [a_1, a_2]$. If further we can indicate a value a_M in $[a_1, a_2]$ as most plausible to represent the uncertain value, then the peak will be the point $(a_M, 1)$. Hence with the three values a_1, a_2 and a_M, one can construct a triangular number and write down its membership function (1.12). That is why the triangular number is also denoted by

$$\mathbf{A} = (a_1, a_M, a_2). \tag{1.14}$$

A central triangular number is *symmetrical* with respect to the axis μ if in (1.13) $a_1 = -a, a_2 = a$, hence $a_M = 0$ (see Fig. 1.18(b)). According to (1.14) it is denoted by

$$\mathbf{A} = (-a, 0, a).$$

It is very suitable to express the word *small*. The right branch (segment) of $\mathbf{A} = (-a, 0, a)$, i.e. when $0 \leq x \leq a$, can be used to describe *positive small* (**PS**), for instance *young age, small profit, small risk*, etc. We can denote it by $\mathbf{A}^r = (0, 0, a)$.

More generally, the left and right branches of the triangular number (1.14) can be denoted correspondingly by $\mathbf{A}^l = (a_1, a_M, a_M)$ and $\mathbf{A}^r = (a_M, a_M, a_2)$. They will be considered as triangular numbers and called correspondingly *left* and *right triangular numbers*. The left triangular number $\mathbf{A}^l$ (see Fig. 1.17) is suitable to represent *positive large* (**PL**) or words with similar meaning, for instance *old age, big profit, high risk*, etc. provided that a_M is large number.

1.6   Trapezoidal Fuzzy Numbers

A *trapezoidal fuzzy number* $\mathbf{A}$ or shortly trapezoidal number (see Fig. 1.19) is defined on R by

$$
\mathbf{A} \triangleq \mu_{\mathbf{A}}(x) = \begin{cases} \frac{x-a_1}{b_1-a_1} & \text{for } a_1 \leq x \leq b_1, \\ 1 & \text{for } b_1 \leq x \leq b_2, \\ \frac{x-a_2}{b_2-a_2} & \text{for } b_2 \leq x \leq a_2, \\ 0 & \text{otherwise.} \end{cases} \tag{1.15}
$$

It is a particular case of a fuzzy number with a flat.

The supporting interval is $\mathbf{A} = [a_1, a_2]$ and the flat segment on level $\alpha = 1$ has projection $[b_1, b_2]$ on the x-axis. With the four values a_1, a_2, b_1, and b_2, we can construct the trapezoidal number (1.15). It can be denoted by

$$
\mathbf{A} = (a_1, b_1, b_2, a_2). \tag{1.16}
$$

If $b_1 = b_2 = a_M$, the trapezoidal number reduces to a triangular fuzzy number and is denoted by (a_1, a_M, a_M, a_2). Hence a triangular number (a_1, a_M, a_2) can be written in the form of a trapezoidal number, i.e. $(a_1, a_M, a_2) = (a_1, a_M, a_M, a_2)$.

If $[a_1, b_1] = [b_2, a_2]$, the trapezoidal number is *symmetrical* with respect to the line $x = \frac{1}{2}(b_1 + b_2)$ (see Fig. 1.20). It is in *central* form and represents the interval $[b_1, b_2]$ and real number close to this interval.

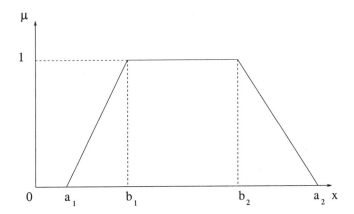

Fig. 1.19. Trapezoidal fuzzy number.

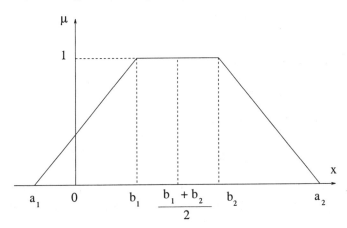

Fig. 1.20. Trapezoidal number in central form.

Similarly to right and left triangular numbers (Section 1.5) we can introduce right and left trapezoidal numbers as parts of a trapezoidal number.

The right trapezoidal number denoted $\mathbf{A}^r = (b_1, b_1, b_2, a_2)$ has supporting interval $[b_1, a_2]$ and the left denoted $\mathbf{A}^l = (a_1, b_1, b_2, b_2)$ has supporting interval $[a_1, b_2]$. Especially they are suitable to represent $small \overset{\triangle}{=} \mathbf{A}^r = (0, 0, b_2, a_2)$ (Fig. 1.21(a)) and $large \overset{\triangle}{=} \mathbf{A}^l = (a_1, b_1, b_2, b_2)$ where b_1 is a large number (Fig. 1.21(b)).

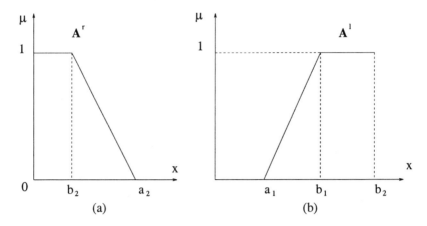

Fig. 1.21 (a) Right trapezoidal number $\mathbf{A}^r$ representing *small*; (b) Left trapezoidal number $\mathbf{A}^l$ representing *large*.

1.7   Fuzzy Relations

Definition of Fuzzy Relation

Consider the Cartesian product

$$A \times B = \{(x, y) \ \mid \ x \in A, y \in B\},$$

where A and B are subsets of the universal sets U_1 and U_2, respectively.

A *fuzzy relation* on $A \times B$ denoted by $\mathcal{R}$ or $\mathcal{R}(x, y)$ is define as the set

$$\mathcal{R} = \{((x, y), \mu_\mathcal{R}(x, y)) | (x, y) \in A \times B, \mu_\mathcal{R}(x, y) \in [0, 1]\}, \qquad (1.17)$$

where $\mu_\mathcal{R}(x, y)$ is a function in two variables called *membership function*. It gives the degree of membership of the ordered pair (x, y) in $\mathcal{R}$ associating with each pair (x, y) in $A \times B$ a real number in the interval $[0, 1]$. The degree of membership indicates the degree to which x is in relation with y. We assume that $\mu_R(x, y)$ is piecewise continuous or discrete in the domain $A \times B$; it describes a surface. Formally, the fuzzy relation $\mathcal{R}$ is a classical trinary relation; it is a set of ordered triples.

The definition (1.17) is a generalization of definition (1.6) for fuzzy set from two-dimensional space $(x, \mu_A(x))$ to three-dimensional space $(x, y, \mu_A(x, y))$.[6] Here we also identify a relation with its membership function.

The fuzzy relation in comparison to the classical relation possesses stronger expressive power while relating x and y due to the membership function $\mu_R(x, y)$ which assigns specific values (grades) to each pair (x, y).

Common *linguistic relations* that can be described by appropriate fuzzy relations are: x is *much greater than y*, x *is close to y*, x is *relevant to y*, x and y are *almost equal*, x and y are *very far*, etc.

Example 1.12

Consider the fuzzy relation which consists of finite number of ordered pairs,
$$
\begin{aligned}
\mathcal{R} \;=\; & \{((x_1, y_1), 0), ((x_1, y_2), 0.1), ((x_1, y_3, 0.2), \\
& ((x_2, y_1), 0.7), ((x_2, y_2, 0.2, ((x_2, y_3, 0.3), \\
& ((x_3, y_1), 1), (x_3, y_2), 0.6), ((x_3, y_3), 0.2))\};
\end{aligned}
$$
it can be described also by the table (or matrix)

$\mathcal{R} \overset{\triangle}{=}$	y x	y_1	y_2	y_3
	x_1	0	0.1	0.2
	x_2	0.7	0.2	0.3
	x_3	1	0.6	0.2

where the numbers in the cells located at the intersection of rows and columns are the values of the membership function:

$\mu_R(x_1, y_1) = 0$, $\mu_R(x_1, y_2) = 0.1$, $\mu_R(x_1, y_3) = 0.2$,
$\mu_R(x_2, y_1) = 0.7$, $\mu_R(x_2, y_2) = 0.2$, $\mu_R(x_2, y_3) = 0.3$,
$\mu_R(x_3, y_1) = 1$, $\mu_R(x_3, y_2) = 0.6$, $\mu_R(x_3, y_3) = 0.2$.

Assuming that $x_1 = 1, x_2 = 2, x_3 = 3, y_1 = 1, y_2 = 2, y_3 = 3$, we can present schematically $\mathcal{R}$ by points in the three-dimensional space (x, y, μ) (see Fig. 1.22).

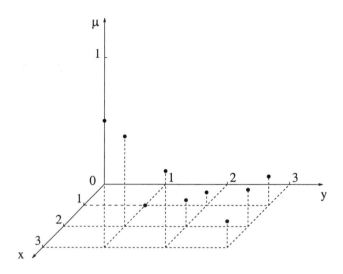

Fig. 1.22. Fuzzy relation $\mathcal{R}$ describing x is greater than y.

Since the values of the membership function 0.7, 1, 0.6 in the direction of x below the major diagonal (0, 0.2, 0.2) in the table are greater than those above in the direction of y, 0.1, 0.2, 0.3, we say that the relation $\mathcal{R}$ describes x *is greater than* y.

The fuzzy relation $\mathcal{R}$ can be expressed also as a fuzzy graph (Fig. 1.23). The numbers at the segments are the degrees of membership.

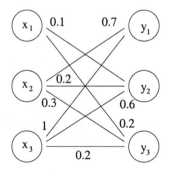

Fig. 1.23. Fuzzy relation $\mathcal{R}$ presented as a fuzzy graph.

□

Example 1.13

Consider the following two sets whose elements are business companies: $A = \{\text{company } a_1, \text{company } a_2, \text{company } a_3\}$, $B = \{\text{company } b_1, \text{company } b_2\}$. Let $\mathcal{R}$ be a fuzzy relation between the two sets that represents the linguistic relation *very far* concerning distance between companies:

$$
\begin{aligned}
\mathcal{R} = \{ &((\text{company} a_1, \text{company} b_1), 0.9), \\
&((\text{company} a_1, \text{company} b_2), 0.6), \\
&((\text{company} a_2, \text{company} b_1), 1), \\
&((\text{company} a_2, \text{company} b_2), 0.4), \\
&((\text{company} a_3, \text{company} b_1), 0.5), \\
&((\text{company} a_3, \text{company} b_2), 0.1)\}.
\end{aligned}
$$

The relation can also be presented by the table

		company b_1	company b_2
$\mathcal{R} \triangleq$	company a_1	0.9	0.6
	company a_2	1	0.4
	company a_3	0.5	0.1

The membership values indicate to what degree the corresponding companies are *very far* from each other. For instance, company a_2 and company b_1 are very far (degree of membership 1) while companies a_3 and b_2 are not very far (degree of membership 0.1).

□

1.8 Basic Operations on Fuzzy Relations

Let $\mathcal{R}_1$ and $\mathcal{R}_2$ be two fuzzy relations on $A \times B$,

$$
\begin{aligned}
\mathcal{R}_1 &= \{((x,y), \mu_{\mathcal{R}_1}(x,y))\}, & (x,y) \in A \times B, \\
\mathcal{R}_2 &= \{((x,y), \mu_{\mathcal{R}_2}(x,y))\}, & (x,y) \in A \times B.
\end{aligned}
$$

We use the membership functions $\mu_{\mathcal{R}_1}(x,y)$ and $\mu_{\mathcal{R}_2}(x,y)$ in order to introduce operations with $\mathcal{R}_1$ and $\mathcal{R}_2$ similarly to operations with fuzzy sets in Section 1.3.

Equality

$\mathcal{R}_1 = \mathcal{R}_2$ if and only if for every pair $(x, y) \in A \times B$,

$$\mu_{\mathcal{R}_1}(x, y) = \mu_{\mathcal{R}_2}(x, y).$$

Inclusion

If for every pair $(x, y) \in A \times B$,

$$\mu_{\mathcal{R}_1}(x, y) \leq \mu_{\mathcal{R}_2}(x, y),$$

the relation $\mathcal{R}_1$ is *included* in $\mathcal{R}_2$ or $\mathcal{R}_2$ is larger than $\mathcal{R}_1$, denoted by $\mathcal{R}_1 \subseteq \mathcal{R}_2$.

If $\mathcal{R}_1 \subseteq \mathcal{R}_2$ and in addition if for at least one pair (x, y),

$$\mu_{\mathcal{R}_1}(x, y) < \mu_{\mathcal{R}_2}(x, y),$$

then we have the proper inclusion $\mathcal{R}_1 \subset \mathcal{R}_2$.

Complementation

The *complement* of a relation $\mathcal{R}$, denoted by $\overline{\mathcal{R}}$, is defined by

$$\mu_{\overline{\mathcal{R}}}(x, y) = 1 - \mu_{\mathcal{R}}(x, y), \tag{1.18}$$

which must be valid for any pair $(x, y) \in A \times B$.

Intersection

The *intersection* of $\mathcal{R}_1$ and $\mathcal{R}_2$ denoted $\mathcal{R}_1 \bigcap \mathcal{R}_2$ is defined by

$$\mu_{\mathcal{R}_1 \cap \mathcal{R}_2}(x, y) = \min\{\mu_{\mathcal{R}_1}(x, y), \mu_{\mathcal{R}_2}(x, y)\}, \quad (x, y) \in A \times B. \tag{1.19}$$

Union

The *union* of $\mathcal{R}_1$ and $\mathcal{R}_2$ denoted $\mathcal{R}_1 \bigcup \mathcal{R}_2$ is defined by

$$\mu_{\mathcal{R}_1 \cup \mathcal{R}_2}(x, y) = \max\{\mu_{\mathcal{R}_1}(x, y), \mu_{\mathcal{R}_2}(x, y)\}, \quad (x, y) \in A \times B. \tag{1.20}$$

The operations intersection and union are illustrated in the following example.

Example 1.14

Consider the relations $\mathcal{R}_1$ and $\mathcal{R}_2$ given by the tables

$$\mathcal{R}_1 \overset{\triangle}{=} \begin{array}{c|ccc} & y_1 & y_2 & y_3 \\ \hline x_1 & 0 & 0.1 & 0.2 \\ x_2 & 0 & 0.7 & 0.3 \\ x_3 & 0.2 & 0.8 & 1 \end{array} \qquad \mathcal{R}_2 \overset{\triangle}{=} \begin{array}{c|ccc} & y_1 & y_2 & y_3 \\ \hline x_1 & 0.3 & 0.3 & 0.2 \\ x_2 & 0.5 & 0 & 1 \\ x_3 & 0.7 & 0.3 & 0.1 \end{array}$$

Using definitions (1.19) and (1.20) for each ordered pair $(x_i, y_j), i, j = 1, 2, 3$, gives

$$\mathcal{R}_1 \cap \mathcal{R}_2 \overset{\triangle}{=} \begin{array}{c|ccc} & y_1 & y_2 & y_3 \\ \hline x_1 & 0 & 0.1 & 0.2 \\ x_2 & 0 & 0 & 0.3 \\ x_3 & 0.2 & 0.3 & 0.1 \end{array} \; ; \qquad \mathcal{R}_1 \cup \mathcal{R}_2 \overset{\triangle}{=} \begin{array}{c|ccc} & y_1 & y_2 & y_3 \\ \hline x_1 & 0.3 & 0.3 & 0.2 \\ x_2 & 0.5 & 0.7 & 1 \\ x_3 & 0.7 & 0.8 & 1 \end{array}$$

A comparison between the corresponding membership values in $\mathcal{R}_1 \cap \mathcal{R}_2$ and $\mathcal{R}_1 \cup \mathcal{R}_2$ shows that $\mathcal{R}_1 \cap \mathcal{R}_2 \subset \mathcal{R}_1 \cup \mathcal{R}_2$ (proper inclusion). □

Direct Product

Consider the fuzzy sets $\mathcal{A}$ and $\mathcal{B}$

$$\mathcal{A} = \{(x, \mu_\mathcal{A}(x)), \quad \mu_\mathcal{A}(x) \in [0, 1]\},$$

$$\mathcal{B} = \{(y, \mu_\mathcal{B}(y)), \quad \mu_\mathcal{B}(y) \in [0, 1]\}.$$

defined on $x \in A \subset U_1$ and $y \in B \subset U_2$, correspondingly.

We introduce two types of *direct products* which will be used in the next chapter.

Direct min product of the fuzzy sets $\mathcal{A}$ and $\mathcal{B}$ denoted $\mathcal{A} \overset{\times}{\cdot} \mathcal{B}$ with membership functions $\mu_{\mathcal{A} \times \mathcal{B}}$ is a fuzzy relation defined by

$$\mathcal{A} \overset{\times}{\cdot} \mathcal{B} = \{(x, y), \min(\mu_\mathcal{A}(x), \mu_\mathcal{B}(y)), (x, y) \in A \times B\}, \qquad (1.21)$$

which means that we have to perform the Cartesian product $A \times B$ and at each pair (x, y) to attach as membership value the smaller between $\mu_\mathcal{A}(x)$ and $\mu_\mathcal{B}(y)$.

Direct max product of the fuzzy sets $\mathcal{A}$ and $\mathcal{B}$ denoted $\mathcal{A}\dot\times\mathcal{B}$ with membership function $\mu_{(\mathcal{A}\dot\times\mathcal{B})}(x,y)$ is a fuzzy relation defined by

$$\mathcal{A}\dot\times\mathcal{B} = \{(x,y), \max(\mu_{\mathcal{A}}(x), \mu_{\mathcal{B}}(y)), (x,y) \in A \times B\}. \qquad (1.22)$$

Here each pair (x,y) has for membership value the larger between $\mu_{\mathcal{A}}(x)$ and $\mu_{\mathcal{B}}(y)$.

Example 1.15

Given the fuzzy sets

$$\mathcal{A} = \{(x_1, 0), (x_2, 0.1), (x_3, 1)\},$$

$$\mathcal{B} = \{(y_1, 0.3), (y_2, 1), (y_3, 0.2), (y_4, 0.1)\},$$

the direct min product and the direct max product according to (1.21) and (1.22) are the fuzzy relations

$$\mathcal{A} \overset{\times}{\cdot} \mathcal{B} \overset{\triangle}{=}$$

y	y_1	y_2	y_3	y_4
x				
x_1	0	0	0	0
x_2	0.1	0.1	0.1	0.1
x_3	0.3	1	0.2	0.1

$$\mathcal{A}\dot\times\mathcal{B} \overset{\triangle}{=}$$

y	y_1	y_2	y_3	y_4
x				
x_1	0.3	1	0.2	0.1 .
x_2	0.3	1	0.2	0.1
x_3	1	1	1	1

□

1.9   Notes

1. The formal development of set theory began in the late 19th century with the work of George Cantor (1845–1918), one of the most original mathematicians in history. Set theory has been used to establish the foundations of mathematics and modern methods of

mathematical proof. Cantor's sets are crisp. Each element under consideration either belongs to a set or it does not; hence there is a line drawn between the elements of the set and those which are not. The boundary of a set is rigid and well defined (see Example 1.5). However in reality things are rather fuzzy than crisp.

2. A paradox coming from ancient Greece has caused serious problems to logicians and mathematicians. Consider a heap of grains of sand. Take a grain and the heap is still there. Take another grain, and another grain, and continue the process. Eventually ten grains are left, then nine, and so on. When one grain is left, what happens with the heap. Is it still a heap? When the last grain is removed and there is nothing, does the heap cease to be a heap? There are many paradoxes of similar nature called "sorites." This word comes from "soros" which is the Greek word for heap. For instance let us apply the above procedure to the cash (say, one million) of a rich person. He/she spends one dollar and is still rich; then another dollar and so on. When one hundred dollars are left, what happens to his/her richness? When does that person cease to be rich? In the crisp set theory such dilemmas are solved by sort of appropriate assumptions (as in Example 1.5) or by decree. In the case of the heap a certain natural number n is to be selected; if the number of sand grains is $\geq n$, then the grains constitute a heap; $n-1$ sand grains does not form a heap anymore. This defies common sense. Also how to select the number n? Is it 100, 1000, or 1,000,000, or larger? Common sense hints that the concept *heap* is a *vague* one. Hence a tool that can deal with vagueness is necessary. The concept of fuzzy set, a generalization of Cantor's sets, is such a tool (see Example 1.7).

The following thoughts by Bertrand Russell (1923) are quoted very often: "All traditional logic habitually assumes that precise symbols are being employed. It is therefore not applicable to this terrestrial life, but only to an imagined celestial one. The law of excluded middle is true when precise symbols are employed but it is not true when symbols are vague, as, in fact, all symbols are." "All language is vague." "Vagueness, clearly, is a matter of degree."

An important step towards dealing with vagueness was made by the philosopher Max Black (1937) who introduced the concept of vague set.

3. The concept of fuzziness was introduced first in the form of fuzzy sets by Zadeh (1965).

According to dictionaries (see for instance *Merriam-Webster's Collegiate Dictionary* and *The Heritage Illustrated Dictionary of the English Language*) and also use in everyday language the words *fuzzy, vague, ambiguous, uncertain, imprecise,* and their adverbs, are more or less closely related in terms of meaning. This statement is supported by the following brief explanations.

Fuzzy: not sharply focused, clearly reasoned or expressed; confused; lacking of clarity; blurred.

Vague: not clearly expressed, defined, or understood; not sharply outlined (hazy); lack of definite form.

Ambiguous: capable of being understood in two or more possible ways; doubtful or uncertain (synonym: vague).

Uncertain: not certain to occur; not clearly identified or defined; lack of sureness about something; lack of knowledge about an outcome or result.

Imprecise: not precise, inexact, vague.

There are various opinions on the meaning of these words and their use and misuse in common language, philosophy, and in fuzzy logic. We leave it to philosophers and linguistists to debate and deliberate on the subject if they choose to do it. Poper (1979) for instance sounds quite discouraging: "One should never quarrel about words, and never get involved in questions of terminology. One should always keep away from discussing concepts. What we are really interested in, our real problems, are factual problems, or in other words, problems of theories and their truth." There is some truth in Poper although he goes to an extreme. We think it will be useful for the better understanding of this book to provide a clarification.

Fuzzy, adv. *fuzziness*, in fuzzy logic is associated with the concept of graded membership which can be interpreted as degree of truth (see Section 2.6). The objects under study in fuzzy logic admit of degrees expressed by the membership functions of fuzzy sets (see Section 1.2). Problems and events in reality involving components labeled as vague, ambiguous, uncertain, imprecise are considered in this book as fuzzy problems and events if graded membership is the tool for their description. In other words, when gradation is involved, vagueness, ambiguity, uncertainty, imprecision are included into the concept of fuzziness.

Beside the fundamental volume *Fuzzy Sets and Applications: Selected Papers by L.A. Zadeh* (1987), here we list several important books dealing with fuzzy sets and fuzzy logic used in this text: Kaufmann (1975), Dubois and Prade (1980), Zimmermann (1984), Kandel (1986), Klir and Folger (1988), Novák (1989), Terano, Asai, Sugeno (1992).

Fascinating popular books on fuzzy logic are written by McNeill and Freiberger (1993) and Kosko (1993).

4. The notion of fuzzy set is sometimes incorrectly considered as a type of probability. Although there are similarities and links between fuzzy sets and probability, there are also substantial differences. For instance, *grade* or *degree of membership* is not a probablistic concept. In Example 1.8 (*tall men*), a man who is 180 cm tall has a degree of membership 0.78 (or 78%) in the set *tall men*. We can say this person is 78% tall (almost tall), but we can not say that there is a probability of 78% that he is tall.

5. The concept of fuzzy number was introduced after that of fuzzy set. Valuable contributions to fuzzy numbers were made by Nahmias (1977), Dubois and Prade (1978), and Kaufmann and Gupta (1985) (see also G. Bojadziev and M. Bojadziev (1995)).

In many applications both fuzzy numbers and fuzzy sets can be used equally well although presentations with fuzzy numbers are somewhat simpler. For general studies and also for facilitating *fuzzy logic*, fuzzy set theory is a very suitable tool.

6. Fuzzy relations were introduced by Zadeh (1971) as a generalization of both classical relations and fuzzy sets.

Chapter 2

Fuzzy Logic

The chapter gives first a short description of classical and many-valued logics. Classical (two-valued) logic deals with propositions that are either true or false. In many-valued logic, a generalization of the classical logic, the propositions have more than two truth values. Fuzzy logic is an extension of the many-valued logic in the sense of incorporating fuzzy sets and fuzzy relations as tools into the system of many-valued logic. Fuzzy logic provides a methodology for dealing with linguistic variables and describing modifiers like very, fairly, not, etc. Fuzzy logic facilitates common sense reasoning with imprecise and vague propositions dealing with natural language and serves as a basis for decision analysis and control actions.

2.1 Basic Concepts of Classical Logic

Here, some basic concepts of the classical[1] (mathematical) or two-valued logic are briefly reviewed.

Propositions

A *proposition*, also called *statement*, is a declarative sentence that is logically either *true* (T) denoted by 1 or *false* (F) denoted by 0. The set $T_2 = \{0, 1\}$ is called *truth value set* for the proposition. In other words a proposition may be considered as a quantity which can assume one of two values: *truth* or *falsity*.

Example 2.1

Consider the sentences:

(a) The stock market is independent of inflation rates (false proposition);

(b) Money supply is an economic indicator (true proposition);

(c) The price of a product is x dollars where $x > 100$ (contains a variable; neither true nor false, it is not a proposition);

(d) Is the stock market going up? (it is not a proposition).

□

We use letters, $p, q, r, \ldots$, to represent propositions.

The propositions (a) and (b) in Example 2.1 are *simple*.

Compound propositions consist of two or more simple propositions joined by one or more *logical connectives*.

Consider the propositions p and q whose truth values belong to the truth value set $\{0, 1\}$. The meaning of the logical connectives is given by definitions and expressed by equations in which p and q stand for the truth values of the propositions p and q.[2]

Negation

Negation or *denial* of p, denoted $\bar{p}$ (read *not p*) is true when p is false and vice versa, hence

$$\bar{p} = 1 - p. \tag{2.1}$$

Conjunction

Conjunction of p and q, denoted $p \wedge q$ (read *p and q*) is true when p and q are both true (*and* is the common and in English);

$$p \wedge q = \min(p, q). \tag{2.2}$$

Disjunction

Disjunction of p and q, denoted $p \vee q$ (read *p or q*) is true when p or q is true or both p and q are true;

$$p \vee q = \max(p, q). \tag{2.3}$$

Implication (*Conditional proposition*)

The proposition p *implies* q, denoted $p \to q$ (also read *if p then q*) is true except when p is true and q is false; p and q are called *premise* (*antecedent*) and *conclusion* (*consequent*) , correspondingly;

$$p \to q = \min(1, 1 + q - p). \tag{2.4}$$

It should be emphasized that the truth or falsity of a compound proposition (formulas (2.1)–(2.4)) is determined only by the truth values of its simpler propositions p and q.

Truth tables

A very useful device to deal with the truth values of compound propositions is the truth table.[3]

The truth values of the operations (2.1)–(2.4) under all possible truth value for p and q are presented in Table 2.1 (1 stands for truth(T) and 0 for false(F)). The right hand sides of (2.1)–(2.4) can be used to calculate the truth values in a straightforward manner.

Table 2.1. Truth values in the set $T_2 = \{0, 1\}$ of negation, conjunction, disjunction, and implication.

p	q	$\overline{p}$ $1 - p$	$p \wedge q$ $\min(p, q)$	$p \vee q$ $\max(p, q)$	$p \to q$ $\min(1, 1 + q - p)$
1	1	0	1	1	1
1	0	0	0	1	0
0	1	1	0	1	1
0	0	1	0	0	1

Tautology

Tautology is a compound proposition form that is *true* under all possible truth values for its simple propositions.

Contradiction

Contradiction or *fallacy* is a compound proposition form that is *false* under all possible truth values for its simple propositions.

Example 2.2

The truth values for the proposition forms $p \wedge \bar{p}$ and $p \vee \bar{p}$ are presented on Table 2.2.

Table 2.2. Truth values for $p \wedge \bar{p}$ and $p \vee \bar{p}$.

p	$\bar{p}$	$p \wedge \bar{p}$	$p \vee \bar{p}$
1	0	0	1
0	1	0	1

Hence $p \wedge \bar{p}$ with truth value 0 is a *contradiction* (it is called *law of contradiction*), while $p \vee \bar{p}$ with truth value 1 is a *tautology* (it is called the *law of excluded middle: every proposition is either true or false*).
□

The branch of classical logic dealing with compound propositions is known as *propositional calculus*. Its extension is the *predicate calculus*.

Predicate

Predicate is a declarative sentence containing one or more variables or unknowns. A predicate is neither true nor false, hence it is not a proposition. Predicates are denoted by $p(x), q(x, y), \cdots$, where $x, y, \cdots$ are unknowns; they are called also *logical functions*. If in a predicate numbers are substituted for variables, the predicate becomes a proposition. For instance sentence (c) in Example 2.1 is a predicate. If x is substituted by a number, say 150, then (c) reduces to a proposition. Hence predicates are closely related to propositions; they can be considered as generalized propositions or indefinite propositions.

Correspondence between the classical logic and set theory

There is a correspondence between the logical connectives *and, or, not, implication* and the set operations *intersection, union, complement, inclusion* (subset), correspondingly, expressed in Table 2.3

It is established that this correspondence (called *isomorphism*) guarantees that every theorem or result in set theory has a counterpart in two-valued logic and vice versa. They can be obtained from one another by exchanging the corresponding symbols given in Table 2.3.

Table 2.3. Correspondence between logical connectives and set operations.

Logic	Set theory
∨	∪
∧	∩
$^-$	$^-$
→	⊆

2.2   Many-Valued Logic

Since the time when in logic the principle *every proposition is either true or false* has been declared, there have always been some doubts about it. One reason for questioning the above principle is the difficulty arising with estimating truth values of propositions expressing future events, for instance *tomorrow will rain*.[4] Future events are not yet true or false. Their truth value is unknown; it will be determined when the events happen. The classical (two-valued) logic is not sufficient to describe the truth value of these type of events. Hence it looks natural to allow a third truth value other than pure truth or falsity which leads to a three-valued logic. Depending on how the third value is defined, several three-valued logics were introduced.

Here we discuss the three-valued logic[5] proposed by Łukasiewicz (1920).

Suppose that a proposition has three truth values: *true* denoted by 1, *false* denoted by 0, and *neutral* or *indeterminate* denoted by $\frac{1}{2}$. They form the truth value set

$$T_3 = \{0, \frac{1}{2}, 1\}.$$

If p and q are propositions, the logical connectives *negation* ($^-$), *conjunction* ($\land$), *disjunction* ($\lor$), and *implication* ($\to$) are defined as in classical logic by (2.1)–(2.4) with the difference that the truth values of p and q belong to T_3.

The truth values of (2.1)–(2.4) with T_3 are given in Table 2.4.

Table 2.4. Truth values in T_3 for negation, conjunction, disjunction, implication.

p	q	$\overline{p}$	$\overline{q}$	$p \wedge q$	$p \vee q$	$p \rightarrow q$
1	1	0	0	1	1	1
1	$\frac{1}{2}$	0	$\frac{1}{2}$	$\frac{1}{2}$	1	$\frac{1}{2}$
1	0	0	1	0	1	0
$\frac{1}{2}$	1	$\frac{1}{2}$	0	$\frac{1}{2}$	1	1
$\frac{1}{2}$	$\frac{1}{2}$	$\frac{1}{2}$	$\frac{1}{2}$	$\frac{1}{2}$	$\frac{1}{2}$	1
$\frac{1}{2}$	0	$\frac{1}{2}$	1	0	$\frac{1}{2}$	$\frac{1}{2}$
0	1	1	0	0	1	1
0	$\frac{1}{2}$	1	$\frac{1}{2}$	0	$\frac{1}{2}$	1
0	0	1	1	0	0	1

Example 2.3

Let us construct the truth table for the compound propositions $p \wedge \overline{p}$ and $p \vee \overline{p}$. The result is presented on Table 2.5.

Table 2.5. Truth values in T_3 for $p \wedge \overline{p}$ and $p \vee \overline{p}$.

p	$\overline{p}$	$p \wedge \overline{p}$	$p \vee \overline{p}$
1	0	0	1
$\frac{1}{2}$	$\frac{1}{2}$	$\frac{1}{2}$	$\frac{1}{2}$
0	1	0	1

Since the value $\frac{1}{2}$ appears in the third and forth columns in Table 2.5, unlike the two-valued logic (see Table 2.3), $p \wedge \overline{p}$ and $p \vee \overline{p}$, respectively, *do not satisfy the law of contradiction and the law of excluded middle.*
□

On the basis of Example 2.3 we may say that $p \wedge \overline{p}$ expresses a more general law of *quasi-contradiction*; $p \vee \overline{p}$ is a *quasi-tautology*.

The three-valued logic is a generalization of the two-valued logic. If the rows in which the truth value $\frac{1}{2}$ appears are removed from Table 2.4, then the result will be Table 2.1.

A further generalization allows a proposition to have more than three truth values. If for any given natural number $n \geq 3$, the truth values are represented by rational numbers in the interval $[0, 1]$ that subdivide $[0, 1]$ into equal parts, then they form the truth set T_n,

$$T_n = \{0, \frac{1}{n-1}, \frac{2}{n-1}, \ldots, \frac{n-2}{n-1}, \frac{n-1}{n-1} = 1\}.$$

In the Łukasiewicz n-valued logic the formulas (2.1)–(2.4) for logical connectives remain valid provided that p and q are substituted by their truth values in T_n.

If the truth values are represented by all real numbers in $[0, 1]$, i.e. the truth set is $T_\infty = [0, 1]$, the many-valued logic[6] is called *infinite-valued logic*; it is referred as the *standard Łukasiewicz logic*. There is a correspondence (isomorphism) between the fuzzy set theory and the infinite-valued logic. Complementation (1.14), intersection (1.15), and union (1.16) in fuzzy sets correspond respectively to negation (2.1), conjunction (2.2), and disjunction (2.2) in the infinite-valued logic provided that p and q are substituted by their truth values from T_∞.

2.3 What is Fuzzy Logic?

The founder of fuzzy logic is Lotfi Zadeh (1973, 1975, 1976, 1978, 1983). He made significant advancement in the establishment of fuzzy logic as a scientific discipline.

There is not a unique system of knowledge called fuzzy logic but a variety of methodologies proposing logical consideration of imperfect and vague knowledge. It is an active area of research with some topics still under discussion and debate.

We have seen that there is a correspondence (isomorphism) between classical sets and classical logic (Table 2.4).

Fuzzy sets are a generalization of classical sets and infinite-valued logic is a generalization of classical logic. There is also a correspondence (isomorphism) between these two areas (Section 2.2).

Fuzzy logic uses as a major tool—fuzzy set theory. Basic mathematical ideas for fuzzy logic evolve from the infinite-valued logic, thus there is a link between both logics. Fuzzy logic can be considered as an extension of infinite-valued logic in the sense of incorporating fuzzy sets and fuzzy relations into the system of infinite-valued logic.[7]

Fuzzy logic focuses on linguistic variables in natural language and aims to provide foundations for approximate reasoning with imprecise propositions. It reflects both the rightness and vagueness of natural language in common-sense reasoning.

The relations between classical sets, classical logic, fuzzy sets (in particular fuzzy numbers), infinite-valued logic, and fuzzy logic are schematically shown on Fig. 2.1.

Major parts of fuzzy logic deal with linguistic variables and linguistic modifiers, propositional fuzzy logic, inferential rules, and approximate reasoning.

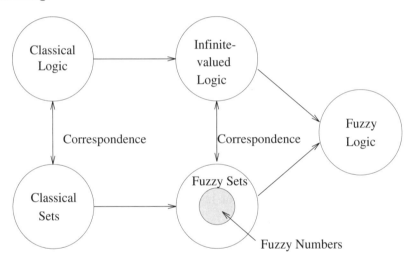

Fig. 2.1. Evolvement of Fuzzy Logic.

2.4   Linguistic Variables

Variables whose values are words or sentences in natural or artificial languages are called *linguistic variables*.

To illustrate the concept of *linguistic variable* consider the word *age* in a natural language; it is a summary of the experience of enormously large number of individuals; it cannot be characterized precisely. Employing fuzzy sets (usually fuzzy numbers), we can describe *age* approximately. *Age* is a *linguistic variable* whose values are words like *very young, young, middle age, old, very old.* They are called *terms* or *labels* of the linguistic variable *age* and are expressed by fuzzy sets on a universal set $U \subset R_+$ called also *operating domain* measured in years. It represents the *base variable* age. Each term is defined by an appropriate membership function. Good candidates for membership functions are triangular, trapezoidal, or bell-type shapes, without or with a flat, or parts of these (Chapter 1, Sections 1.4–1.6).

Example 2.4

Let us describe the linguistic variable *age* on the universal set $U = [0, 100]$ or operating domain of x (base variable) representing age in years (see Fig. 2.2) by triangular and part of trapezoidal numbers which specify the terms very young, young, middle age, old, and very old.

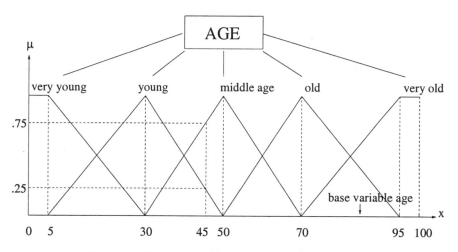

Fig. 2.2. Terms of the linguistic variable *age*.

The membership functions of the terms are:

$$\mu_{very\ young}(x) = \begin{cases} 1 & \text{for } 0 \leq x \leq 5, \\ \frac{30-x}{25} & \text{for } 5 \leq x \leq 30, \end{cases}$$

$$\mu_{young}(x) = \begin{cases} \frac{x-5}{25} & \text{for } 5 \leq x \leq 30, \\ \frac{50-x}{20} & \text{for } 30 \leq x \leq 50, \end{cases}$$

$$\mu_{middle\ age}(x) = \begin{cases} \frac{x-30}{20} & \text{for} \quad 30 \leq x \leq 50, \\ \frac{70-x}{20} & \text{for} \quad 50 \leq x \leq 70, \end{cases}$$

$$\mu_{old}(x) = \begin{cases} \frac{x-50}{20} & \text{for} \quad 50 \leq x \leq 70, \\ \frac{95-x}{25} & \text{for} \quad 70 \leq x \leq 95, \end{cases}$$

$$\mu_{very\ old}(x) = \begin{cases} \frac{x-70}{25} & \text{for} \quad 70 \leq x \leq 95, \\ 1 & \text{for} \quad 95 \leq x \leq 100. \end{cases}$$

For instance, a person whose age is 45 is young to degree 0.25 and middle age to degree 0.75. The degrees are found by substituting 45 for x into the second equation of the term $\mu_{young}(x)$ and first equation of the term $\mu_{middleage}(x)$, correspondingly. Hence a person whose age is 45 is less *young* (degree 0.25) and more *middle age* (degree 0.75). □

Linguistic variables play an important role in applications and in particular in financial and management systems. For example, *truth*,[8] *confidence, stress, income, profit, inflation, risk, investment*, etc. can be understood to be linguistic variables.

2.5   Linguistic Modifiers

Let $x \in U$ and $\mathcal{A}$ is a fuzzy set with membership function $\mu_{\mathcal{A}}(x)$. We denote by m a *linguistic modifier*, for instance *very, not, fairly* (more or less), etc. Then by $m\mathcal{A}$ we mean a modified fuzzy set by m with membership function $\mu_{m\mathcal{A}}(x)$.

The following selections for $\mu_{m\mathcal{A}}(x)$ are often used to describe the modifiers *not, very,* and *fairly*:

$$\text{not,} \quad \mu_{not\mathcal{A}}(x) = 1 - \mu_{\mathcal{A}}(x), \tag{2.5}$$

$$\text{very,} \quad \mu_{very\mathcal{A}}(x) = [\mu_{\mathcal{A}}(x)]^2, \tag{2.6}$$

$$\text{fairly,} \quad \mu_{fairly\mathcal{A}}(x) = [\mu_{\mathcal{A}}(x)]^{\frac{1}{2}}. \tag{2.7}$$

Example 2.5

Consider the fuzzy set $\mathcal{A}$ describing the linguistic value *high score* (*high*) related to a loan scoring model defined as

x	0	20	40	60	80	100
$\mu_{high}(x)$	0	0.2	0.5	0.8	0.9	1

where x is a base variable over $U_1 = \{0, 20, 40, 60, 80, 100\}$, the universal set; it is numerical in nature and represents a discrete scale of the scores used in the model.

The graph of $\mu_{high}(x)$ is shown in Fig. 2.3. by dots.

The linguistic value *high score* can be modified to become *not high score, very high score,* and *fairly high score* by using (2.5)–(2.7). First let us find *not high score*:

$$\mu_{not\ high}(x) = 1 - \mu_{high}(x).$$

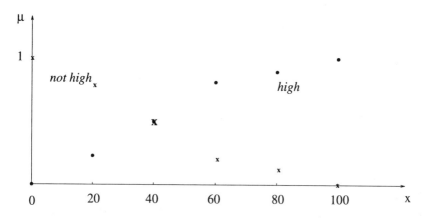

Fig. 2.3. Fuzzy sets *high score* (dots) and *not high score* (crosses).

Using the table for $\mu_{high}(x)$ we calculate

$$\mu_{not\ high}(0) = 1 - \mu_{high}(0) = 1 - 0 = 1,$$
$$\mu_{not\ high}(20) = 1 - \mu_{high}(20) = 1 - 0.2 = 0.8,$$
$$\mu_{not\ high}(40) = 1 - \mu_{high}(40) = 1 - 0.5 = 0.5,$$
$$\mu_{not\ high}(60) = 1 - \mu_{high}(60) = 1 - 0.8 = 0.2,$$
$$\mu_{not\ high}(80) = 1 - \mu_{high}(80) = 1 - 0.9 = 0.1,$$
$$\mu_{not\ high}(100) = 1 - \mu_{high}(100) = 1 - 1 = 0.$$

Hence for the fuzzy set *not high score* we obtain the table (see Fig. 2.3)

x	0	20	40	60	80	100
$\mu_{not\ high}(x)$	1	0.8	0.5	0.2	0.1	0

Similarly we construct the tables for the fuzzy sets *very high score* and *fairly high score*. The results are presented in Fig. 2.4.

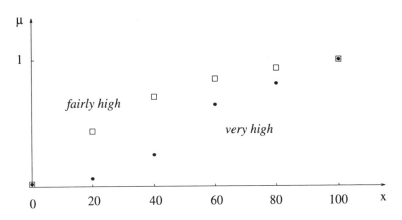

Fig. 2.4. Fuzzy sets *very high score* (dots) and *fairly high score* (squares).

$$\mu_{very\ high}(x) = [\mu_{high}(x)]^2.$$

x	0	20	40	60	80	100
$\mu_{very\ high}(x)$	0	0.04	0.25	0.64	0.81	1

$$\mu_{fairly\ high}(x) = [\mu_{fast}(x)]^{\frac{1}{2}}.$$

x	0	20	40	60	80	100
$\mu_{fairly\ high}(x)$	0	0.447	0.707	0.894	0.949	1

□

Example 2.6

The fuzzy set $\mathcal{B}$ describes the linguistic value *good credit* (*good*). The membership function of $\mathcal{B}$ is (see Fig. 2.5)

y	0	20	40	60	80	100
$\mu_{good}(y)$	0	0.2	0.4	0.7	1	1

where y is a base variable over $U_2 = \{0, 20, 40, 60, 80, 100\}$, the universal set; it is a discrete scale for credit rating similar to that in Example 2.5 concerning *high score*.

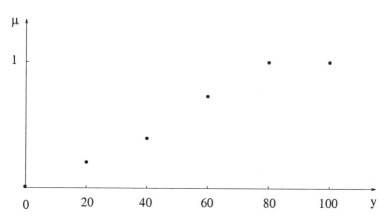

Fig. 2.5. Fuzzy set *good credit*.

Following Example 2.5 we modify *good credit* using (2.5)–(2.7). The results are given below.

y	0	20	40	60	80	100
$\mu_{not\ good}(y)$	1	0.8	0.6	0.3	0	0
$\mu_{very\ good}(y)$	0	0.04	0.16	0.49	1	1
$\mu_{fairly\ good}(y)$	0	0.45	0.63	0.84	1	1

□

The representation of $m\mathcal{A}$ should express the meaning of the linguistic modifier adequately. However there is no unique way to do this.

For instance the modifier *very* described by (2.6) can be expressed differently by a shift of the membership function $\mu_{\mathcal{A}}(x)$ to the right,

$$\mu_{very\mathcal{A}}(x) = \mu_{\mathcal{A}}(x - c), \quad a + c \leq x \leq b + c,$$

where $c > 0$ is a suitable constant (Fig. 2.6). Similarly *fairly* can be described by a shift of $\mu_{\mathcal{A}}(x)$ to the left.

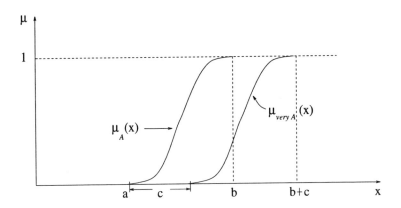

Fig. 2.6. Modifier *very* expressed by a shift.

Also $\mu_A(x)$ and $\mu_{very\ A}(x)$ can be defined as terms of a linguistic variable; this was already demonstrated in Example 2.1, Fig. 2.2 (*old* and *very old, young* and *very young*).

2.6   Composition Rules for Fuzzy Propositions

In two-valued logic a proposition p is true or false (Section 2.1). In many-valued logic and fuzzy logic the concept of proposition is considered in a broader context, i.e. a proposition is *true to a degree* in the interval [0, 1]. The truth of a proposition p in fuzzy logic is expressed by a fuzzy set, hence by its membership function.

Below are listed some important propositions involving the fuzzy sets $A = \{(x, \mu_A(x))\}$ and $B = \{(y, \mu_B(y))\}$.

(i) x is A,   proposition in *canonical form*;
(ii) x is mA,   *modified* proposition;
(iii) If x is A then y is B,   *conditional* proposition.

The propositions (i)–(iii) are illustrated in the following example.

Example 2.7

Let *high score* and *good credit* be described by the fuzzy sets defined in Examples 2.5 and 2.6.

(i) Client loan score is *high score* (canonical form).

(ii) Client loan score is a *very high score* (modified proposition).
(iii) If client loan score is *high score* then client loan credit is *good credit* (conditional proposition).

□

Operation *composition* consists of two propositions p and q joined by logical connectives.

The propositions are defined by

$$p \stackrel{\triangle}{=} x \text{ is } \mathcal{A}, \qquad q \stackrel{\triangle}{=} y \text{ is } \mathcal{B}, \qquad (2.8)$$

where $\mathcal{A}$ and $\mathcal{B}$ are the fuzzy sets (see Fig. 2.7)

$$\mathcal{A} = \{(x, \mu_{\mathcal{A}}(x)) | x \in A \subset U_1\}, \quad \mathcal{B} = \{(y, \mu_{\mathcal{B}}(y)) | y \in B \subset U_2\}. \quad (2.9)$$

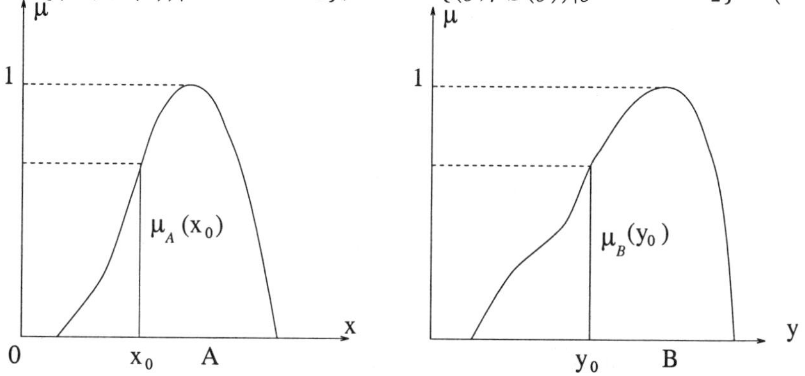

Fig. 2.7. Truth values $\mu_{\mathcal{A}}(x_0), \mu_{\mathcal{B}}(y_0)$.

We can give here the following interpretation. The membership grades $\mu_{\mathcal{A}}(x)$ and $\mu_{\mathcal{B}}(y)$ represent the truth values of the propositions (2.8), correspondingly. Conversely, the truth values of (2.8) are expressed by the membership functions $\mu_{\mathcal{A}}(x)$ and $\mu_{\mathcal{B}}(y)$. If x_0 and y_0 are specified values on the universes U_1 and U_2, respectively, then the truth values $\mu_{\mathcal{A}}(x_0), \mu_{\mathcal{B}}(y_0)$ of propositions x_0 is $\mathcal{A}$, y_0 is $\mathcal{B}$ are shown in Fig. 2.7 where the membership functions are assumed continuous.

Composition conjunction $p \wedge q$

The truth value (tr) of $p \wedge q$ (p *and* q) is defined by

$$\operatorname{tr}(p \wedge q) = \mu_{A \overset{\times}{\cdot} B}(x, y) = \min(\mu_A(x), \mu_B(y)), (x, y) \in A \times B, \quad (2.10)$$

where $\mu_{A \overset{\times}{\cdot} B}(x, y)$ is the membership function of the direct min product (Section 1.8 (1.21)).

Composition disjunction $p \vee q$

The truth value of $p \vee q$ (p *or* q) is defined by

$$\operatorname{tr}(p \vee q) = \mu_{A \overset{\cdot}{\times} B}(x, y) = \max(\mu_A(x), \mu_B(y)), (x, y) \in A \times B, \quad (2.11)$$

where $\mu_{A \overset{\cdot}{\times} B}(x, y)$ is the membership function of the direct max product (Section 1.8 (1.22)).

Composition implication $p \rightarrow q$

The truth value of $p \rightarrow q$ (*if* p ... *then* q) is defined by

$$\operatorname{tr}(p \rightarrow q) = \min(1, 1 - \mu_A(x) + \mu_B(y)), (x, y) \in A \times B, \quad (2.12)$$

meaning that to each pair (x, y) in the Cartesian product $A \times B$ we have to attach as a membership value the smaller between 1 and $1 - \mu_A(x) + \mu_B(y)$.

There are also several other definitions for composition implication (see for instance Mizumoto (1985)).

The rules (2.10)–(2.12) originate from the classical logic and many-valued logics of Łukasiewicz (see (2.2)–(2.4)).

The right hand sides of (2.10)–(2.12) are membership functions of *fuzzy relations* since (x, y) belongs to the Cartesian product $A \times B \subset U_1 \times U_2$. Hence the truth values of composition rules are presented by *fuzzy relations*.

In formulas (2.10)–(2.12) the notation tr which stands for truth could be omitted similarly to Chapter 1, Section 2.1.

It should be stressed that the membership functions of $\mathcal{A}$ and $\mathcal{B}$ (see 2.9) have different arguments, x and y, correspondingly. From this point of view the operations min (2.10) and max (2.11) expressing the logical connectives *and* and *or* differ from the operations min (1.9) and max (1.10) in Section 1.3.

Example 2.8

Consider two propositions p and q of the type (2.8) in canonical form defined by

$$p \overset{\triangle}{=} x \text{ is } high \text{ } score, \qquad q \overset{\triangle}{=} y \text{ is } good \text{ } credit,$$

related to a loan scoring model where *high score* is the fuzzy set $\mathcal{A}$ in Example 2.5 defined on the universe U_1 (operating domain of x representing client loan score) and *good credit* is the fuzzy set $\mathcal{B}$ in Example 2.6, defined on the universe U_2 (operating domain of y representing client credit rating).

(i) The truth value of composition conjunction (2.10) is the membership function $\mu_{A \times B}(x, y)$ of the relation $\mathcal{R}$ presented on Table 2.6.

Table 2.6. Truth value of x *is high score and* y *is good credit.*

		B				
	y $\\$ 0	20	40	60	80	100
x						
0	0	0	0	0	0	0
20	0	0.2	0.2	0.2	0.2	0.2
40	0	0.2	0.4	0.5	0.5	0.5
60	0	0.2	0.4	0.7	0.8	0.8
80	0	0.2	0.4	0.7	0.9	0.9
100	0	0.2	0.4	0.7	1	1

(with A labelling the rows $x = 0,20,40,60,80,100$)

To construct the table we use the direct min product (2.10), i.e. consider all ordered pairs $(x_i, y_j), x_i \in A, y_j \in B$ in the Cartesian product $A \times B$ and in the cell (x_i, y_j), located at the intersection of row x_i and column y_j, write the smaller value of $\mu_A(x_i)$ and $\mu_B(y_j)$. For instance let us calculate the truth values in the third row in Table 2.6 when $x = 40$ and y takes the values in B:

$$\mu_{high}(40) = 0.5 > \mu_{good}(0) = 0, \quad \mu_{A \times B}(40, 0) = 0$$
$$\mu_{high}(40) = 0.5 > \mu_{good}(20) = 0.2, \quad \mu_{A \times B}(40, 40) = 0.2$$
$$\mu_{high}(40) = 0.5 > \mu_{good}(40) = 0.4, \quad \mu_{A \times B}(40, 40) = 0.4$$
$$\mu_{high}(40) = 0.5 < \mu_{good}(60) = 0.7, \quad \mu_{A \times B}(40, 60) = 0.5$$

$$\mu_{high}(40) = 0.5 < \mu_{good}(80) = 1, \quad \mu_{A \times B}(40, 80) = 0.5$$
$$\mu_{high}(40) = 0.5 < \mu_{good}(100) = 1, \quad \mu_{A \times B}(40, 100) = 0.5.$$

(ii) To find the truth value of composition disjunction (2.11) we use the direct max product and proceed like in case (i) with the only difference that in the cell (x_i, y_i) we write the larger value of $\mu_A(x_i)$ and $\mu_B(y_i)$.

(iii) To find the truth value of composition implication (2.12) for each pair $(x_i, y_j) \in A \times B$ we calculate $1 - \mu_A(x_i) + \mu_B(y_j)$ and then take this value if it is smaller than 1; otherwise we take 1.

□

2.7 Semantic Entailment

Semantic entailment concerns *inclusion* of fuzzy sets taking part in propositions. Consider the propositions

$$p \stackrel{\triangle}{=} x \text{ is } \mathcal{A}, \qquad q \stackrel{\triangle}{=} x \text{ is } \mathcal{B},$$

both defined on the same universe U. We say that proposition p *semantically entails* proposition q (or q is *semantically entailed* by p), denoted by

$$p \to q \tag{2.13}$$

if and only if

$$\mu_A(x) \leq \mu_B(x), \quad x \in U. \tag{2.14}$$

The meaning of (2.13), based upon the concept of subset (2.14) introduced in Section 1.3, is that p brings as an inevitable consequence q in the sense that q is less specific than p.

Example 2.9

The proposition

$$p \stackrel{\triangle}{=} \text{Client loan score is a very high score}$$

semantically entails the proposition

$$q \stackrel{\triangle}{=} \text{Client loan score is a high score}$$

no matter how the linguistic variable *high score* is defined. Hence from
the proposition *Client loan score is a very high score* we may infer that
Client loan score is a high score. We say that the *semantic entailment
is strong.*

To be more specific assume that *high* and *very high* are defined as
they appear in Examples 2.5 (see Figs. 2.3 and 2.4). Clearly (2.14) is
satisfied since

$$\mu_{very\ high}(x) \leq \mu_{high}(x).$$

□

Example 2.10

The proposition

$$p \overset{\triangle}{=} Client\ loan\ score\ is\ not\ a\ high\ score$$

may or may not *semantically entail* the proposition

$$q \overset{\triangle}{=} Client\ loan\ score\ is\ a\ low\ score$$

depending on how the fuzzy sets *high* and *low* are defined. In this case
we say the *semantic entailment is not strong.*

Let us assume that *not high* is defined as in Example 2.5 (Fig. 2.3)
and *low* is defined below (the universe U is the same) in two slightly
different ways

x	0	20	40	60	80	100
$\mu_{low}^{(1)}(x)$	1	0.85	0.6	0.3	0.2	0.1
$\mu_{low}^{(2)}(x)$	1	0.7	0.4	0.2	0.15	0.1

Clearly (see Fig. 2.8)

$$\mu_{not\ high}(x) \leq \mu_{low}^{(1)}(x), \qquad \mu_{not\ high}(x) \approx \mu_{low}^{(2)}(x),$$

hence the semantic entailment is not strong; if *low* is defined by $\mu_{low}^{(1)}(x)$,
(2.14) is satisfied; if *low* is defined by $\mu_{low}^{(2)}(x)$, (2.14) is not satisfied.

From the proposition *Client loan score is not a high score* we may
or may not infer that *Client loan score is a low score.*

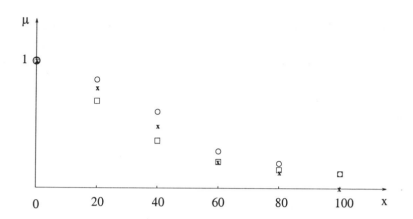

Fig. 2.8. Fuzzy sets *not high* (crosses), *low* (1) (circles), *low* (2) (squares).

□

Semantic entailment plays an important role in fuzzy logic as a main *rule of inference* known as *entailment principle* in the sense that the validity of proposition q is inferred from the validity of proposition p (see (2.13)) if and only if (2.14) holds.

The entailment principle can be generalized for more that two proposition. For instance, if $p \overset{\triangle}{=} x$ is $\mathcal{A}$, $q \overset{\triangle}{=} x$ is $\mathcal{B}$, $r \overset{\triangle}{=} x$ is $\mathcal{C}$, and $\mu_{\mathcal{A}}(x), \mu_{\mathcal{B}}(x), \mu_{\mathcal{C}}(x)$ are the corresponding membership functions, we have

$$p \to q \to r$$

if and only if

$$\mu_{\mathcal{A}}(x) \leq \mu_{\mathcal{B}}(x) \leq \mu_{\mathcal{C}}(x).$$

2.8   Notes

1. Classical (two-valued) logic has its roots in the work of George Boole (1815–1864) after whom *Boolean algebra*, a branch of classical logic, is named.

   The modern two-valued logic started with the book *Begriffsschrift* (1879) by Gottlob Frege (1848–1925), for whom the meaning of logic is based on the rules for manipulating symbols and the propositional connectives *not, or, and, if . . . then.*

Charles Peirce (1839–1914) who made important contributions to the two-valued logic in his study *On the Algebra of Logic* (1880) may be considered as one of the pioneers of many-valued logic. He wrote: "Vagueness is no more to be done away with in the world of logic than friction in mechanics."

Further advancement in two-valued logic and its use to formalize mathematics was made by Bertrand Russell (logician and philosopher) and Alfread Whitehead (mathematician and philosopher) in their fundamental work *Principia Mathematica* which appeared in three volumes between 1910–1913.

2. In order to be more precise while denoting propositions and their truth values in this Chapter we may use $tr\ p$ to express the truth value of p. Then for instance formula (2.2) will take the form

$$tr(p \wedge q) = \min(tr\ p,\ tr\ q),$$

where $tr\ p$ and $tr\ q$ belong to the set $\{0, 1\}$.

3. The truth tables were introduced by the philosopher Ludwig Wittgenstein (1889–1951) in *Tractatus Logico-Philosophicus* (1922). He made significant contributions to the philosophy of mathematics.

4. The origins of many-valued logics can be traced back to ancient Greek philosophy. Aristotle (384–322 B.C.) himself, the father of logic, made remarks about the problematic truth values of propositions expressing future events. In *Metaphysics* he wrote *"The more and less are still present in the nature of things."*

5. The three-valued logic was established independently by J. Łukasiewicz (1920) and E. Post (1921). They also introduced many-valued logics.

6. The many-valued logic is a generalization, not a rejection, of the classical two-valued logic. The many-valued logic only dismantles the philosophical illusions about the absoluteness of classical logic and proposes a more general approach towards solving logical problems.

7. A part of fuzzy logic is *possibility theory* introduced by Zadeh (1978). The basic concept of possibility theory is that of *possibility distribution*. The membership function $\mu_A(x)$ of a fuzzy set A can be considered as a constraint or restriction on the values (grades, degrees of membership) that can be assigned to $x \in U$. In other words, the degree of membership $\mu \in [0,1]$ is interpreted as a possibility level $\pi \in [0,1]$. The fuzzy set A is interpreted as a possibility distribution $\Pi(x)$; to the membership function $\mu_A(x)$ corresponds the function $\pi(x)$ describing the possibility distribution $\Pi(x)$; $\pi(x) \in [0,1]$; actually $\pi(x) = \mu_A(x)$.

8. Perhaps the most important linguistic variable is *truth*. It is described by a fuzzy set with membership function $\mu_{true}(x)$, $\mu \in [0,1]$ (we are using *true* instead of *truth*). *False* is interpreted as *not true*.

Truth and its terms have been defined differently in fuzzy logic. We consider first the simplest definition introduced by Baldwin (1979)

$$true \triangleq \{(x, \mu_{true}(x)) \mid x \in [0,1], \mu_{true}(x) = x, \mu \in [0,1]\}.$$

The modifiers (2.5)–(2.7) applied to $\mu_{true}(x) = x$ give that

$$\mu_{not\ true}(x) = \mu_{false}(x) = 1 - x,$$
$$\mu_{very\ true}(x) = [\mu_{true}(x)]^2 = x^2,$$
$$\mu_{fairly\ true}(x) = [\mu_{true}(x)]^{\frac{1}{2}} = x^{\frac{1}{2}}.$$

Similarly one can define

$$\mu_{very\ false}(x) = (1 - x)^2, \quad \mu_{fairly\ false}(x) = (1 - x)^{\frac{1}{2}}.$$

The extreme case $x = 1$ in $\mu_{true}(x) = x$ gives the singleton $\mu_{absolute\ true}(1) = 1$; then it follows that $\mu_{absolute\ false}(0) = 1$.

The linguistic variables *truth* and *false* are shown in Fig. 2.9. On the same figure are shown also their modifications and the modified modifications:

$$\mu_{very\ very\ true}(x) = [\mu_{very\ true}(x)]^2 = x^4,$$
$$\mu_{very\ very\ false}(x) = [\mu_{very\ false}(x)]^2 = (1 - x)^4.$$

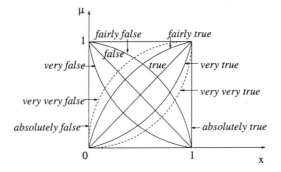

Fig. 2.9. Linguistic variable *truth* and various modifications.

Zadeh (1975) defined *truth* by the membership function (Fig. 2.10)

$$\mu_{true}(x) = \begin{cases} 0 & \text{for } 0 \leq x \leq a, \\ 2\left(\frac{x-a}{1-a}\right)^2 & \text{for } a \leq x \leq \frac{a+1}{2}, \\ 1 - \left(\frac{x-1}{1-a}\right)^2 & \text{for } \frac{a+1}{2} \leq x \leq 1. \end{cases}$$

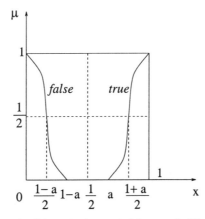

Fig. 2.10. Linguistic variable *truth* (Zadeh).

Here $1 + \frac{a}{2}$ is the crossover point. The parameter $a \in [0,1]$ indicates the subjective selection of the minimum value of a in such a way that for $x > a$ the degree of truth is positive, i.e. $\mu_{true}(a) > 0$. The membership function of *false* is defined by $\mu_{false}(x) = \mu_{true}(1-x)$. The terms $\mu_{very\ true}(x)$ and $\mu_{fairly\ true}(x)$ can be calculated from (2.6) and (2.7).

Chapter 3

Fuzzy Averaging for Forecasting

Forecasting[1] provides the basis for any production activity. The ability to predict and estimate future events requires the study of imprecise data information coming from a rapidly changing environment, a task for which fuzzy logic is better suited to deal with than classical methods. Analysis of complex situations needs the efforts and opinions of many experts. The experts opinions, almost never identical, are either more or less close or more or less conflicting. They have to be combined or aggregated in order to produce one conclusion. In this chapter the methodology of fuzzy averaging is introduced. It is used as a major tool for aggregation in various forecasting models (fuzzy Delphi, project management, forecasting demand). In Chapter 4 fuzzy averaging is applied to decision making.

3.1 Statistical Average

One of the most important concepts in statistics is the *average* or *mean* of n measurements, readings, or estimates expressed by real numbers $r_1, \ldots, r_n$. It is defined by

$$r_{ave} = \frac{r_1 + \cdots + r_n}{n} = \frac{\sum_{i=1}^{n} r_i}{n};$$

(3.1)

the measurements are considered of equal importance. The average which is typical or representative of n measurements is also known as a *measure of central tendency*.

If the measurements $r_1, \ldots, r_n$ have different importance expressed by the real numbers $\lambda_1, \ldots, \lambda_n$, correspondingly, then the concept of *weighted average* or *weighted mean* is introduced by the formula

$$r_{ave}^w = \frac{\lambda_1 r_1 + \cdots + \lambda_n r_n}{\lambda_1 + \cdots + \lambda_n} = w_1 r_1 + \cdots + w_n r_n = \sum_{i=1}^{n} w_i r_i. \quad (3.2)$$

Here w_i called *weights* are given by

$$w_i = \frac{\lambda_i}{\lambda_1 + \cdots + \lambda_n}, \quad i = 1, \ldots, n, \quad w_1 + \cdots + w_n = \sum_{i=1}^{n} w_i = 1. \quad (3.3)$$

The weights reflect the relative importance or strength of the measurements r_i.

The concept of average, we may call it *crisp average*, can be generalized by substituting fuzzy numbers for the real numbers r_i in formulas (3.1) and (3.2). For that purpose arithmetic operations with fuzzy numbers have to be performed, which in general requires complicated computations. Here we restrict the generalization procedure to triangular and trapezoidal numbers. They are used very often in applications and besides, it is easy to perform arithmetic operations with them; this is demonstrated in the next section.[2]

3.2   Arithmetic Operations with Triangular and Trapezoidal Numbers

Addition of triangular numbers

It can be proved that the sum of two triangular numbers $\mathbf{A}_1 = (a_1^{(1)}, a_M^{(1)}, a_2^{(1)})$ and $\mathbf{A}_2 = (a_1^{(2)}, a_M^{(2)}, a_2^{(2)})$, is also a triangular number,

$$
\begin{aligned}
\mathbf{A}_1 + \mathbf{A}_2 &= (a_1^{(1)}, a_M^{(1)}, a_2^{(1)}) + (a_1^{(2)}, a_M^{(2)}, a_2^{(2)}) \\
&= (a_1^{(1)} + a_1^{(2)}, a_M^{(1)} + a_M^{(2)}, a_2^{(1)} + a_2^{(2)}). \quad (3.4)
\end{aligned}
$$

This summation formula can be extended for n triangular numbers. Also it can be applied for left and right triangular numbers (Section 1.5). For instance:

$$
\begin{aligned}
\mathbf{A}_1^r + \mathbf{A}_2 &= (a_M^{(1)}, a_M^{(1)}, a_2^{(1)}) + (a_1^{(2)}, a_M^{(2)}, a_2^{(2)}) \\
&= (a_M^{(1)} + a_1^{(2)}, a_M^{(1)} + a_M^{(2)}, a_2^{(1)} + a_2^{(2)}),
\end{aligned}
$$

$$
\begin{aligned}
\mathbf{A}_1^l + \mathbf{A}_2^l &= (a_1^{(1)}, a_M^{(1)}, a_M^{(1)}) + (a_1^{(2)}, a_M^{(2)}, a_M^{(2)}) \\
&= (a_1^{(1)} + a_1^{(2)}, a_M^{(1)} + a_M^{(2)}, a_M^{(1)} + a_M^{(2)}).
\end{aligned}
$$

Example 3.1

The sum of the triangular numbers

$$
\mathbf{A}_1 = (-5, -2, 1), \qquad \mathbf{A}_2 = (-3, 4, 12),
$$

according to (3.4) is the triangular number

$$
\mathbf{A}_1 + \mathbf{A}_2 = (-5 + (-3), -2 + 4, 1 + 12) = (-8, 2, 13)
$$

shown on Fig. 3.1.

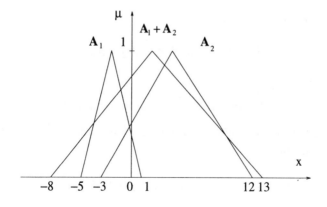

Fig. 3.1. Sum of two triangular numbers.

Figure 3.1 can be interpreted as follows. If $\mathbf{A}_1$ describes real numbers close to -2 and $\mathbf{A}_2$ describes real numbers close to 4, then $\mathbf{A}_1 + \mathbf{A}_2$ represents real numbers close to $-2 + 4 = 2$.

$\square$

Example 3.2

Now let us find the sum of three triangular numbers:

$$\mathbf{A}_1^r = (0, 0, 2), \quad \mathbf{A}_2 = (1, 3, 4), \quad \mathbf{A}_3^l = (3, 6, 6);$$

$\mathbf{A}_1^r$ and $\mathbf{A}_3^l$ are right and left triangular numbers. The extended formula (3.4) gives (see Fig. 3.2)

$$\mathbf{A}_1^r + \mathbf{A}_2 + \mathbf{A}_3^l = (0 + 1 + 3, 0 + 3 + 6, 2 + 4 + 6) = (4, 9, 12).$$

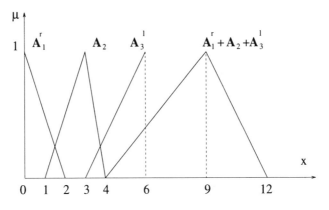

Fig. 3.2. Sum of $\mathbf{A}_1^r$, $\mathbf{A}_2$, and $\mathbf{A}_3^l$.

$\square$

Multiplication of a triangular number by a real number

The product of a triangular number $\mathbf{A}$ with a real number r is also a triangular number,

$$\mathbf{A}r = r\mathbf{A} = r(a_1, a_M, a_2) = (ra_1, ra_M, ra_2). \quad (3.5)$$

Division of a triangular number by a real number

This operations is defined as multiplication of **A** by $\frac{1}{r}$ provided that $r \neq 0$. Hence (3.5) gives

$$\frac{\mathbf{A}}{r} = \frac{1}{r}(a_1, a_M, a_2) = (\frac{a_1}{r}, \frac{a_M}{r}, \frac{a_2}{r}). \tag{3.6}$$

Example 3.3

(a) The product of **A** $= (2, 4, 5)$ by 2 according to (3.5) is (see Fig. 3.3)

$$2\mathbf{A} = 2(2, 4, 5) = (4, 8, 10).$$

(b) The division of **A** $= (2, 4, 5)$ by 2 using (3.6) produces (Fig. 3.3)

$$\frac{\mathbf{A}}{2} = \frac{1}{2}(2, 4, 5) = (1, 2, 2.5).$$

(c) Also

$$\frac{2\mathbf{A}}{2} = \frac{(4, 8, 10)}{2} = \mathbf{A}, \quad 2(\frac{\mathbf{A}}{2}) = 2(1, 2, 2.5) = \mathbf{A}.$$

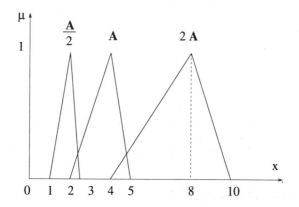

Fig. 3.3. Triangular number **A** $= (2, 4, 5)$; product 2**A**; quotient $\frac{\mathbf{A}}{2}$.

□

Operations with trapezoidal numbers can be performed similarly to those with triangular numbers.

Addition of trapezoidal numbers

The sum of the trapezoidal numbers $\mathbf{A}_1 = (a_1^{(1)}, b_1^{(1)}, b_2^{(1)}, a_2^{(1)})$ and $\mathbf{A}_2 = (a_1^{(2)}, b_1^{(2)}, b_2^{(2)}, a_2^{(2)})$ is also a trapezoidal number,

$$
\begin{aligned}
\mathbf{A}_1 + \mathbf{A}_2 &= (a_1^{(1)}, b_1^{(1)}, b_2^{(1)}, a_2^{(1)}) + (a_1^{(2)}, b_1^{(2)}, b_2^{(2)}, a_2^{(2)}) \\
&= (a_1^{(1)} + a_1^{(2)}, b_1^{(1)} + b_1^{(2)}, b_2^{(1)} + b_2^{(2)}, a_2^{(1)} + a_2^{(2)}). \quad (3.7)
\end{aligned}
$$

Formula (3.7) can be generalized for n trapezoidal numbers and also for left and right trapezoidal numbers.

Multiplication of a trapezoidal number by a real number

$$
\mathbf{A}r = r\mathbf{A} = (ra_1, rb_1, rb_2, ra_2). \quad (3.8)
$$

Division of a trapezoidal number by a real number

$$
\frac{\mathbf{A}}{r} = \frac{1}{r}\mathbf{A} = \left(\frac{a_1}{r}, \frac{b_1}{r}, \frac{b_2}{r}, \frac{a_2}{r}\right), \quad r \neq 0. \quad (3.9)
$$

Sum of triangular and trapezoidal numbers

Consider the triangular number $\mathbf{A}_1 = (a_1^{(1)}, a_M^{(1)}, a_2^{(1)})$ which can be presented as a trapezoidal number $(a_1^{(1)}, a_M^{(1)}, a_M^{(1)}, a_2^{(1)})$ and the trapezoidal number $\mathbf{A}_2 = (a_1^{(2)}, b_1^{(2)}, b_2^{(2)}, a_2^{(2)})$. Using (3.7) gives

$$
\begin{aligned}
\mathbf{A}_1 + \mathbf{A}_2 &= (a_1^{(1)}, a_M^{(1)}, a_M^{(1)}, a_2^{(1)}) + (a_1^{(2)}, b_1^{(2)}, b_2^{(2)}, a_2^{(2)}) \\
&= (a_1^{(1)} + a_1^{(2)}, a_M^{(1)} + b_1^{(2)}, a_M^{(1)} + b_2^{(2)}, a_2^{(1)} + a_2^{(2)}). \quad (3.10)
\end{aligned}
$$

3.3 Fuzzy Averaging

Triangular average formula

Consider n triangular numbers $\mathbf{A}_i = (a_1^{(i)}, a_M^{(i)}, a_2^{(i)}), i = 1, \ldots, n$. Using addition of triangular numbers and division by a real number (see (3.4) and (3.6)) gives the *triangular average (mean)* $\mathbf{A}_{ave}$,

$$\mathbf{A}_{ave} = \frac{\mathbf{A}_1 + \cdots + \mathbf{A}_n}{n}$$

$$= \frac{(a_1^{(1)}, a_M^{(1)}, a_2^{(1)}) + \cdots + (a_1^{(n)}, a_M^{(n)}, a_2^{(n)})}{n}$$

$$= \frac{(\sum_{i=1}^{n} a_1^{(i)}, \sum_{i=1}^{n} a_M^{(i)}, \sum_{i=1}^{n} a_2^{(i)})}{n},$$

which is a triangular number,

$$\mathbf{A}_{ave} = (m_1, m_M, m_2) = (\frac{1}{n} \sum_{i=1}^{n} a_1^{(i)}, \frac{1}{n} \sum_{i=1}^{n} a_1^{(i)}, \frac{1}{n} \sum_{i=1}^{n} a_2^{(i)}). \qquad (3.11)$$

Example 3.4

(a) The triangular numbers $\mathbf{A}_1$ and $\mathbf{A}_2$ in Example 3.1 have average

$$\mathbf{A}_{ave} = \frac{\mathbf{A}_1 + \mathbf{A}_2}{2} = \frac{(-8, 2, 13)}{2} = (-4, 1, 6.5).$$

(b) The triangular numbers $\mathbf{A}_1^r, \mathbf{A}_2$, and $\mathbf{A}_3^l$ in Example 3.2 have average

$$\mathbf{A}_{ave} = \frac{\mathbf{A}_1^r + \mathbf{A}_2 + \mathbf{A}_3^l}{3} = \frac{(4, 9, 12)}{3} = (1.33, 3, 4).$$

$\square$

Weighted triangular average formula

If the real numbers λ_i represent the importance of $\mathbf{A}_i = (a_1^{(i)}, a_M^{(i)}, a_2^{(i)})$, $i = 1, \ldots, n$, then following (3.2), using (3.3), and similarly to (3.11) we obtain the *weighted triangular average (mean)*,

$$\mathbf{A}_{ave}^w = \frac{\lambda_1 \mathbf{A}_1 + \cdots + \lambda_n \mathbf{A}_n}{\lambda_1 + \cdots + \lambda_n}$$

$$= w_1(a_1^{(1)}, a_M^{(1)}, a_2^{(1)}) + \cdots + w_n(a_1^{(n)}, a_M^{(n)}, a_2^{(n)})$$

$$= (w_1 a_1^{(1)}, w_1 a_M^{(1)}, w_1 a_2^{(1)}) + \cdots + (w_n a_1^{(n)}, w_n a_M^{(n)}, w_2^{(n)})$$

$$= (w_1 a_1^{(1)} + \cdots + w_n a_1^{(n)}, w_1 a_M^{(1)} + \cdots + w_n a_M^{(n)},$$

$$w_1 a_2^{(1)} + \cdots + w_n a_2^{(n)}),$$

which can be written as

$$\mathbf{A}_{ave}^w = (m_1^w, m_M^w, m_2^w) = (\sum_{i=1}^{n} w_i a_1^{(i)}, \sum_{i=1}^{n} w_i a_M^{(i)}, \sum_{i=1}^{n} w_i a_2^{(i)}). \quad (3.12)$$

Average formulas for trapezoidal numbers which can be derived similarly to (3.11) and (3.12) are presented below.

Trapezoidal average formula

If $\mathbf{A}_i = (a_1^{(i)}, b_1^{(i)}, b_2^{(i)}, a_2^{(i)}), i = 1, \ldots, n$, are trapezoidal numbers, then

$$
\begin{aligned}
\mathbf{A}_{ave} &= (m_1, m_{M_1}, m_{M_2}, m_2) \\
&= \frac{(a_1^{(1)}, b_1^{(1)}, b_2^{(1)}, a_2^{(1)}) + \cdots + (a_1^{(n)}, b_1^{(n)}, b_2^{(n)}, a_2^{(n)})}{n} \\
&= \frac{(\sum_{i=1}^{n} a_1^{(i)}, \sum_{i=1}^{n} b_1^{(i)}, \sum_{i=1}^{n} b_2^{(i)}, \sum_{i=1}^{n} a_2^{(i)})}{n}. \quad (3.13)
\end{aligned}
$$

Weighted trapezoidal average formula

$$
\begin{aligned}
\mathbf{A}_{ave}^w &= (m_1^w, m_{M_1}^w, m_{M_2}^w, m_2^w) \\
&= w_1(a_1^{(1)}, b_1^{(1)}, b_2^{(1)}, a_2^{(1)}) + \cdots + w_n(a_1^{(n)}, b_1^{(n)}, b_2^{(n)}, a_2^{(n)}) \\
&= (\sum_{i=1}^{n} w_i a_1^{(i)}, \sum_{i=1}^{n} w_i b_1^{(i)}, \sum_{i=1}^{n} w_i b_2^{(i)}, \sum_{i=1}^{n} w_i a_2^{(i)}). \quad (3.14)
\end{aligned}
$$

The triangular and trapezoidal average and weighted average formulas (3.11)–(3.14) produce a result which can be interpreted as follows. It is a *conclusion* or *aggregation* of all combined meanings expressed by triangular and trapezoidal numbers $\mathbf{A}_1, \ldots, \mathbf{A}_n$ considered either of equal importance or of different importance expressed by weights w_i.

Based on the arithmetic operations in Section 3.2, we can state that:

1) Formulas (3.11)–(3.14) remain valid when some of $\mathbf{A}_i$ are left or right triangular or trapezoidal numbers.

2) Formulas (3.13) and (3.14) for trapezoidal numbers remain valid when some $\mathbf{A}_i$ are triangular numbers since they can be expressed in the form of trapezoidal numbers.

The process of averaging presented here is a cross section of classical statistics and fuzzy sets theory; it belongs to a new branch of science— *fuzzy statistics*.

Defuzzification of fuzzy average

The aggregation defined by a triangular or trapezoidal average number ((3.11)–(3.14)) very often has to be expressed by a crisp value which represent best the corresponding average. This operation is called *defuzzification*.

First consider the defuzzification of $\mathbf{A}_{ave} = (m_1, m_M, m_2)$ given in (3.11). It looks plausible to select for that purpose the value m_M in the supporting interval $[m_1, m_2]$ of $\mathbf{A}_{ave}$; m_M has the highest degree (one) of membership in $\mathbf{A}_{ave}$. In other words, $\mathbf{A}_{ave}$ attains its maximum at

$$x_{\max} = m_M \tag{3.15}$$

which we call *maximizing value*.

However the operation defuzzification can not be defined uniquely. Here we present three options for defuzzifying $\mathbf{A}_{ave} = (m_1, m_M, m_2)$ which are essentially statistical average formulas:

$$
\begin{aligned}
(1) \quad & x_{\max}^{(1)} = \frac{m_1 + m_M + m_2}{3}, \\[6pt]
(2) \quad & x_{\max}^{(2)} = \frac{m_1 + 2m_M + m_2}{4}, \\[6pt]
(3) \quad & x_{\max}^{(3)} = \frac{m_1 + 4m_M + m_2}{6}.
\end{aligned}
\tag{3.16}
$$

Contrary to (3.15), the values (3.16) take into consideration the contribution of m_1 and m_2 but give different weight to m_M.

If the triangular number $\mathbf{A}_{ave}$ is close to a central triangular number (see Fig. 1.18 (a)) meaning that m_M is almost in the middle of $[m_1, m_2]$, then (3.15) gives a good crisp value $x_{\max} = m_M$. Then the three average formulas (1)–(3) in (3.16) also produce numbers (maximizing values) close to m_M hence there is no need to be used. Usually in applications the triangular average numbers appear to be in central form. However, the experts dealing with a given situation have to use their judgement when selecting a maximizing value.

The defuzzification procedure is presented as a block diagram in Fig. 3.4.

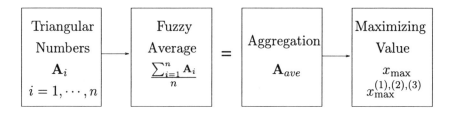

Fig. 3.4. Defuzzification of fuzzy average $\mathbf{A}_{ave} = (m_1, m_2, m_3)$.

For the defuzzification of $\mathbf{A}_{ave}^{w} = (m_1^{w}, m_M^{w}, m_2^{w})$ formulas (3.15) and (3.16) remains valid provided $m_1^{w}, m_M^{w}, m_2^{w}$ are substituted for m_1, m_M, m_2 correspondingly.

The defuzzification of the trapezoidal average $\mathbf{A}_{ave} = (m_1, m_{M_1}, m_{M_2}, m_2)$ can be performed by an extension of (3.15) and (3.16) using instead of m_M the midpoint of the flat segment $m_{M_1} m_{M_2}$ at maximum level $\alpha = 1$. The maximizing values are as follows:

$$x_{\max} = \frac{m_{M_1} + m_{M_2}}{2}, \tag{3.17}$$

and

$$(1) \quad x_{\max}^{(1)} = \frac{m_1 + \frac{m_{M_1} + m_{M_2}}{2} + m_2}{3},$$

$$(2) \quad x_{\max}^{(2)} = \frac{m_1 + m_{M_1} + m_{M_2} + m_2}{4}, \tag{3.18}$$

$$(3) \quad x_{\max}^{(3)} = \frac{m_1 + 2(m_{M_1} + m_{M_2}) + m_2}{6}.$$

For the defuzzification of $\mathbf{A}_{ave}^{w} = (m_1^{w}, m_{M_1}^{w}, m_{M_2}^{w}, m_2^{w})$ formulas (3.17) and (3.18) hold but $m_1^{w}, m_{M_1}^{w}, m_{M_2}^{w}, m_2^{w}$ have to be substituted for $m_1, m_{M_1}, m_{M_2}, m_2$.

Similar block diagrams like that on Fig. 3.4. can be constructed to illustrate defuzzification for the fuzzy averages (3.12)–(3.14).

3.4 Fuzzy Delphi Method for Forecasting

Fuzzy Delphi method is a generalization of the classical method for long range forecasting in management science known as *Delphi method.* It was developed in the sixties by the Rand Corporation at Santa Monica, California. The name comes from the ancient Greek oracles of Delphi who were famous for forecasting the future.

The essence of Delphi method can be described as follows:

(i) Experts with high qualification regarding a subject are requested to give their opinion separately and independently of each other about the realization dates of a certain event, say in science, technology, or business. They may be asked to forecast the general state of the market, economy, technological advances, etc.

(ii) The data which have subjective character are analyzed statistically by finding their average (see (3.1)) and the results are communicated to the experts.

(iii) The experts review the results and provide new estimates which are analyzed statistically and sent again to the experts for estimation.

(iv) This process could be repeated again and again until the outcome converges to a reasonable solution from the point of view of a manager or a governing body. Usually two or three repetitions are sufficient.

However, long range forecasting problems involve imprecise and incomplete data information. Also the decisions made by the experts rely on their individual competence and are subjective. Therefore it is more appropriate the data to be presented by fuzzy numbers instead of crisp numbers. Especially triangular numbers are very suitable for that purpose since they are constructed easily by specifying three values, the smallest, the largest, and the most plausible (see Section 1.5). Instead of crisp average, the analysis will be based on fuzzy average.

The Fuzzy Delphi method was introduced by Kaufman and Gupta (1988). It consists of the following steps.

Step 1. Experts $E_i, i = 1, \ldots, n$, are asked to provide the possible realization dates of a certain event in science, technology, or business, namely: the earlist date $a_1^{(i)}$, the most plausible date $a_M^{(i)}$, and the latest date $a_2^{(i)}$. The data given by the experts E_i are presented in the form of triangular numbers

$$\mathbf{A}_i = (a_1^{(i)}, a_M^{(i)}, a_2^{(i)}), \quad i = 1, \ldots, n. \tag{3.19}$$

Step 2. First, the average (mean) $\mathbf{A}_{ave} = (m_1, m_M, m_2)$ of all $\mathbf{A}_i$ is computed (see (3.11)).

Then for each expert E_i the *deviation* between $\mathbf{A}_{ave}$ and $\mathbf{A}_i$ is computed. It is a triangular number defined by

$$\mathbf{A}_{ave} - \mathbf{A}_i = (m_1 - a_1^{(i)}, m_M - a_M^{(i)}, m_2 - a_2^{(i)})$$
$$= \left(\frac{1}{n} \sum_{i=1}^n a_1^{(i)} - a_1^{(i)}, \frac{1}{n} \sum_{i=1}^n a_M^{(i)} - a_M^{(i)}, \frac{1}{n} \sum_{i=1}^n a_2^{(i)} - a_2^{(i)} \right). \tag{3.20}$$

The deviation $\mathbf{A}_{ave} - \mathbf{A}_i$ is sent back to the expert E_i for reexamination.

Step 3. Each expert E_i presents a new triangular number

$$\mathbf{B}_i = (b_1^{(i)}, b_M^{(i)}, b_2^{(i)}), \quad i = 1, \ldots, n. \tag{3.21}$$

This process starting with *Step 2* is repeated. The triangular average $\mathbf{B}_m$ is calculated according to formula (3.11) with the difference that now $a_1^{(i)}, a_M^{(i)}, a_2^{(i)}$ are substituted correspondingly by $b_1^{(i)}, b_M^{(i)}, b_2^{(i)}$. If necessary, new triangular numbers $\mathbf{C}^{(i)} = (c_1^{(i)}, c_M^{(i)}, c_2^{(i)})$ are generated and their average $\mathbf{C}_m$ is calculated. The process could be repeated again and again until two successive means $\mathbf{A}_{ave}, \mathbf{B}_{ave}, \mathbf{C}_{ave}, \ldots$ become reasonably close.

Step 4. At a later time the forecasting may be reexamined by the same process if there is important information available due to new discoveries.

Fuzzy Delphi method is a typical multi-experts forecasting procedure for combining views and opinions.

Case Study 1 *Time Estimation for Technical Realization of an Innovative Product*[3]

A group of 15 computer experts are asked to give estimation using Fuzzy Delphi method for the technical realization of a brand new product, say a cognitive information processing computer. They are ranked equally hence their opinions carry the same weight. The triangular numbers $\mathbf{A}_i, i = 1, \ldots, 15$ (see (3.19)) presented by the experts are shown on Table 3.1.

Table 3.1. Triangular numbers $\mathbf{A}_i$ presented by experts (first request).

E_i	$\mathbf{A}_i$	Earliest date	Most plausible date	Lates date
E_1	$\mathbf{A}_1$	$a_1^{(1)} = 1995$	$a_M^{(1)} = 2003$	$a_2^{(1)} = 2020$
E_2	$\mathbf{A}_2$	$a_1^{(2)} = 1997$	$a_M^{(2)} = 2004$	$a_2^{(2)} = 2010$
E_3	$\mathbf{A}_3$	$a_1^{(3)} = 2000$	$a_M^{(3)} = 2005$	$a_2^{(3)} = 2010$
E_4	$\mathbf{A}_4$	$a_1^{(4)} = 1998$	$a_M^{(4)} = 2003$	$a_2^{(4)} = 2008$
E_5	$\mathbf{A}_5$	$a_1^{(5)} = 2000$	$a_M^{(5)} = 2005$	$a_2^{(5)} = 2015$
E_6	$\mathbf{A}_6$	$a_1^{(6)} = 1995$	$a_M^{(6)} = 2010$	$a_2^{(6)} = 2015$
E_7	$\mathbf{A}_7$	$a_1^{(7)} = 2010$	$a_M^{(7)} = 2018$	$a_2^{(7)} = 2020$
E_8	$\mathbf{A}_8$	$a_1^{(8)} = 1995$	$a_M^{(8)} = 2007$	$a_2^{(8)} = 2013$
E_9	$\mathbf{A}_9$	$a_1^{(9)} = 1995$	$a_M^{(9)} = 2002$	$a_2^{(9)} = 2007$
E_{10}	$\mathbf{A}_{10}$	$a_1^{(10)} = 2008$	$a_M^{(10)} = 2009$	$a_2^{(10)} = 2020$
E_{11}	$\mathbf{A}_{11}$	$a_1^{(11)} = 2010$	$a_M^{(11)} = 2020$	$a_2^{(11)} = 2024$
E_{12}	$\mathbf{A}_{12}$	$a_1^{(12)} = 1996$	$a_M^{(12)} = 2002$	$a_2^{(12)} = 2006$
E_{13}	$\mathbf{A}_{13}$	$a_1^{(13)} = 1998$	$a_M^{(13)} = 2006$	$a_2^{(13)} = 2010$
E_{14}	$\mathbf{A}_{14}$	$a_1^{(14)} = 1997$	$a_M^{(14)} = 2005$	$a_2^{(14)} = 2012$
E_{15}	$\mathbf{A}_{15}$	$a_1^{(15)} = 2002$	$a_M^{(15)} = 2010$	$a_2^{(15)} = 2020$

To find the average $\mathbf{A}_{ave}$ the sums of the numbers in the last three columns are calculated

$$\sum_{i=1}^{15} a_1^{(i)} = 29996, \quad \sum_{i=1}^{15} a_M^{(i)} = 30109, \quad \sum_{i=1}^{15} a_2^{(i)} = 30210$$

and substituted into (3.11) which gives

$$\mathbf{A}_{ave} = (\frac{29996}{15}, \frac{30109}{15}, \frac{30210}{15}) = (1999.7, 2007.3, 2014)$$

or approximately

$$\mathbf{A}_{ave}^a = (2000, 2007, 2014).$$

The deviations (3.20) between $\mathbf{A}^a_{ave}$ and $\mathbf{A}_i$ are presented in Table 3.2.

Table 3.2. Deviation $\mathbf{A}^a_{ave} - \mathbf{A}_i$.

E_i	$m_1 - a_1^{(i)}$	$m_M - a_M^{(i)}$	$m_2 - a_2^{(i)}$
E_1	5	4	-6
E_2	3	3	4
E_3	0	2	4
E_4	2	4	6
E_5	0	2	-1
E_6	5	-3	-1
E_7	-10	-11	-6
E_8	5	0	1
E_9	5	5	7
E_{10}	-8	-2	-6
E_{11}	-10	-13	-10
E_{12}	4	5	8
E_{13}	2	1	4
E_{14}	3	2	2
E_{15}	-2	-3	-6

Table 3.2 shows the divergence of each expert's opinion from the average. A quick glance gives that the experts $E_3, E_5, E_8, E_{13}, E_{14}$ are close to the average while E_7, E_{11} are not.

Since the word *close* is fuzzy a more detailed study requires some clarification. It can be based on the concept of distance d_{ij} between two triangular numbers $\mathbf{A}_i$ and $\mathbf{A}_j$. If all d_{ij} are calculated and recorded in a table (in our case consisting of 15 rows and columns), then we will have a better grasp on how close are various pairs of $\mathbf{A}_i$ and $\mathbf{A}_j$. Here we do not give a formula for calculating the distance d_{ij} (there are several),[4] but refer to Kaufmann and Gupta (1988).

Suppose the manager is not satisfied with the average (2000, 2007, 2014). Then the deviation $(m_1 - a_1^{(i)}, m_M - a_M^{(i)}, m_2 - a_2^{(i)})$ is given to each expert E_i for reconsideration. The experts suggest new triangular numbers $\mathbf{B}_i$ (see (3.21)) presented on Table 3.3.

Table 3.3. Triangular numbers presented by experts (second request).

E_i	B_i	Earliest date	Most plausible date	Lates date
E_1	$\mathbf{B}_1$	$b_1^{(1)} = 1996$	$b_M^{(1)} = 2004$	$b_2^{(1)} = 2018$
E_2	$\mathbf{B}_2$	$b_1^{(2)} = 1997$	$b_M^{(2)} = 2004$	$b_2^{(2)} = 2011$
E_3	$\mathbf{B}_3$	$b_1^{(3)} = 2000$	$b_M^{(3)} = 2005$	$b_2^{(3)} = 2011$
E_4	$\mathbf{B}_4$	$b_1^{(4)} = 1998$	$b_M^{(4)} = 2003$	$b_2^{(4)} = 2010$
E_5	$\mathbf{B}_5$	$b_1^{(5)} = 2000$	$b_M^{(5)} = 2005$	$b_2^{(5)} = 2015$
E_6	$\mathbf{B}_6$	$b_1^{(6)} = 1997$	$b_M^{(6)} = 2009$	$b_2^{(6)} = 2015$
E_7	$\mathbf{B}_7$	$b_1^{(7)} = 2005$	$b_M^{(7)} = 2015$	$b_2^{(7)} = 2016$
E_8	$\mathbf{B}_8$	$b_1^{(8)} = 1996$	$b_M^{(8)} = 2007$	$b_2^{(8)} = 2013$
E_9	$\mathbf{B}_9$	$b_1^{(9)} = 1997$	$b_M^{(9)} = 2004$	$b_2^{(9)} = 2010$
E_{10}	$\mathbf{B}_{10}$	$b_1^{(10)} = 2004$	$b_M^{(10)} = 2009$	$b_2^{(10)} = 2017$
E_{11}	$\mathbf{B}_{11}$	$b_1^{(11)} = 2004$	$b_M^{(11)} = 2015$	$b_2^{(11)} = 2016$
E_{12}	$\mathbf{B}_{12}$	$b_1^{(12)} = 1996$	$b_M^{(12)} = 2004$	$b_2^{(12)} = 2006$
E_{13}	$\mathbf{B}_{13}$	$b_1^{(13)} = 1998$	$b_M^{(13)} = 2006$	$b_2^{(13)} = 2010$
E_{14}	$\mathbf{B}_{14}$	$b_1^{(14)} = 1997$	$b_M^{(14)} = 2004$	$b_2^{(14)} = 2012$
E_{15}	$\mathbf{B}_{15}$	$b_1^{(15)} = 2001$	$b_M^{(15)} = 2009$	$b_2^{(15)} = 2015$

The experts E_5, E_{12}, and E_{13} have not change their first estimate. Other experts, for instance E_2, E_3, E_8, E_{14}, made very small changes. Using again (3.11), this time to find $\mathbf{B}_{ave}$, gives

$$\mathbf{B}_{ave} = (1999.07, 2006.9, 2013.2)$$

which is approximately $\mathbf{B}_{ave}^a = (1999, 2007, 2013)$.

The manager is satisfied that $\mathbf{A}_{ave}$ and $\mathbf{B}_{ave}$, also $\mathbf{A}_{ave}^a$ and $\mathbf{B}_{ave}^a$, are very close (see Fig. 3.5), stops the fuzzy Delphi process, and accepts the triangular number $\mathbf{B}_{ave}^a$ as a combined conclusion of experts' opinions. The interpretation is that the realization of the invention will occur in the time interval [1999, 2013], the supporting interval of the triangular number $\mathbf{B}_{ave}^a$ which is almost in central form. The most likely year for the realization according to the defuzzification formula (3.15) is 2007. Formulas (3.16) produce numbers close to 2007.

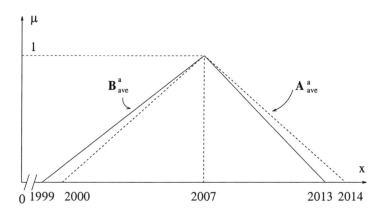

Fig. 3.5. Average triangular numbers $\mathbf{A}^a_{ave}$ and $\mathbf{B}^a_{ave}$.

3.5 Weighted Fuzzy Delphi Method

In business, finance, management, and science, the knowledge, experience, and expertise of some experts is often preferred to the knowledge, experience, and expertise of other experts. This is expressed by weights w_i assigned to the experts (Section 3.3). The experts using Fuzzy Delphi Method (Section 3.4) were considered of equal importance, hence there was no need to introduce weights. Now we consider the case when expert judgements or opinions carry different weights. That leads to *Weighted Fuzzy Delphi Method.*

Assume that to expert $E_i, i = 1, \ldots, n$, is attached a weight $w_i, i = 1, \ldots, n, w_1 + \cdots + w_n = 1$. The four steps in Fuzzy Delphi Method remain valid with some modifications, namely: in *Steps* 2 and 3 the weighted triangular average $\mathbf{A}^w_{ave}$ (see (3.12)) appears instead of the triangular average $\mathbf{A}_{ave}$; in Step 4 similarly $\mathbf{A}^w_{ave}, \mathbf{B}^w_{ave}, \mathbf{C}^w_{ave} \ldots$ take part instead of $\mathbf{A}_{ave}, \mathbf{B}_{ave}, \mathbf{C}_{ave} \ldots$.

Case Study 2 *Weighted Time Estimation for Technical Realization of an Innovative Product*

Consider Case Study 1 where 15 experts present their opinions expressed by triangular numbers $\mathbf{A}_i$ given on Table 3.1. Assume now that the experts $\mathbf{E}_1, \mathbf{E}_3, \mathbf{E}_5, \mathbf{E}_8$, and $\mathbf{E}_{13}$ are ranked higher (weight 0.1) than the rest (weight 0.05); the sum of all weights is one. To facilitate the calculation of the weighted triangular average we construct Table 3.4.

Table 3.4. Experts, weights, and weighted data.

E_i	w_i	$w_i \times a_l^{(i)}$	$w_i \times a_M^{(i)}$	$w_i \times a_2^{(i)}$
E_1	0.1	199.5	200.3	202
E_2	0.05	99.85	100.2	100.5
E_3	0.5	200	200.5	201
E_4	0.05	99.9	100.15	100.4
E_5	0.1	200	200.5	201.5
E_6	0.05	99.75	100.5	100.75
E_7	0.05	100.5	100.9	101
E_8	0.1	199.5	200.7	201.3
E_9	0.05	99.75	100.1	100.35
E_{10}	0.05	100.4	100.45	101
E_{11}	0.05	100.5	101	101.2
E_{12}	0.05	99.8	100.1	100.3
E_{13}	0.1	199.8	200.6	201
E_{14}	0.05	99.85	100.25	100.6
E_{15}	0.05	100.1	100.5	101
Total	1	1999.2	2006.75	2013.9

Substituting the totals from the last row in Table 3.4 into (3.12) gives the weighted triangular average

$$\mathbf{A}_{ave}^w = (1999.2, 2006.75, 2013.9)$$

or approximately $\mathbf{A}_{ave}^{wa} = (1999, 2007, 2014)$. It is almost the same result obtained in Case Study 1. The defuzzification of $\mathbf{A}_{ave}^{wa}$ according to (3.15) produces the year 2007. Formulas (3.16) give close result. If the average $\mathbf{A}_{ave}^w$ is defuzzied instead of $\mathbf{A}_{ave}^{wa}$ and then the maximizing value is rounded up, the same year 2007 is obtained.

□

3.6 Fuzzy PERT for Project Management

Project management is a complicated enterprise involving planning of various activities which have to be performed in the process of development of a new product or technology.

Projects have a specified beginning and end. For convenience they are subdivided into activities which also have specified beginnings and ends. The activities have to be performed in order, some before others, some simultaneously. The time required for completion of each activity has to be *estimated*.

Classical PERT and CPM

Two important classical techniques have been developed to facilitate planning and controlling projects: "Project Evaluation and Review Technique" (PERT) and "Critical Path Method" (CPM).

Table 3.5. Material handling system design, fabrication, and assembly planning data.

	Activity Description	Activities Preceding	Activities Concurrent	Activities Following	Completion time required (days)
A	Mechanical Design	–	–	B, C	35
B	Electrical Design	A	C	D	35
C	Mechanical Fabrication	A	B	E	55
D	Electrical Fabrication	B	C, E	F	35
E	Mechanical Subassembly	C	D	F	50
F	Electrical Installation	D, E	–	G	30
G	Piping Installation	F	–	G	30
H	Start-up, Test, Ship	F	–	–	10

PERT was developed by the U.S.A. Navy while planning the production of Polaris, the nuclear submarine. CPM was developed about the same time by researchers from Remington Rand and DuPont for chemical plant maintenance. There are some similarities between PERT and CPM and often they are used together as one technique.

To illustrate PERT and CPM we present a simplified and modified version of a real project considered by Fogarty and Hoffmann (1983). It is schematically given in Table 3.5. The project, called *Material handling system design*, involves design, fabrication, assembly, and testing. The project is subdivided into eight activities labeled A, B, C, D, E, F, G, H. The completion time for each activity in the last column in Table 3.5 is estimated by managers in charge of activities.

Network planning model

PERT and CPM construct a network planning model from the data in a table. The model corresponding to Table 3.5 is shown in Fig. 3.6. Each activity is represented by a square, rectangle, or circle inside of which is its label and completion time in days.

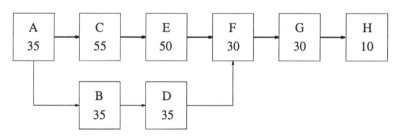

Fig. 3.6. Network planning model for *Material handling system*.

The network planning model gives explicit representation of the sequential relationship between the activities.

Critical path

Critical path is defined as the path of connected-in-sequence activities from beginning to the end of the project that requires the longest completion time. Hence the total time for completion of the project is the time needed to complete the activities on the critical path.

The network planning model helps to determine the critical path. The critical path on Fig. 3.6 is shown by tick arrows connecting activities A, C, E, F, G, and H. The total time for project completion is $35 + 55 + 50 + 30 + 30 + 10 = 210$ days. From Fig. 3.6 one can also see that activities B and D are not on the critical path. They may not be completed as planned, but delay should be no more than 35 days. Otherwise activity F on the critical path will be delayed.

Probabilistic PERT

Time estimation or forecasting for activities completion is inherently uncertain. To deal with uncertainty, researchers extended the capability of PERT by employing statistics and probability. PERT requires from experts three estimates for each activity time completion: the *optimistic time* t_1, the time required to complete the activity if everything goes very well; the *most likely time* t_M, the time required to complete the activity if everything goes according to the plan; the *pessimistic time* t_2, the time for completion if there are difficulties or things go wrong. The single time for activity completion is calculated by the weighted average formula

$$t_e = \frac{t_1 + 4t_M + t_2}{6} \tag{3.22}$$

applied for each activity. Formula (3.22) is exactly (3.16) (3) when t is substituted for m. The total time T_e for completion of the project is the time for completion the activities on the critical path. The times calculated from (3.22) for the network planning model on Fig. 3.6 will be close to those presented in the squares and in general will provide a better estimate. The total time T_e (close to 210 days) will be more realistic than 210 days. Further PERT proceeds with calculation of standard deviation for t_e and other probabilistic analysis. We will propose an alternative to the probabilistic PERT which is less complicated.

The three time estimates t_1, t_M, t_2 for each activity come from experts who use their knowledge, experience, and whatever relevant information is available; they are subjective, but not arbitrary. Hence the nature of uncertainties involved in those types of problems is rather fuzzy than probabilistic. PERT does not suggest a technique for finding

t_1, t_M, t_2; only states that they have to be estimated and combined by the statistical weighted average formula (3.22).

Fuzzy PERT for time forecasting

We propose to improve PERT by using Fuzzy Delphi (Section 3.4) for estimating t_1, t_M, t_2 for each activity. Experts represent each time for activity completion by triangular numbers of the type (t_1, t_M, t_2). For each activity the triangular average number is calculated. To find a crisp activity time value we have to use defuzzification (Section 3.3). Simply we may take the maximizing value (formula (3.15)) or resort to the average formulas (3.16)(1)–(3).

The Fuzzy PERT is illustrated in the following case study.

Case Study 3 (Part 1) *Time Forecasting for Project Management of a Material Handling System*

Let us consider the material handling system design on Table 3.5 and Fig. 3.6 and discard the time estimates obtained by the classical PERT. Now each time activity is to be estimated by three experts; some may participate in the estimation time for several activities. The top manager of the project may take part in all group estimates.

The experts are asked to estimate the optimistic, most likely, and pessimistic completion time of activities $A, B, \ldots, H$, expressed as triangular numbers $\mathbf{T}_i^A, \mathbf{T}_i^B, \ldots, \mathbf{T}_i^H, i = 1, 2, 3$.

Suppose that the experts designated to estimate the completion time for activity A produce the results on Table 3.6.

Table 3.6. Estimated completion time for activity A.

Expert	$\mathbf{T}_i^A$	Optimistic time	Most likely time	Pesimistic time
E_1	$\mathbf{T}_1^A$	33	35	38
E_2	$\mathbf{T}_2^A$	33	34	37
E_3	$\mathbf{T}_3^A$	32	36	39
Total	$\sum_{i=1}^{3} \mathbf{T}_i^A$	98	105	114

The aggregated experts opinions (see (3.11)) give the average time for completion of A in days

$$\mathbf{T}_{ave}^A = (\frac{98}{3}, \frac{105}{3}, \frac{114}{3}) = (32.67, 35, 38) \approx (33, 35, 38).$$

To find a crisp time for completion we have to defuzzify $\mathbf{T}_{ave}^A$. Observing that $\mathbf{T}_{ave}$ is almost a central triangular number (the midpoint of the interval [32.67, 38] is 35.335, close to 35, we use formula (3.15) which gives $t_{max} = 35$.

Just for comparison let us apply to $\mathbf{T}_{ave}^A$ the three defuzzification formulas (3.16). We get

$$(1) \quad t_{max}^{(1)} = \frac{32.67 + 35 + 38}{3} = 35.22,$$

$$(2) \quad t_{max}^{(2)} = \frac{32.67 + 2(35) + 38}{4} = 35.17,$$

$$(3) \quad t_{max}^{(3)} = \frac{32.67 + 4(35) + 38}{6} = 35.11,$$

numbers close to 35. Besides, when counting days in those type of projects, it is irrelevant to keep decimals; we round them off and work with full days. Usually decimals appear when working with average formulas.

Similarly the other seven groups of experts can give estimates and construct tables like Table 3.6. We do not give details but assume that the rounded average times $\mathbf{T}_{ave}^B, \ldots, \mathbf{T}_{ave}^H$ are those presented in Table 3.7 ($\mathbf{T}_{ave}^A$ is also included).

Table 3.7. Average times for activities completion.

Activity	Average activity time	Optimistic time t_1	Most likely time t_M	Pesimistic time t_2
A	$\mathbf{T}_{ave}^A$	33	35	38
B	$\mathbf{T}_{ave}^B$	32	35	38
C	$\mathbf{T}_{ave}^C$	51	54	58
D	$\mathbf{T}_{ave}^D$	32	34	36
E	$\mathbf{T}_{ave}^E$	46	50	53
F	$\mathbf{T}_{ave}^F$	27	30	33
G	$\mathbf{T}_{ave}^G$	27	29	32
H	$\mathbf{T}_{ave}^H$	7	10	12

Each triangular number representing the average activity time (the second column in Table 3.7) has to be defuzzified to produce a crisp number expressing the activity completion time. These triangular numbers are almost in central form, hence we can apply formula (3.15) for defuzzification which produces the numbers in the fourth column labeled t_M. The use of formulas (3.16) gives close results.

The defuzzified times can be presented in an improved network planning model (see Fig. 3.7)

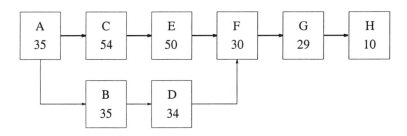

Fig. 3.7. Improved network planning model by using Fuzzy PERT.

The total time for project completion expressed by the triangular number **T** is the time for completion the activities on the critical path. Adding the numbers in the three columns in Table 3.7 designated by t_1, t_M, t_2, excluding those belonging to activities B and D, gives

$$\mathbf{T} = \mathbf{T}_{ave}^A + \mathbf{T}_{ave}^C + \mathbf{T}_{ave}^E + \mathbf{T}_{ave}^F + \mathbf{T}_{ave}^G + \mathbf{T}_{ave}^H = (192, 208, 226).$$

Hence the project duration will be between 192 days and 226 days, most likely 208 days. The last number 208 is the result of defuzzification of **T** using (3.15). The application of formulas (3.16) for defuzzification generates the crisp numbers $\mathbf{T}_{max}^{(1)} = 208.67, \mathbf{T}_{max}^{(2)} = 208.50$, and $\mathbf{T}_{max}^{(3)} = 208.33$; they are close to 208. As a conclusion the completion time for the project is forecasted to be 208 days.

□

Schedule allocation of resources

Activity time duration and allocation of resources, material and human, are in a close relationship.

It is accepted as common practice that prior to allocation of resources to a project the critical path network should be established. The forecasting of activity completion times assumes implicitly that the needed resources are available and could be allocated to activities at an efficient rate so that the project proceeds without interruption. In reality various difficulties may arise and complicate the work.

Often management has the option to apply additional resources to reduce the activity completion time. This may increase the cost. Shortening project length may be desirable because of rewards; late completion may be penalized.

PERT helps the analysis of issues like those mentioned above and others concerned with scheduling resources (see for instance, Fogarty and Hoffmann (1983)). For issues requiring estimations, PERT could be combined with Fuzzy Delphi in a fashion similar to activity time forecasting and finding the critical path.

Case Study 3 (Part 2) *Fuzzy PERT for Shortening Project Length*

Following PERT we introduce the notations: t_n—*normal time* for completing an activity as planned, t_c—*crash time* (shorten time) for completing an activity, C_n—*normal cost* for completing an activity, C_c—*crash cost* (increased cost) for completing an activity in crash time. For each activity, t_c, t_n, C_n, and C_c have to be estimated.

We illustrate here Fuzzy PERT for shortening project length on the material handling system discussed in Case Study 3 (Part 1).

To shorten project length means to shorten the time for completion the critical path., i.e. to shorten the total time $T_{\max} = 208$ days. Shortening duration time of activities not on the critical path (B and D, see Fig. 3.6) will not reduce $T_{\max}$. However, some resources allocated to B and D could be reallocated to activities C and D in order to shorten their completion time (internal reallocation). Here we consider shortening activities time on the critical path without internal reallocation of resources.

The normal time t_n for each activity is already estimated; it is the time $t_{\max} = t_M$ shown in Table 3.7, the fourth column.

The crash time t_c, the normal cost C_n, and the crash cost C_c for each activity could be forecasted similarly to the normal time t_n applying

Fuzzy Delphi. The defuzzified values based on formula (3.15) will be denoted by $t_{c\ max}$, $C_{n\ max}$, and $C_{c\ max}$, correspondingly.

Here estimation is presented for the normal cost C_n for activity A; t_c and C_c can be estimated similarly.

Three experts are asked to estimate the normal cost for completion activity A in the form of a triangular number $\mathbf{C}_n = (C_{n1}, C_{nM}, C_{n2})$, where C_{n1} is the lowest cost, C_{nM} is the most likely cost, and C_{n2} is the highest cost. Assume the experts estimates are those in Table 3.8.

Table 3.8. Experts estimate for completion activity A at normal cost C_n.

Expert	Lowest cost C_{n1}	Most likely cost C_{nM}	Highest cost C_{n2}
E_1	18,000	20,000	22,000
E_2	19,500	21,000	22,000
E_3	17,000	19,500	21,000
Total	54,500	60,500	65,000

Using formula (3.11) gives the average normal cost $\mathbf{C}^A_{n\ ave}$ for completing activity A,

$$\mathbf{C}^A_{n\ ave} = (18,166.67,\ \ 20,166.67,\ \ 21,666.67).$$

Neglecting in $\mathbf{C}^A_{n\ ave}$ the decimals and rounding off the last three digits to 000, 500, or 1000, gives

$$\mathbf{C}^A_{n\ ave} = (18,000,\ \ 20,000,\ \ 21,500).$$

The defuzzification of $\mathbf{C}^A_{n\ ave}$ according to (3.15) produces 20,000 (formulas (3.16) give numbers close to 20,000).

Further, groups of experts forecast t_c, C_n, and C_c for the other activities on the critical path, then defuzzify, and round off as above. Assume that the defuzzified results for the activities on the critical path are those presented in Table 3.9.

To select activities for shortening duration time, PERT uses the notion of *cost slope*. With our notations it is presented as (see Fig. 3.8)

$$k = cost\ slope = \left| \frac{C_{n\ max} - C_{c\ max}}{t_{n\ max} - t_{c\ max}} \right|. \tag{3.23}$$

Figure 3.8 shows that as normal time $t_{n\ max}$ decreases approaching the crash time $t_{c\ max}$, the normal cost $C_{n\ max}$ increases approaching the crash cost $C_{c\ max}$.

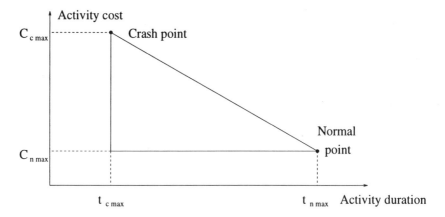

Fig. 3.8. Cost slope for shortening activity time.

Table 3.9. Defuzzified normal and crash times and costs for activities in Material Handling System.

Activity	Normal time $t_{n\ max}$	Crash time $t_{c\ max}$	Normal cost $C_{n\ max}$	Crash cost $C_{c\ max}$	Cost slope $ per day
A	35	25	20,000	26,000	600
C	54	30	30,500	40,500	417
E	50	32	28,000	35,000	389
F	30	22	18,500	25,000	813
G	29	20	15,000	19,000	444
H	10	8	7,000	8,000	500

The cost slope coefficient (3.23) calculated for activity A gives

$$k_A = \left| \frac{C_{n\ max} - C_{c\ max}}{t_{n\ max} - t_{c\ max}} \right| = \left| \frac{20,000 - 26,000}{35 - 25} \right| = \left| \frac{-6000}{10} \right| = 600.$$

The cost slope coefficients for the other activities are calculated similarly. The results are displayed in the last column of Table 3.9.

In general additional resources should be applied first to activities with the smallest cost slope.

The activities in Table 3.9 are ranked in Table 3.10 according to their cost slopes—from the smallest to the largest.

Table 3.10. Ranked activities according to cost slope.

Rank	Activity	Reduced time $t_{n\ max} - t_{c\ max}$	Additional cost $C_{c\ max} - C_{n\ max}$	Cost slope $ per day
1	E	18	7,000	389
2	C	24	10,000	417
3	G	9	4,000	444
4	H	2	1,000	500
5	A	10	6,000	600
6	A	8	6,500	813

Assume that the management wants to reduce the length of the project from 208 days to 180 days, a reduction of 28 days. Of the activities on the critical path, activity E ranked first (Table 3.10) has the smallest k, $ 389 per day. By investing $ 7,000 the time duration for activity E can be reduced by 18 days, meaning that the project can be reduced by 18 days. A further reduction of 10 days must be found. A good candidate is activity C ranked second on Table 3.10. A 10-day reduction will cost $10 \times 417 = 4,170$ dollars. However, if there are some reasons against shortening the activity time for E or for C, or for both, other options must be examined.

□

3.7 Forecasting Demand

The concept of demand is basic in business and economics. Essentially *demand* is composed of two components expressing: (1) the quantity of a product wanted at a specified price and time; (2) willingness and ability to purchase a product.

Demand for a new product should be forecasted. Forecasting succeeds better when history of demand for a similar product is available.

Unless the product is innovative, even in today's rapidly changing environment, some basic links between the past and the future are present. The demand for a given inventory item is subdivided into *independent demand* and *dependent demand* (Orlicky, 1975). Demand is independent when it is not related or derived from demand for other items or products. Otherwise demand is called dependent. Independent demand must be forecasted while dependent demand should be determined from the demand of related items.

Example 3.5

Five experts are asked to forecast the annual demand for a new product using Fuzzy Delphi technique which requires use of triangular numbers $\mathbf{A}_i = (a_1^{(i)}, a_M^{(i)}, a_2^{(i)}), i = 1, \ldots, 5$. Here $a_1^{(i)}$ is the smallest number of units to be produced, $a_M^{(i)}$ is the most likely number of units, and $a_2^{(i)}$ is the largest number of units. The experts opinions are shown on Table 3.11.

Table 3.11. Experts estimates for annual demand for a new product.

E_i	$\mathbf{A}_i$	Smallest number $a_1^{(i)}$	Most likely number $a_M^{(i)}$	Largest number $a_2^{(i)}$
E_1	$\mathbf{A}_1$	10,000	12,000	13,000
E_2	$\mathbf{A}_2$	11,000	13,000	15,000
E_3	$\mathbf{A}_3$	10,000	11,000	14,000
E_4	$\mathbf{A}_4$	12,000	13,000	14,000
E_5	$\mathbf{A}_5$	11,000	12,000	13,000
Total		54,000	61,000	69,000

Substituting the total values into (3.11) gives

$$\mathbf{A}_{ave} = \left(\frac{54,000}{5}, \frac{61,000}{5}, \frac{69,000}{5} \right) = (10800, 12200, 13800).$$

The defuzzified $\mathbf{A}_{ave}$ according to (3.15) is 12200. Hence this number can be adopted to represent the annual demand for the new product.

□

3.8 Notes

1. Forecasting in business, finance, and management, regardless of the methodology used, is a controversial subject. A wide range of opinions exist, from claims that forecasting is impossible, to categorical statement that it is a must. Here we present some quotations on the matter by experts and scientists well acquainted with classical techniques for forecasting; there is no evidence that they have knowledge of fuzzy theory.

   "The ability to forecast accurately is central to effective planning strategies. If the forecasts turn out to be wrong, the real cost and opportunity costs ... can be considerable. On the other hand, if they are correct they can provide a great deal of benefit—if the competitors have not followed similar planning strategies"(Makridakis, 1990).

   "To produce an accurate forecast under conditions of stability, the forecaster has merely to conclude that the future will be just like the past. Forecasting may also come out reasonably well if trends change in a way favorable to the organization, for example, if markets grow faster than predicted. Then at least extrapolation does little harm. Typically is overestimation that causes the problems, for example, by projecting a higher demand for a company's products than actually materializes" (Mintzberg, 1994).

   "To claim that forecast is impossible is, of course, a rather extreme way of drawing attention to the frequency with which decision-makers are prone to suffer expensive surprise"(Earl, 1995).

   "The significance of science lies precisely in this: To know in order to foresee .... There is a difference in the degree of foresight and precision achieved in the various sciences." (Leon Trotsky, in *The Age of Permanent Revolution: A Trotsky Anthology*, 1964). The last sentence written in 1940 shows that Trotsky was intuitively close to the concept of fuzziness.

2. Arithmetic operations with fuzzy numbers and in particular with triangular and trapezoidal numbers can be defined by using op-

erations with α-level intervals, level by level (see Kaufmann and Gupta (1985) and G. Bojadziev and M. Bojadziev (1995)).

3. Case Study 1 is based on Kaufmann and Gupta (1988).

4. A simple approximate formula for distance between triangular numbers is given by G. Bojadziev and M. Bojadziev (1995).

Chapter 4

Decision Making in a Fuzzy Environment

Decision making is a process of problem solving which results in an action. It is a choice between various ways of getting an end accomplished. Decision making plays an important role in business, finance, management, economics, social and political science, engineering and computer science, biology, and medicine. It is a difficult process due to factors like incomplete and imprecise information, subjectivity, linguistics, which tend to be presented in real-life situations to lesser or greater degree. These factors indicate that a decision-making process takes place in a fuzzy environment. The main objective of this chapter is to consider two methods for decision making based on fuzzy sets and fuzzy logic. First to be introduced is the Bellman–Zadeh (1970) approach, according to which decision making is defined as intersection of goals and constraints described by fuzzy sets. The second approach for making decisions combines goals and constraints using fuzzy averaging. Applications are made to various real-life situations requiring selection or evaluation type decisions and to pricing models. Also a budget allocation procedure is discussed.

4.1   Decision Making by Intersection of Fuzzy Goals and Constraints

Decision making is characterized by *selection* or choice from *alternatives* which are available, i.e. they are found or discovered. In the process of decision making, specified goals have to be reached and specified constraints have to be kept.

Consider a simple decision-making model consisting of a goal described by a fuzzy set $\mathcal{G}$ with membership function $\mu_{\mathcal{G}}(x)$ and a constraint described by a fuzzy set $\mathcal{C}$ with membership function $\mu_{\mathcal{C}}(x)$, where x is an element of the crisp set of alternatives A_{alt}.

By definition (Bellman and Zadeh (1970)) the decision is a fuzzy set $\mathcal{D}$ with membership function $\mu_{\mathcal{D}}(x)$, expressed as intersection of $\mathcal{G}$ and $\mathcal{C}$,

$$\mathcal{D} = \mathcal{G} \cap \mathcal{C} = \{(x, \mu_{\mathcal{D}}(x) | x \in [d_1, d_2], \quad \mu_{\mathcal{D}}(x) \in [0, h \le 1]\}. \quad (4.1)$$

It is a multiple decision resulting in selection the crisp set $[d_1, d_2]$ from the set of alternatives A_{alt}; $\mu_{\mathcal{D}}(x)$ indicates the degree to which any $x \in [d_1, d_2]$ belongs to the decision $\mathcal{D}$. A schematic presentation is shown on Fig. 4.1 when $x \in A_{alt} \subset R$ and $\mathcal{G}$ and $\mathcal{C}$ have monotone continuous membership functions.

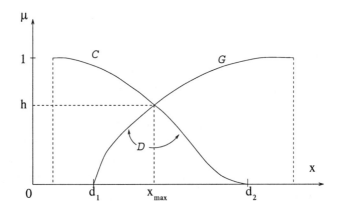

Fig. 4.1. Fuzzy goal $\mathcal{G}$, constraint $\mathcal{C}$, decision $\mathcal{D}$, max decision $x_{\max}$.

Using the membership functions and operation intersection (1.9), formula (4.1) gives

$$\mu_{\mathcal{D}}(x) = \min(\mu_{\mathcal{G}}(x), \mu_{\mathcal{C}}(x)), \qquad x \in A_{alt}. \tag{4.2}$$

The operation intersections is commutative, hence the goal and constraint in (4.1) can be formally interchanged, i.e. $\mathcal{D} = \mathcal{G} \cap \mathcal{C} = \mathcal{C} \cap \mathcal{D}$. Actually there are real situations in which, depending on the point of view, goal could be considered as constraint and vice versa. Sometimes there is no need to specify the goal and constraint; we simply call them objectives or aspects of a problem.

Usually the decision makers want to have a crisp result, a value among the elements of the set $[d_1, d_2] \subset A_{alt}$ which best or adequately represents the fuzzy set $\mathcal{D}$. That requires *defuzzification* of $\mathcal{D}$. It is natural to adopt for that purpose the value x from the selected set $[d_1, d_2]$ with the highest degree of membership in the set $\mathcal{D}$. Such a value x maximizes $\mu_{\mathcal{D}}(x)$ and is called *maximizing decision* (Fig. 4.1). It is expressed by

$$x_{\max} = \{x | \max \mu_{\mathcal{D}}(x) = \max \min(\mu_{\mathcal{G}}(x), \mu_{\mathcal{C}}(x))\}. \tag{4.3}$$

The process of decision making is shown as a block diagram on Fig. 4.2.

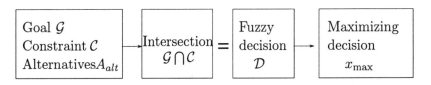

Fig. 4.2. Process of decision making by intersection.

Formulas (4.1)–(4.3) have been generalized for decision-making models with many goals and constraints (Bellman and Zadeh (1970)). For n goals $\mathcal{G}_i, i = 1, \ldots, n$, and m constraints $\mathcal{C}_j, j = 1, \ldots, m$, the decision is

$$\mathcal{D} = \mathcal{G}_1 \cap \cdots \mathcal{G}_n \cap \mathcal{C}_1 \cap \cdots \cap \mathcal{C}_m, \tag{4.4}$$

the membership function of $\mathcal{D}$ is

$$\mu_{\mathcal{D}}(x) = \min(\mu_{\mathcal{G}_1}(x), \ldots, \mu_{\mathcal{G}_m}(x), \mu_{\mathcal{C}_1}(x), \ldots, \mu_{\mathcal{C}_m}(x)), \tag{4.5}$$

and the maximizing decision is given by

$$x_{\max} = \{x | \mu_{\mathcal{D}}(x) \text{ is max}\}. \tag{4.6}$$

If A_{alt} is not a continuous set, for instance a subset of $\mathbf{N}$, the set of integers, formulas (4.1)–(4.6) remain valid.

Example 4.1

On the set of alternatives $A_{alt} = \{1, 2, 3, 4, 5, 6\}$ consider the goal $\mathcal{G}$ and constraint $\mathcal{C}$ given by the discrete fuzzy sets

$$\mathcal{G} = \{(1,0), (2,0.2), (3,0.4), (4,0.6), (5,0.8), (6,1)\},$$
$$\mathcal{C} = \{(1,1), (2,0.9), (3,0.7), (4,0.6), (5,0.2), (6,0)\}.$$

Using the decision formula (4.2) gives (see Fig. 4.3)

$$
\begin{aligned}
\mathcal{D} = \mathcal{G} \cap \mathcal{C} &= \{(1, \min(0,1)), (2, \min(0.2, 0.9)), (3, \min(0.4, 0.7)), \\
&\quad (4, \min(0.6, 0.6)), (5, \min(0.8, 0.2)), (6, \min(1, 0))\} \\
&= \{(1,0), (2,0.2), (3,0.4), (4,0.6), (5,0.2), (6,0)\}.
\end{aligned}
$$

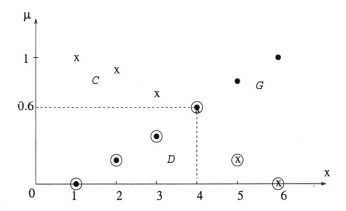

Fig. 4.3. Goal $\mathcal{G}$ (dot), constraint $\mathcal{C}$ (cross), fuzzy decision $\mathcal{D}$ (circle).

Here $[d_1, d_2] = \{1, 2, 3, 4, 5, 6\}, h = 0.6$; the maximizing decision (see (4.3)) is $x_{\max} = 4$ with the highest degree of membership 0.6 in $\mathcal{D}$.

□

We would like to stress that Bellman and Zadeh (1970) made an important comment according to which the definition (4.4) expressing a decision as intersection of goals and constraints is not the only one possible:

"In short, a broad definition of the concept of decision may be stated as *Decision* = Confluence of Goals and Constraints."

Instead of operation intersection (and) defined as *min*, other operations of fuzzy theory could be used to define a decision (see for instance Zimmermann (1984) and Novak (1989)).

We will come back to this point in Section 4.4 where fuzzy averaging is used for decision making.

4.2 Various Applications

Case Study 4 *Dividend Distribution*

In a company the board of directors is willing to pay an attractive dividend to the shareholders but on the other hand, it should be modest. *Attractive dividend*, a linguistic value, is regarded as a goal $\mathcal{G}$ described by a fuzzy set defined on a certain set of alternatives $A_{alt} = \{x | 0 < x \le a\}$, where x is measured in dollars. The membership function $\mu_{\mathcal{G}}(x)$ is increasing on the interval A_{alt}. *Modest dividend* is a constraint $\mathcal{C}$ described by a fuzzy set on A_{alt} with a decreasing membership function $\mu_{\mathcal{C}}(x)$. Good candidate for membership functions are part of triangular or trapezoidal members; also bell-shaped curves could be used.

Assume that the fuzzy set goal $\mathcal{G}$, *attractive dividend*, is defined on the set of alternatives $A_{alt} = \{x | 0 < x \le 8\}$ as

$$\mathcal{G} \triangleq \mu_{\mathcal{G}}(x) = \begin{cases} 0 & \text{for } 0 < x \le 1, \\ \frac{x-1}{4} & \text{for } 1 \le x \le 5, \\ 1 & \text{for } 5 \le x \le 8, \end{cases}$$

and the fuzzy set constraint $\mathcal{C}$, *modest dividend*, is given on A_{alt} by

$$\mathcal{C} \triangleq \mu_{\mathcal{C}}(x) = \begin{cases} 1 & \text{for } 0 < x \le 2, \\ -\frac{x-6}{4} & \text{for } 2 \le x \le 6, \\ 0 & \text{for } 6 \le x \le 8. \end{cases}$$

According to (4.1) the fuzzy set decision $\mathcal{D}$ is represented by its membership function shown on Fig. 4.4. The crisp set $[d_1, d_2]$ is the interval $[1, 6]$. The intersection point of the straight lines $\mu = \frac{x-1}{4}$ and $\mu = -\frac{x-6}{4}$ is $(3.5, 0.625)$, i.e. $x_{\max} = 3.5, h = \max \mu_{\mathcal{D}}(x) = 0.625$. The dividend to be paid is \$3.5.

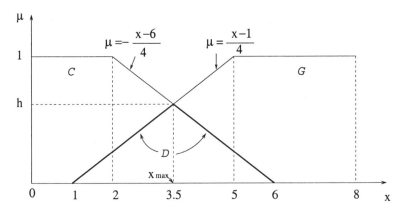

Fig. 4.4. Goal $\mathcal{G}$, constraint $\mathcal{C}$, decision $\mathcal{D}$, maximizing decision $x_{\max}$.

□

Case Study 5 *Job Hiring Policy*

A company advertises a position for which candidates x_k, $k = 1, \ldots, p$, apply; they form the discrete set of alternatives $A_{alt} = \{x_1, \ldots, x_p\}$. The hiring committee requires candidates to possess certain qualities like experience, knowledge in specified areas, etc.[1] which are considered as goals $\mathcal{G}_i, i = 1, \ldots, n$. The committee also wants to impose some constraints $\mathcal{C}_j, j = 1, \ldots, m$, like modest salary, etc.. At the end of the interviewing process each candidate x_k is evaluated from point of view of goals and constraints on a scale from 0 to 1. The score (grade) given to the candidate x_k concerning the goals $\mathcal{G}_i$ is denoted by a_{k_i} and that concerning the constraints $\mathcal{C}$ is denoted by b_{k_j}. Using the scores, committee members construct discrete fuzzy sets $\mathcal{G}_i$ and $\mathcal{C}_j$ on the set of alternatives A_{alt}:

$$
\begin{aligned}
\mathcal{G}_i &= \{(x_1, a_{1i}), \ldots, (x_p, a_{pi})\}, \quad i = 1, \ldots, n, \\
\mathcal{C}_j &= \{(x_1, b_{1j}), \ldots, (x_p, b_{pj})\}, \quad j = 1, \ldots, m.
\end{aligned} \tag{4.7}
$$

The decision formula (4.4) gives

$$\mathcal{D} = \mathcal{G}_1 \cap \cdots \mathcal{G}_n \cap \mathcal{C}_1 \cap \cdots \cap \mathcal{C}_m,$$

which with (4.5) produces

$$\mathcal{D} = \{(x_1, \mu_1), \dots, (x_p, \mu_p)\}, \tag{4.8}$$

where

$$\mu_k = \min(a_{k1}, \dots, a_{kn}, b_{k1}, \dots, b_{km}), \quad k = 1, \dots, p.$$

The candidate with the highest membership grade among $\mu_1, \dots, \mu_p$ will be considered as the best candidate for the job.

The decision in the numerical Example 4.1 is a particular case of formula (4.8).

Assume that the company wants to fill a position for which there are five candidates $x_i, i = 1, \dots, 5$, who form the set of alternatives, $\mathcal{A}_{alt} = \{x_1, x_2, x_3, x_4, x_5\}$. The hiring committee has three objectives (goals) which the candidates have to satisfy: (1) experience, (2) computer knowledge, (3) young age. Also the committee has a constraint, the salary offered should be modest. After a serious discussion each candidate is evaluated from point of view of the goals and the constraint. The committee constructs the following fuzzy sets on the set of alternatives (they are a particular case of (4.7) when $n = 3$ and $m = 1$):

$$\mathcal{G}_1 = \{(x_1, 0.8), (x_2, 0.6), (x_3, 0.3), (x_4, 0.7), x_5, 0.5)\},$$
$$\mathcal{G}_2 = \{(x_1, 0.7), (x_2, 0.6), (x_3, 0.8), (x_4, 0.2), x_5, 0.3)\},$$
$$\mathcal{G}_3 = \{(x_1, 0.7), (x_2, 0.8), (x_3, 0.5), (x_4, 0.5), x_5, 0.4)\},$$
$$\mathcal{C} = \{(x_1, 0.4), (x_2, 0.7), (x_3, 0.6), (x_4, 0.8), x_5, 0.9)\}.$$

Here $\mathcal{G}_1$ represents *experience*; $\mathcal{G}_2$, *computer knowledge*; $\mathcal{G}_3$, *young age*; and $\mathcal{C}$ gives the readiness of the candidates to accept a *modest salary*.

The use of the decision formula (4.8) gives

$$\mathcal{D} = \{(x_1, 0.4), (x_2, 0.6), (x_3, 0.3), (x_4, 0.2), x_5, 0.3)\}.$$

The candidate x_2 has the largest membership grade 0.6, hence he/she is the best candidate for the job.

The decision model for job hiring, formulas (4.7) and (4.8), can be applied to similar situations framed formally into the same model. The following three case studies fall into that category.

□

Case Study 6 *Selection for Building Construction*

Four buildings are planned for construction consequently in a city, but the order is not determined.[2]

A construction company wants to select the building which will be constructed first. The buildings labeled $b_i, i = 1, \ldots, 4$, form the set of alternatives A_{alt}. The company prefers (has goals) to construct a building which is *not very important* but is *highly profitable* and the construction time is *rather long*. The company is also aware that the city council prefers the first building to be *very important*, with *short construction time*, and *reasonable construction cost*; these are constraints for the company. The management of the company describes the goals and constraints by the following fuzzy sets (b stays for building):

$$\mathcal{G}_1 \triangleq \text{ not very important } b = \{(b_1, 0), (b_2, 0.4), (b_3, 0.3), (b_4, 0.8)\},$$

$$\mathcal{G}_2 \triangleq \text{ hightly profitable } b = \{(b_1, 0.5), (b_2, 0.6), (b_3, 0.7), (b_4, 0.3)\},$$

$$\mathcal{G}_3 \triangleq \text{ long construction time } = \{(b_1, 0.8), (b_2, 0.7), (b_3, 1), (b_4, 0.2)\},$$

$$\mathcal{C}_1 \triangleq \text{ very important } b = \{(b_1, 1), (b_2, 0.6), (b_3, 0.7), (b_4, 0.2)\},$$

$$\mathcal{C}_2 \triangleq \text{ short construction time } = \{(b_1, 0.3), (b_2, 0.4), (b_3, 0.5), (b_4, 0.7)\},$$

$$\mathcal{C}_3 \triangleq \text{ reasonable cost } = \{(b_1, 0.3), (b_2, 0.4), (b_3, 0.7), (b_4, 0.2)\}.$$

The decision according to (4.8) is

$$\begin{aligned}
\mathcal{D} &= \mathcal{G}_1 \cap \mathcal{G}_2 \cap \mathcal{G}_3 \cap \mathcal{C}_1 \cap \mathcal{C}_2 \cap \mathcal{C}_3 \\
&= \{(b_1, 0), (b_2, 0.4), (b_3, 0.3), (b_4, 0.2)\}.
\end{aligned}$$

The company management decision is to propose for construction to the city council the building b_2 with maximum membership value

0.4 in the set $\mathcal{D}$. This decision meets best the goals and constraints. If the proposal is not accepted by the city council, the management is ready to propose for construction building b_3 which is a second choice (membership value 0.3 in $\mathcal{D}$).

Note that $\mathcal{G}_1 \stackrel{\triangle}{=}$ *not very important b* is a complement to $\mathcal{C}_1 \stackrel{\triangle}{=}$ *very important b*, i.e. $\mu_{\mathcal{C}_1}(b) = 1 - \mu_{\mathcal{G}_1}(b)$ (see (1.8)). However, $\mathcal{C}_2 \stackrel{\triangle}{=}$ *short duration* is close but not equal to the complement of $\mathcal{G}_3 \stackrel{\triangle}{=}$ *long duration*, i.e. $\mu_{\mathcal{C}_2}(b) \approx 1 - \mu_{\mathcal{G}_3}(b)$. The linguistic values *short* and *long* are words with opposite meaning and could be described by fuzzy sets which almost complement each other, i.e. *short* $\approx$ *not long*; $\mu_{short}(x) \approx 1 - \mu_{long}(x) = \mu_{notlong}(x)$. However, one has to be careful with the interpretation of words with opposite meaning. □

Case Study 7 *Housing Policy for Low Income Families*

A city council wants to introduce a housing policy for low income families living in an old apartment building located on a big lot. Three alternative projects are under discussion: p_1 (renovation and housing management), p_2 (ownership transfer program), and p_3 (new construction). The set of alternatives is $A_{alt} = \{p_1, p_2, p_3\}$. Projects p_1 and p_3 will require partial and full relocation of families.

The city council, using the analysis of experts and various interested groups, after long discussions states three goals and one constraint described by fuzzy sets on A_{alt} as follows:

$\mathcal{G}_1 \stackrel{\triangle}{=}$ *improved quality of housing* $= \{(p_1, 0.2), (p_2, 0.4), (p_3, 0.8)\}$,

$\mathcal{G}_2 \stackrel{\triangle}{=}$ *more housing units* $= \{(p_1, 0.1), (p_2, 0), (p_3, 0.9)\}$,

$\mathcal{G}_3 \stackrel{\triangle}{=}$ *better living enviromnent* $= \{(p_1, 0.4), (p_2, 0.5), (p_3, 0.8)\}$,

$\mathcal{C}_1 \stackrel{\triangle}{=}$ *reasonable cost* $= \{(p_1, 0.8), (p_2, 0.9), (p_3, 0.4)\}$.

The decision according to (4.8) is

$$\mathcal{D} = \{(p_1, 0.1), (p_2, 0), (p_3, 0.4)\}.$$

Project p_3 with the greatest membership degree 0.4 is preferred over p_1 and p_2; it is superior when goals are concerned, but not that satisfactory as far as cost is concern. □

Case Study 8 *Job Selection Strategy*

A professional person, say Mary, is offered jobs by several compa-
nies $c_1, \ldots, c_n$; they form the set of alternatives $A_{alt} = \{c_1, \ldots, c_n\}$. The
salaries differ, but Mary while having the goal to earn a high salary, also
has in mind certain requirements such as interesting job, job within
close driving distance, company with future, opportunity for fast advancement, etc. Those requirements are aspects of the problem and
could be considered as constraints (see Section 4.1). Mary expresses
the goal of a high salary by a set $\mathcal{G}$ with membership function $\mu_{\mathcal{G}}(x)$
which is continuously increasing in the universal set of salaries located
in R_+ measured in dollars. She constructs also the set of constraints
on the set of alternatives A_{alt} by attaching to each company a membership value according to her judgement. However the decision making
formulas in Section 4.1 are valid for goals and constraints defined on
the same set of alternatives. Here the goal is defined on R_+ while the
constraints are defined on the set A_{alt} of companies, hence an adjustment is necessary. The set of salaries can be converted to a set located
in A_{alt}. For that purpose the salaries $s_1, \ldots, s_n$ offered by companies
$c_1, \ldots, c_n$, correspondingly, are substituted into $\mu_{\mathcal{G}}(x)$ and the values
$\mu_{\mathcal{G}}(s_1), \ldots, \mu_{\mathcal{G}}(s_m)$, attached to $c_1, \ldots, c_n$, form the set high salary on
A_{alt}:

$$\mathcal{G}_{alt} = \{(c_1, \mu_{\mathcal{G}}(s_1)), \ldots, (c_m, \mu(s_m))\}.$$

Assume that Mary must choose one of three jobs[3] offered to her by
three different companies c_1, c_2, and c_3; hence the set of alternatives is
$A_{alt} = \{c_1, c_2, c_3\}$. The salaries in dollars per year are given on the table

Company	c_1	c_2	c_3
Salary	40,000	35,000	30,000

Mary has the goal to earn a high salary subject to the constraints (aspects): (1) interesting job, (2) job within close driving distance, and
(3) company with future. Mary uses her subjective judgement to define
the goal and the first two constraints. Regarding the third, she uses
her knowledge accumulated by reading the book, *Excelarate: Growing
in the New Economy*, by Beck (1995). She describes the constraints by

the discrete fuzzy sets

$$
\begin{aligned}
C_1 &= \{(c_1, 0.5), (c_2, 0.7), (c_3, 0.8)\}, \\
C_2 &= \{(c_1, 0.3), (c_2, 0.8), (c_3, 1)\}, \\
C_3 &= \{(c_1, 0.3), (c_2, 0.7), (c_3, 0.5)\},
\end{aligned}
$$

on the set of alternatives (this is the universal set for C_1, C_2, and C_3) and the goal $\mathcal{G}$ of a high salary by the continuous membership function

$$
\mathcal{G} \triangleq \mu_\mathcal{G}(x) = \begin{cases} 0 & \text{for} \quad 0 < x < 25000, \\ \frac{x - 25000}{20000} & \text{for} \quad 25000 \le x \le 45000, \\ 1 & \text{for} \quad 45000 \le x \end{cases}
$$

on the universal set R_+ of salaries (see Fig. 4.5).

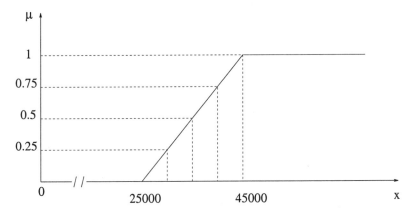

Fig. 4.5. Goal $\mathcal{G}$—high salary.

In order to apply a decision-making formula of the type (4.4) Mary has to deal with one universal set, that of the alternatives. For that purpose she generates membership values by substituting in $\mu_\mathcal{G}(x)$, for x, the salaries corresponding to the alternatives,

$$\mu_\mathcal{G}(40,000) = 0.75, \qquad \mu_\mathcal{G}(35,000) = 0.5, \qquad \mu_\mathcal{G}(30,000) = 0.25.$$

As a consequence, the fuzzy set goal $\mathcal{G}$ on the universe R_+ is now substituted by the fuzzy set goal $\mathcal{G}_{alt}$ on the set of the alternatives,

$$\mathcal{G}_{alt} = \{(c_1, 0.75), (c_2, 0.5), (c_3, 0.25)\}.$$

The decision is then (see (4.4))

$$\mathcal{D} = \mathcal{G}_{alt} \cap \mathcal{C}_1 \cap \mathcal{C}_2 \cap \mathcal{C}_3 = \{(c_1, 0.3), (c_2, 0.5), (c_3, 0.25)\}.$$

The maximum membership value in $\mathcal{D}$ is 0.5, hence Mary has to take the job with company c_2 if she wants to satisfy best her objectives.

□

Case Study 9 *Evaluation of Learning Performance*[4]

The management of a company established an annual university undergraduate scholarship to support a high school student with excellent performance in science (Mathematics, Physics, Chemistry) and in English. *Excellent* is a linguistic label which the management described separately for science (**ES**) and English (**EE**) on Fig. 4.6 (a) and (b), correspondingly, using part of trapezoidal numbers on the universe $[0, 100]$ of scores.

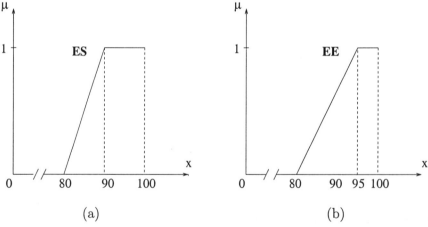

(a)   (b)

Fig. 4.6. (a) *Excellent* in Science; (b) *Excellent* in English.

The using of (1.15) gives the membership functions

$$\mathbf{ES} \triangleq \mu_{\mathbf{ES}}(x) = \begin{cases} 0 & \text{for } 0 \leq x \leq 80, \\ \frac{x-80}{10} & \text{for } 80 \leq x \leq 90, \\ 1 & \text{for } 90 \leq x \leq 100; \end{cases} \qquad (4.9)$$

$$\mathbf{EE} \stackrel{\triangle}{=} \mu_{\mathbf{EE}}(x) = \begin{cases} 0 & \text{for} \quad 0 \le x \le 80, \\ \frac{x-80}{15} & \text{for} \quad 80 \le x \le 95, \\ 1 & \text{for} \quad 95 \le x \le 100. \end{cases} \quad (4.10)$$

A student's score of 90 in Science has grade of membership 1 in the set **ES** while the same score in English has grade of membership of only 0.67 in the set **EE**.

Five students are candidates for the scholarship, x_1 = Henry, x_2 = Lucy, x_3 = John, x_4 = George, x_5 = Mary. The students' scores are presented in the table bellow.

Table 4.1. Students' scores in Science and English.

	Mathematics	Physics	Chemistry	English
Henry(x_1)	86	91	95	93
Lucy(x_2)	98	89	93	90
John(x_3)	90	92	96	88
George(x_4)	96	90	88	89
Mary(x_5)	90	87	92	94

The set of alternatives is $A_{alt} = \{x_1, x_2, x_3, x_4, x_5\}$.

Substituting the students scores in Mathematics, Physics, Chemistry into (4.9) and those in English into (4.10) gives the degrees of excellence corresponding to the scores. They are shown on Table 4.2.

Table 4.2. Students' degrees of excellence in Science and English.

	Mathematics	Physics	Chemistry	English
Henry(x_1)	0.6	1	1	0.87
Lucy(x_2)	1	0.9	1	0.67
John(x_3)	1	1	1	0.53
George(x_4)	1	1	0.8	0.60
Mary(x_5)	1	0.7	1	0.93

The degrees of excellence, attached to each student, produce the fuzzy sets of excellence in Science and English which form the objectives or aspects of the problem:

Excellent in Mathematics $\stackrel{\triangle}{=} \mathcal{G}_1$

$= \{(x_1, 0.6), (x_2, 1), (x_3, 1), (x_4, 1), (x_5, 1)\},$

Excellent in Physics $\overset{\triangle}{=} \mathcal{G}_2$

$= \{(x_1, 1), (x_2, 0.9), (x_3, 1), (x_4, 1), (x_5, 0.7)\}$,

Excellent in Chemistry $\overset{\triangle}{=} \mathcal{G}_3$

$= \{(x_1, 1), (x_2, 1), (x_3, 1), (x_4, 0.8), (x_5, 1)\}$,

Excellent in English $\overset{\triangle}{=} \mathcal{G}_4$

$= \{(x_1, 0.87), (x_2, 0.67), (x_3, 0.53), (x_4, 0.6), (x_5, 0.93)\}$.

The decision formula (4.4) gives

$$
\begin{aligned}
\mathcal{D} &= \mathcal{G}_1 \cap \mathcal{G}_2 \cap \mathcal{G}_3 \cap \mathcal{G}_4 \\
&= \{(x_1, 0.6), (x_2, 0.67), (x_3, 0.53), (x_4, 0.6), (x_5, 0.7)\},
\end{aligned}
$$

hence the conclusion is that x_5, i.e. Mary with the degree of membership 0.7 in $\mathcal{D}$ is the student with the best performance.

Similar approach could be used to evaluate different types of employee performance in a company or industry.

□

4.3   Pricing Models for New Products

Pricing a new product by a company is a complicated task. It requires the combined efforts of financial, marketing, sales, and management experts to recommend the initial price of a new consumer product. It is also a responsible task since overpricing could create a market for the competitor.

Here we develop a pricing model using the decision method in Section 4.1. The model is based on requirements R_i (rules or objectives) designed by experts. Below are listed some typical requirements[5]:

$R_1 \overset{\triangle}{=}$ The product should have *low price*;

$R_2 \overset{\triangle}{=}$ The product should have *high price*;

$R_3 \overset{\triangle}{=}$ The product should have *close price to double*   (4.11)

 manufacturing cost;

$R_4 \overset{\triangle}{=}$ The product should have *close price to competition price*;

More requirements or rules relevant to a particular situation could be added. For instance,

$$R_5 \triangleq \text{The product should have } slightly \ higher \ price$$
$$\text{than the competition price.}$$

The linguistic values *low price, high price, close price* can be modified by the modifiers *very* and *fairly* (Section 2.3) which leads to modified requirements.

A particular pricing model should contain at least two requirements.

Considering the requirements as objectives or aspects of a problem the decision-making procedure in Section 4.1 can be applied without any need to specify goals and constraints.

The conflicting linguistic values *low price* and *high price* can be described by right and left triangular or trapezoidal numbers on the set of alternatives, a subset of R_+, measured in dollars. The linguistic value *close price* can be described by triangular numbers. We denote the fuzzy number describing the linguistic value in requirement R_i by $\mathbf{A}_i$. To show the use of pricing requirements in establishing pricing policy we discuss three closely related models.

Case Study 10 *Pricing Models with Three Rules*

Model 1. Consider a pricing model consisting of the three rules (requirements) R_1, R_3 and R_4 stated in (4.11). Assume that the competition price is 25 and the double manufacturing cost is 30. Assume also that the set of alternatives A_{alt} is the interval [10, 50], meaning that the price of the product should be selected from the numbers in this interval.

The model is shown on Fig. 4.7. The linguistic values in the rules are described by fuzzy numbers as follows: R_1 is represented by the right triangular number $\mathbf{A}_1$ (*low price*), R_3 and R_4 are represented by the triangular numbers $\mathbf{A}_3$ (*close to competition price*) and $\mathbf{A}_4$ (*close to double manufacturing cost*), correspondingly.

The analytical expressions of $\mathbf{A}_1, \mathbf{A}_2$, and $\mathbf{A}_3$ are

$$\mathbf{A}_1 \triangleq \mu_{\mathbf{A}_1}(x) = \begin{cases} \frac{-x+40}{30} & \text{for} \quad 10 \leq x \leq 40, \\ 0 & \text{otherwise,} \end{cases}$$

$$\mathbf{A}_3 \stackrel{\triangle}{=} \mu_{\mathbf{A}_3}(x) = \begin{cases} \frac{x-20}{5} & \text{for} & 20 \le x \le 25, \\ \frac{-x+30}{5} & \text{for} & 25 \le x \le 30, \\ 0 & \text{otherwise}, \end{cases}$$

$$\mathbf{A}_4 \stackrel{\triangle}{=} \mu_{\mathbf{A}_4}(x) = \begin{cases} \frac{x-25}{5} & \text{for} & 25 \le x \le 30, \\ \frac{-x+35}{5} & \text{for} & 30 \le x \le 35, \\ 0 & \text{otherwise}. \end{cases}$$

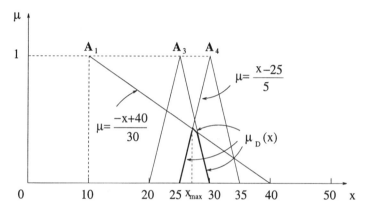

Fig. 4.7. Pricing model with rules R_1, R_3, R_4.

Using (4.5) gives the decision $\mathcal{D}$ (Fig. 4.7) in the interval $[25, 30]$,

$$\mathcal{D} \stackrel{\triangle}{=} \mu_{\mathcal{D}}(x) = \min(\mu_{\mathbf{A}_1}(x), \mu_{\mathbf{A}_3}(x), \mu_{\mathbf{A}_4}(x)).$$

Solving together $\mu = \frac{-x+40}{30}$ and $\mu = \frac{x-25}{5}$ gives the maximizing decision

$$x_{\max} = 27.14,$$

interpreted as price for the product. The experts accept this price as a recommendation. For instance, 14 cents in the price is not customary. The experts may consider a price close to 27.14 in the interval $[25, 30]$, say 27, 26.95, or 26.99.

One can observe from Fig. 4.7 that the triangular number $\mathbf{A}_3$ (*close to competition price*) contributes to the fuzzy decision $\mathcal{D}$, but does not have any impact on the maximizing decision $x_{\max}$. Only the triangular numbers $\mathbf{A}_4$ (*close to double manufacturing cost*) and $\mathbf{A}_1$ (*low price*) contribute to x_{max}. A major role is played by $\mathbf{A}_4$ whose peak with maximum membership grade 1 is at $x = 30$, the double manufacturing cost. Due to the influence of $\mathbf{A}_1$ the maximizing price is 27.14.

Model 2. Now we study the pricing Model 1 when the requirement R_1 defined by $\mathbf{A}_1$ is modified by the modifiers: (a) *very*; (b) *fairly*.

(a) The modified R_1 by *very* reads

$$very R_1 \triangleq \text{The product should have } \textit{very low price.}$$

According to (2.6) the membership function of *very* $\mathbf{A}_1$ is

$$\mu_{very\mathbf{A}_1}(x) = (\mu_{\mathcal{A}_1}(x))^2 = \begin{cases} (\frac{-x+40}{30})^2 & \text{for} & 10 \le x \le 40, \\ 0 & \text{otherwise} & . \end{cases}$$

It is a parabola in the interval $[10, 40]$ (Fig. 4.8).

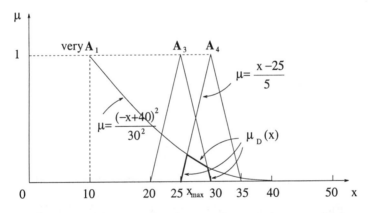

Fig. 4.8. Pricing model with rules *very* R_1, R_3, R_4.

The decision $\mathcal{D}$ has a membership function $\mu_{\mathcal{D}}(x)$ in the interval $[25, 30]$ (Fig. 4.8),

$$\mu_{\mathcal{D}}(x) = \min(\mu_{very\mathbf{A}_1}(x), \mu_{\mathbf{A}_3}(x), \mu_{\mathbf{A}_4}(x)).$$

To find x_{max} here we have to solve together $\mu = (\frac{-x+40}{30})^2$ and $\mu = \frac{x-25}{5}$ which gives the quadratic equation $x^2 - 260x + 6100 = 0$ with solutions 26.08 and 233.92. The solution in $[25, 30]$, i.e. $x_{max} = 26.08 \approx 26$, gives the suggested product price.

The modifier *very* gives more emphasis on *low price*. That is why here we get 26, a smaller price than 27.14 obtained in Model 1 (although both models have the same domain).

Here, similarly to Model 1, $\mathbf{A}_3$ (*close to competition price*) contributes to the fuzzy decision $\mathcal{D}$ but not to the maximizing decision.

(b) The modified R_1 by *fairly* reads

$$fairly \; R_1 \triangleq \text{The product should have } fairly \; low \; price.$$

Using (2.7) gives the membership function of *fairly* A_1.

$$\mu_{fairly}\mathbf{A}_1 = \left(\mu_{\mathbf{A}_1}(x)\right)^{\frac{1}{2}} = \begin{cases} \left(\frac{-x+40}{30}\right)^{\frac{1}{2}} & \text{for} \qquad 10 \le x \le 40, \\ 0 & \text{otherwise} \end{cases}$$

which is a parabola in the interval [10, 40] (Fig. 4.9).

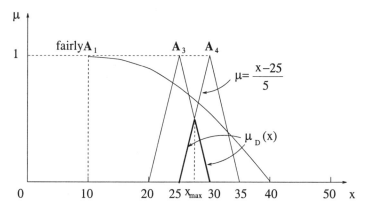

Fig. 4.9. Pricing model with rules *fairly* R_1, R_3, R_4.

From the figure is clear that the rule *fairly* R_1 (fairly *low price*) does not contribute to the fuzzy decision $\mathcal{D}$ with membership function $\mu_{\mathcal{D}}(x)$ on the domain $D = [25, 30]$. Only the rules R_3 and R_4, i.e. $\mathbf{A}_3$ and $\mathbf{A}_4$ contribute to $\mathcal{D}$. The maximizing decision is the midpoint of [25, 30], $x_{\max} = 27.5$.

□

Pricing models like Model 1 and Model 2(a) in Case Study 10 produce maximizing decisions based on *low price* and *doubled manufacturing cost* without reflecting the *competition price* which takes part in the model.[6] A company with such product pricing policy may create favorable market conditions for the competitor. As a consequence the company may incur loses leading to actions as price cutting, redesigning the product, or dropping it from the market. Real-life examples (*Managing in a Time of Great Change*, Drucker[7] (1995)) tell us that it may be more important for a company to consider seriously competition price than to try to make a quick profit of premium pricing. "The only sound way to price is to start out with what the market is willing to pay—and thus, it must be assumed, what competition will charge—and design to that price specification." The next model illustrates Drucker's suggestion: "price-led costing."

Cast Study 11 *A Price-Led Costing Model*

A simple model to reflect "price-led costing" consists of two rules, R_1 (*low price*) and R_3 (*close to competition price*) (see (4.11)). Assume R_1 and R_3 are described by the triangular numbers $\mathbf{A}_1$ and $\mathbf{A}_3$ defined in Model 1 (Case Study 10); they are shown in Fig. 4.10.

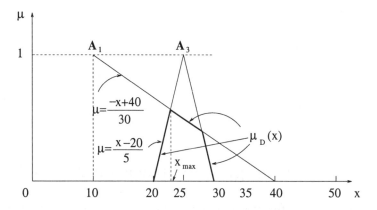

Fig. 4.10. A price-led costing model with rules R_1 and R_3.

The fuzzy decision $\mathcal{D}$ on the domain $\mathcal{D} = [20, 30]$ is

$$\mathcal{D} \overset{\triangle}{=} \mu_{\mathcal{D}}(x) = \min(\mu_{\mathbf{A}_1}(x), \mu_{\mathbf{A}_3}(x)).$$

The maximizing decision in $[20, 30]$ is the solution of equations $\mu = \frac{x-20}{5}$ and $\mu = \frac{-x+40}{30}$; it is $x_{\max} = 22.66$, below the competition price of 25 due to the requirement *low price*.

This pricing model, contrary to the models in Case Study 10, does not include a requirement concerning manufacturing cost. The price 22.66 should be considered as a suggestion. The product should be designed, produced, and marketed at cost to ensure that profit could be made if the price of the product is 22.66 or close to it.

□

If a product is new on the market and there is no competition then a reasonable price which consumers are willing to pay should be suggested. A possible model can be based on rules R_1, R_2, and R_4 in (4.11).

If a product is superior to the product of competition then this should be reflected in the model by including rule R_5. A more sophisticated and general model could contain instead of R_5 rules of the type:

"If the product is *superior to the product of competition*, the product price should be *higher than that of competition*."

This is a conditional statement (Chapter 2, Section 2.3). Models with if ... then rules are discussed in Chapter 6.

We have seen that in some pricing models (Case Study 10) there are rules which do not contribute to the decision. The root of the problem lies in the decision-making procedure based on intersection. Formula (4.3) does not always assure contribution from all rules that participate in the model. In those cases decision making by intersection may not be the most appropriate technique to be used. Another approach towards decision making which takes contribution from all goals and constraints (or rules) is based on fuzzy averaging. It is presented in the next section.

4.4   Fuzzy Averaging for Decision Making

In this section the fuzzy averaging technique (Chapter 3, Section 3.1) is used for making decisions. Goals and constraints, or requirements (rules) are described by triangular or trapezoidal numbers. If they are ranked according to importance, the weighted fuzzy averaging is applied. The result (conclusion, aggregation) is a triangular or trapezoidal number **D** interpreted as *decision*. We call this approach *averaging decision making*. To find a maximizing decision we consider the value in the supporting interval of **D** for which $\mu_{\mathbf{D}}(x)$ has maximum membership degree (it is one)(see (3.15) and (3.17)). Also the statistical averages (3.16) and (3.18) could be used.

Case Study 12 *Dividend Distribution by Fuzzy Averaging and Weighted Fuzzy Averaging*

1. Let us apply the fuzzy averaging technique for the problem discussed in Case Study 4 (Section 4.1). The goal **G** (*attractive dividend*) and the constraint **C** (*modest dividend*) (Fig. 4.3 and Fig. 4.11) are right and left trapezoidal numbers. They can be presented as (see Section 1.6)

$$\mathbf{G} = (1, 5, 8, 8), \qquad \mathbf{C} = (0, 0, 2, 6).$$

Using direct calculations (or the trapezoidal average formula (3.13)) gives the trapezoidal number

$$\mathbf{D} = \mathbf{A}_{ave} \; = \; \frac{\mathbf{G} + \mathbf{C}}{2} = \frac{(1, 5, 8, 8) + (0, 0, 2, 6)}{2}$$

$$= \; \frac{(1, 5, 10, 14)}{2} = (0.5, 2.5, 5, 7)$$

which represents the decision (see Fig. 4.11).

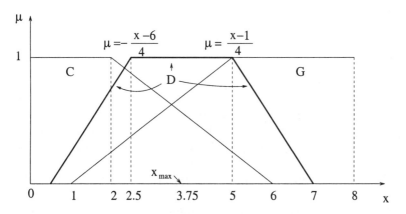

Fig. 4.11. Decision $\mathbf{D}, x_{\max} = 3.75$.

The membership function $\mu_{\mathbf{D}}(x)$ of the decision has a flat segment whose projection on x-axis is the interval [2.5, 5]. The numbers in this interval have the highest degree of membership in $\mathbf{D}$. We define the maximizing decision as the midpoint of the flat interval (see (3.17)), i.e.

$$x_{\max} = \frac{2.5 + 5}{2} = \frac{7.5}{2} = 3.75.$$

The maximizing decision obtained in Case Study 4 by the intersection method is 3.5. It is up to the board of directors to decide which value to take.

2. Assume now that the board of directors gives different weight to $\mathbf{G}$ and $\mathbf{C}$, for instance $w_{\mathbf{G}} = 0.4$ and $w_{\mathbf{C}} = 0.6$, meaning that the constraint (*modest dividend*) is a little more important than the goal (*attractive dividend*). Then following (3.14) gives the decision

$$
\begin{aligned}
\mathbf{D} = \mathbf{A}^w_{ave} &= (0.4)\mathbf{G} + (0.6)\mathbf{C} \\
&= (0.4)(1,5,8,8) + (0.6)(0,0,2,6) \\
&= (0.4, 2, 3.2, 3.2) + (0, 0, 1.2, 3, 6) \\
&= (0.4, 2, 4.4, 6.8)
\end{aligned}
$$

expressed as a trapezoidal number with a flat interval $[2, 4.4]$. The midpoint of the flat (formula (3.17)) gives the maximizing decision

$$x_{\max} = \frac{2 + 4.4}{2} = \frac{6.4}{2} = 3.2$$

which as expected is smaller than 3.75, the case without preference.

Case Study 13 *Two Pricing Models*

Model 1. Consider the pricing Model 1 (Case Study 10) presented on Fig. 4.7 and again on Fig. 4.12. The rules R_1, R_3, and R_4 are described by triangular numbers which can be written in the form of

$$\mathbf{A}_1 = (10, 10, 40), \qquad \mathbf{A}_3 = (20, 25, 30), \qquad \mathbf{A}_4 = (25, 30, 35).$$

Using the triangular average formula (3.13) or direct calculations one gets the decision

$$\mathbf{D} = \mathbf{A}_{ave} = \frac{\mathbf{A}_1 + \mathbf{A}_3 + \mathbf{A}_4}{3}$$

$$= \frac{(10,10,40) + (20,25,30) + (25,30,35)}{3}$$

$$= \frac{(55,65,105)}{3}$$

$$= (18.33, 21.67, 35).$$

It is a triangular number shown in Fig. 4.12.

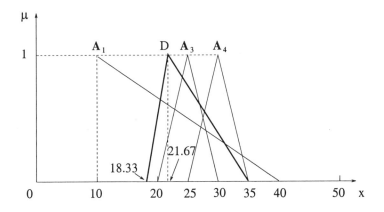

Fig. 4.12. Pricing model with rules R_1, R_3, R_4.

The maximizing decision according to (3.15) is $x_{\max} = 21.67$ since at this value the membership function $\mu_D(x)$ is maximum. The maximizing decision for Model 1, Case Study 10, is 27.14. The difference between the two decisions is not small. Then which value is the correct one? There is no definitive answer to this question. Both decisions should be considered as suggestions. The experts have to make a final decision. The value 27.14 is too high; it does not reflect competition price presented by A_3. On the other hand side, the value 21.67 looks too small; it is not around A_4 although it is influenced by it. A compromise could be to take the number (average) between 21.67 and 27.14 which is 24.405 ≈ 24.4.

Model 2. Let us describe rule R_1 in Model 1 in a slightly different way; the rest remains unchanged. The new right triangular number is $A_1 = (10,10,25)$ (see Fig. 4.13); it has the same peak 1 as the old A_1.

Using the new A_1, and A_3 and A_4 from Model 1, the triangular averaging gives

$$D = A_{ave} = \frac{(10, 10, 25) + (20, 25, 30) + (25, 30, 35)}{3}$$

$$= \frac{(55, 65, 90)}{3}$$

$$= (18.33, 21.67, 30).$$

It is a triangular number shown on Fig. 4.13. The maximizing decision is $x_{max} = 21.67$; the same as in Model 1.

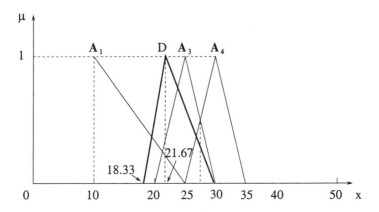

Fig. 4.13. Pricing model with rules R_3, R_4, and slightly different R_1.

Just to make a comparison, let us apply the decision-intersection method to the same model. Noticing that A_1 intersects A_3 but not A_4 above the x-axis, the decision $\mathcal{D}$,

$$\mathcal{D} \triangleq \mu_{\mathcal{D}} = \min(\mu_{A_1}(x), \mu_{A_3}(x), \mu_{A_4}(x)),$$

which is supposed to be a fuzzy set, degenerates into the point (25,0). Recall that when performing operation min the smallest value of μ for each x takes part in $\mathcal{D}$. The number 25 looks like a maximizing decision, but since its degree of membership is zero, the decision intersection method is not the proper tool to be used in this case.

4.5   Multi-Expert Decision Making

Analysis of complex problems requires the efforts and opinions of many experts. Expert opinions are expressed by words from a natural and professional language. They can be considered as linguistic values, hence described and handled by fuzzy sets and fuzzy logic.

It is unlikely that expert opinions are identical. Usually they are either close or conflicting to various degrees. They have to be combined or reconciled in order to produce one decision. We call this multi-expert decision-making procedure *aggregatoin*; it is a conflict resolution when the opinions are confliction. The aggregation is obtained by applying the fuzzy averaging (Section 3.3). It is illustrated on two case studies concerning individual investment planning policy proposed by experts whose opinions are in the first case close and in the second case confliting.

Case Study 14 *Investment Model Under Close Experts Opinions*

Consider a simplified individual investment planning model that produces an *aggressive* or *conservative* policy depending on wheter the interest rates are fallign or rising (see Cox (1995)).

The words *aggresive* and *conservative* are linguistic variables, i.e. fuzzy concepts. The financial experts dealing with the investment model agree to describe *aggressive* (aggressive investment policy) by a suitable left trapezoidal number on a scale from 0 to 100 (universal set – the interval $[0, 100]$) and *conservative* by a right trapezoidal number on a scale from -100 to 0 (universal set $[-100, 0]$). The numbers on the joined scale from -100 to 100 have a certain meaning accepted by the experts. For instance 50 and -50 can be interpreted as indicators for moderately aggressive investment and moderately conservative investment, correspondingly; 70 and -70 as aggressive and conservative investments, etc.

Assume that interest rates are falling and three experts $E_i, i = 1, 2, 3$, have the opinion that the investment policy should be agreessive. Their description of *aggressive* is given in the form of left trapezoidal numbers (see Fig. 4.14)

$$\mathbf{A}_1 = (40, 70, 100, 100), \quad \mathbf{A}_2 = (45, 80, 100, 100), \quad \mathbf{A}_3 = (70, 85, 100, 100).$$

The aggregation of the close experts opinions (assumed of equal importance) according to the trapezoidal average formula (3.13) produces

$$
\begin{aligned}
\mathbf{A}_{ave} &= \frac{\mathbf{A}_1 + \mathbf{A}_2 + \mathbf{A}_3}{3} \\
&= \frac{(40, 70, 100, 100) + (45, 80, 100, 100) + (70, 85, 100, 100)}{3} \\
&= \frac{(155, 235, 300, 300)}{3} = (51.66, 78.33, 100, 100).
\end{aligned}
$$

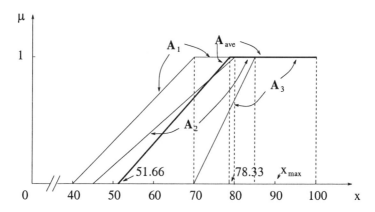

Fig. 4.14 Investment planning policy: three close experts opinions; aggregated decision $\mathcal{A}_{ave}$; maximizing decision x_{max}.

Defuzzification of $\mathbf{A}_{ave}$ using (3.17) gives the maximizing value $\frac{78.33+100}{2} = 89.16 \approx 90$. The interpretation of this number is *very aggressive* investment policy.

Assume now that the three experts are evaluated differently by their peers on a scale from 0 to 10 as follows: $r_1 = 6$ is the ranking of expert $E_1, r_2 = 10$ is the ranking of expert E_2, and $r_3 = 4$ is the ranking of expert E_3. The weights $w_i, i = 1, 2, 3$, which express the relative importance of E_i can be calculated from (3.3):

$$
w_i = \frac{r_i}{r_1 + r_2 + r_3}; \ w_1 = \frac{6}{20} = 0.3; \ w_2 = \frac{10}{20} = 0.5, \ w_3 = \frac{4}{20} = 0.2.
$$

Substituting these values into the weighted trapezoidal average formula (3.14) gives

$$
\begin{aligned}
\mathbf{A}_{ave}^{w} &= 0.3\mathbf{A}_1 + 0.5\mathbf{A}_2 + 0.2\mathbf{A}_3 \\
&= (12, 21, 30, 30) + (22.5, 40, 50, 50) + (14, 17, 20, 20) \\
&= (43.5, 78, 100, 100).
\end{aligned}
$$

Using again (3.17) for defuzzification gives $\frac{78+100}{2} = 89$; this number suggests *very aggressive* investment policy.

There is a little difference between $\mathbf{A}_{ave}$ and $\mathbf{A}_{ave}^{w}$ and also between the maximized (defuzzified) values 89.16 and 89. Hence the ranking of the experts in this case has no significance on the final conclusion. This is mainly due to the fact that the experts opinions are more or less close and also to the fact that the second expert E_2 which opinion is closest to $\mathbf{A}_{ave}$ was ranked as the best ($r_2 = 10$).

If the interest rates are not falling but raising the same methodology can be applied.

$\square$

Case Study 15 *Investment Model Under Conflicting Experts Opinions*

Consider the investment model studied in Case Study 14 when interest rates are falling but assume now that the experts have conflicting opinions.[8] This means that some experts are reccommending *aggressive* policy (scale from 0 to 100) while at the same time others are reccommending *conservative* policy (scale from -100 to 0); also there is a possibility that some experts may express opinions which are almost in the middle between aggressive and conservative policy.

Suppose that three experts present their opinions on the matter (they are of equal importance) by the fuzzy numbers (see Fig. 4.15):

$$
\begin{aligned}
\mathbf{A}_1 &= (-100, -100, -50, -30), \\
\mathbf{A}_2 &= (-10, 10, 30), \\
\mathbf{A}_3 &= (60, 90, 100, 100);
\end{aligned}
$$

$\mathbf{A}_1$ (describing *conservative*) is a right trapezoidal number, $\mathbf{A}_2$ (describing *slightly aggressive*) is a triangular number, and $\mathbf{A}_3$ (describing *aggressive*) is a left trapeziodal number.

To use (3.13) for aggregation of the three conflicting opinions expressed by A_1, A_2, and A_3, first A_2 must be presented as a trapezoidal number, $A_2 = (-10, 10, 10, 30)$ (Section 3.2). The result is (Fig. 4.15)

$$A_{ave} = A_1 + A_2 + A_3$$

$$= \frac{(-100, -100, -50, -30) + (-10, 10, 10, 30) + (60, 90, 100, 100)}{3}$$

$$= \frac{(-50, 0, 60, 100)}{3} = (-16.67, 0, 20, 33.33).$$

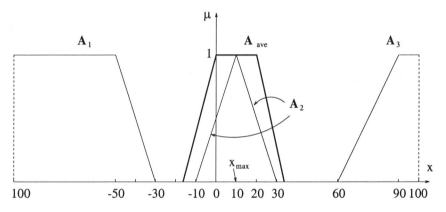

Fig. 4.15. Investment planning policy: three conflicting experts opinions; aggragated decision A_{ave}; maximizing decision x_{max}.

The maximizing value according to (3.17) is $\frac{0+20}{2} = 10$. It suggests a policy on the aggressive side of the scale but a very caustious one.

Now consider the case when the opinions of the three conflicting experts have different importance on a scale from 0 to 10. The ranking of experts E_1, E_2, and E_3 is assumed to be 4, 6, and 10, correspondingly. The weights w_i for E_i calculated from (3.3) are

$$w_i = \frac{\lambda_i}{\lambda_1 + \lambda_2 + \lambda_3}; \quad w_1 = \frac{4}{20} = 0.2, \quad w_2 = \frac{6}{20} = 0.3, \quad w_3 = \frac{10}{20} = 0.5.$$

Using (3.14) to aggragate the conflicting experts opinions gives

$$
\begin{aligned}
A_{ave}^w &= 0.2A_1 + 0.3A_2 + 0.5A_3 \\
&= (-20, -20, -10, -6) + (-3, 3, 3, 9) + (30, 45, 50, 50) \\
&= (7, 28, 43, 53)
\end{aligned}
$$

whose maximizing value (3.15) is $x_{max} = \frac{28+43}{2} = 35.54$. It indicates that the investment policy should be cautiously aggressive.

There is some difference between $\mathbf{A}_{ave}$ and $\mathbf{A}_{ave}^{w}$ and also between the defuzzified values 10 and 35.5 due to the high ranking of expert $\mathbf{E}_3$ who favors aggressive investment policy.

□

4.6 Fuzzy Zero-Based Budgeting

Government agencies and companies often use the *zero-based budgeting* method for budget planning with crisp data. Since the available information is usually imprecise and ambiguous, it is more realistic to use fuzzy data instead of crisp data. This is the justification for the establishment of a more general method known as *fuzzy zero-based budgeting* (Kaufmann and Gupta (1988)).

The fuzzy zero-based budgeting method uses triangular numbers to model fuzziness in budgeting. It is a decision-making procedure different from the two methods discussed in this chapter, decision making by intersection and fuzzy averaging. Since fuzzy zero-based budgeting uses addition of triangular numbers, from this point of view it is close to fuzzy averaging. It will be illustrated on a particular situation.

Consider a company with several decision centers, say A, B, and C. Assume that the decision makers agree on some preliminary budgets using a specified number of budget levels for each center depending on its importance. The budgets are expressed in terms of triangular fuzzy numbers obtained by certain procedure (it might be the Fuzzy Delphi method or some other way).

The following possible budget levels were suggested:

for the center A, $\mathbf{A}_0 < \mathbf{A}_1 < \mathbf{A}_2$,

for the center B, $\mathbf{B}_0 < \mathbf{B}_1$,

for the center C, $\mathbf{C}_0 < \mathbf{C}_1 < \mathbf{C}_2$.

They are schematically presented in Table 4.3.

Table 4.3 Suggested budgets for three centers.

center	A	B	C
level 2	$\mathbf{A_2}$		$\mathbf{C_2}$
level 1	$\mathbf{A_1}$	$\mathbf{B_1}$	$\mathbf{C_1}$
level 0	$\mathbf{A_0}$	$\mathbf{B_0}$	$\mathbf{C_0}$

The budget with a subscript zero (level 0) represents a minimal budget; if a center is given this budget, it might be closed. Budgets with subscript one (level 1) are normal budgets; those with subscript two or greater than two (level 2 or higher levels if such exist) are improved.

The total budget available to the company is limited but it is flexible and could be expressed by a right trapezoidal number **L** of the type shown in Fig. 4.16 with membership function

$$\mu_L(x) = \begin{cases} 1 & \text{for} & 0 < x \leq l_1, \\ \frac{x-l_2}{l_1-l_2} & \text{for} & l_1 \leq x \leq l_2, \\ 0 & \text{otherwise.} \end{cases} \qquad (4.12)$$

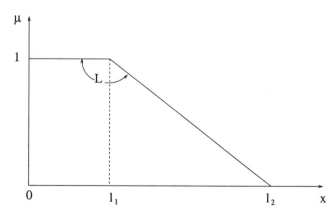

Fig. 4.16. Total available budget.

The decision makers follow a step by step budget allocation procedure according to the importance of each center in their opinion. They select a budget for a center beginning at zero level and continue until all budgets on Table 4.3 are specified. A budget on a higher level includes that on a lower level for the same center. The procedure is shown in Table 4.4; the selected budgets are presented by shaded area. From the table we see that first (Step 1) an initial budget C_0 is allocated to the center C considered to be the most important. After that (Step 2) the center A gets support A_0. Then again (Step 3) the center C is chosen; its budget is increased from C_0 to C_1 before even center B to be selected. Clearly center B is the last priority. The selection procedure continuous (Table 4.4). Step 7 for instance indicates that while centers C and A are selected for allocation at level 2 the center B is given budget on level 0; only in the last Step 8 this center gets budget on level 1.

The cumulative budgets according to Table 4.4 after dropping the lower level budgets from any center when a budget on higher level is selected, listed step by step are:

$$
\begin{aligned}
S_1 &= C_0, \\
S_2 &= A_0 + C_0, \\
S_3 &= A_0 + C_1, \\
S_4 &= A_0 + C_2, \\
S_5 &= A_0 + B_0 + C_2, \\
S_6 &= A_1 + B_0 + C_2, \\
S_7 &= A_2 + B_0 + C_2, \\
S_8 &= A_2 + B_1 + C_2.
\end{aligned}
\tag{4.13}
$$

The budgets $S_i, i = 1, \ldots, 8$ are triangular numbers since they are sums of triangular numbers (Section 3.2 (3.4)). They can be presented in the form $S_i = (s_1^{(i)}, s_M^{(i)}, s_2^{(i)})$.

The final budget has to be selected from (4.13). The company wants to have an optimal fuzzy budget $S_{opt} = (s_1, s_M, s_2)$ with peak $(s_M, 1)$ consistent with the available budget L. Hence it is reasonable and prudent to require

$$
S_{opt} = (s_1, s_M, s_2) \subseteq L,
\tag{4.14}
$$

where

$$s_M = \max s_M^{(i)} \le l_1, \qquad s_2 = \max s_2^{(i)} \le l_2, \qquad (4.15)$$

i.e. s_M is the largest $s_M^{(i)} \le l_1$ and s_2 is the largest $s_2^{(i)} \le l_2, i = 1, \ldots, 8$ (see Fig. 4.16 for l_1 and l_2).

Table 4.4. Procedure for budget selection.

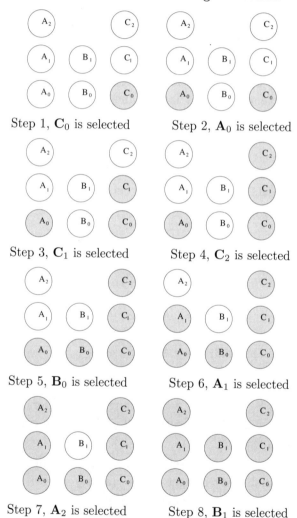

The inclusion (4.14) interpreted as a requirement that the budget $\mathbf{S}_{opt}$ does not exceed the available budget $\mathbf{L}$ essentially means that $\mathbf{S}_{opt}$ entails $\mathbf{L}$ (see Section 2.7 (2.14)).

If a crisp budget is needed, the company could take as such the maximizing value (see (3.15)) $x_{\max} = s_M$ in (4.14).

Condition (4.14) with (4.15) is suitable for a conservative budget. A company expecting additional funding which may or may not materialize or willing to take risk may decide to relax the inclusion (4.14) and substitute it with

$$\mathbf{S}_{opt} \approx \mathbf{L}.$$

In such a case the first condition (4.15) is required, the second is dropped or vise versa, or both conditions (4.15) are dropped but substituted instead by $s_M = \min s_M^{(i)} > l_1$.

Case Study 16 *Application of Fuzzy Zero-Based Budgeting*

Let us assign specified values to the fuzzy numbers in the particular situation considered above.

The limited available budget $\mathbf{L}$ (see (4.12)) given by

$$\mu_L(x) = \begin{cases} 1 & \text{for} & 0 < x \leq 40000, \\ -\frac{x-46000}{6000} & \text{for} & 40000 \leq x \leq 46000, \\ 0 & \text{otherwise} \end{cases} \qquad (4.16)$$

is shown in Fig. 4.17 and the eight budgets on Table 4.3 are selected as follows

$$\begin{aligned}
\mathbf{A}_0 &= (10000, 11000, 12000), \\
\mathbf{A}_1 &= (12000, 13000, 15000), \\
\mathbf{A}_2 &= (14000, 15000, 17000), \\
\mathbf{B}_0 &= (7000, 9000, 11000), \\
\mathbf{B}_1 &= (11000, 12000, 13000), \\
\mathbf{C}_0 &= (7000, 9000, 12000), \\
\mathbf{C}_1 &= (11000, 13000, 15000), \\
\mathbf{C}_2 &= (15000, 18000, 19000).
\end{aligned}$$

For the cumulative budgets (4.13) using addition of triangular fuzzy numbers (Section 3.2) we find

$$
\begin{aligned}
\mathbf{S}_1 &= \mathbf{C}_0 = (7000, 9000, 12000), \\
\mathbf{S}_2 &= \mathbf{A}_0 + \mathbf{C}_0 = (17000, 20000, 24000), \\
\mathbf{S}_3 &= \mathbf{A}_0 + \mathbf{C}_1 = (21000, 24000, 27000), \\
\mathbf{S}_4 &= \mathbf{A}_0 + \mathbf{C}_2 = (25000, 29000, 31000), \\
\mathbf{S}_5 &= \mathbf{A}_0 + \mathbf{B}_0 + \mathbf{C}_2 = (32000, 38000, 42000), \\
\mathbf{S}_6 &= \mathbf{A}_1 + \mathbf{B}_0 + \mathbf{C}_2 = (34000, 40000, 45000), \\
\mathbf{S}_7 &= \mathbf{A}_2 + \mathbf{B}_0 + \mathbf{C}_2 = (36000, 42000, 47000), \\
\mathbf{S}_8 &= \mathbf{A}_2 + \mathbf{B}_1 + \mathbf{C}_2 = (39000, 45000, 49000).
\end{aligned}
$$

The budgets $\mathbf{S}_1, \mathbf{S}_2, \mathbf{S}_3$, and $\mathbf{S}_4$ are too small in comparison to the limiting budget $\mathbf{L}$. Hence the company discards them and considers the rest, $\mathbf{S}_5, \mathbf{S}_6, \mathbf{S}_7$, and $\mathbf{S}_8$ shown in Fig. 4.17 together with $\mathbf{L}$. However the budgets $\mathbf{S}_7$ and $\mathbf{S}_8$ violate condition (4.14).

The budgets $\mathbf{S}_5$ and $\mathbf{S}_6$ have a peak 1 for $s_M^{(5)} = 38000$ and $s_M^{(6)} = 40000$, correspondingly, but since $s_M^{(5)} < s_M^{(6)} = l_1 = 4000$ and $s_2^{(5)} < s_2^{(6)} < l_2 = 4600$, the optimal budget (see (4.14) and (4.15)) is $\mathbf{S}_6 = (34000, 40000, 45000)$ and the crisp budget is $x_{\max} = s_M^{(6)} = 40000$. If the company accepts this budget, recalling that $\mathbf{S}_6 = \mathbf{A}_1 + \mathbf{B}_0 + \mathbf{C}_2$, the center A gets budget $\mathbf{A}_1$ (crisp 13000), the center B gets budget $\mathbf{B}_0$ (crisp 9000), and the center C gets budget $\mathbf{C}_2$ (crisp 18000).

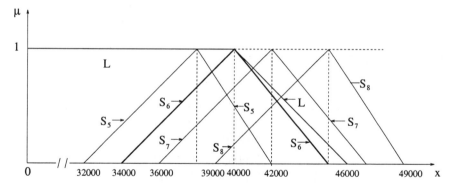

Fig. 4.17. Cumulative budgets.

The budget of center B is at level 0 (smaller than normal); the decision makers may consider the option to close this center and redistribute the money to the other two centers which are more important.

If the company management wants to be more flexible and have reasons to be more optimistic, then the budget $\mathbf{S}_7 = (36000, 42000, 47000)$ could be considered (crisp 42000). This budget satisfies the condition that $s_M^{(7)}$ is the smallest $s_M^{(i)} > l_1 = 4000$.

□

4.7 Notes

1. According to Nuala Beck (1995) "the skills that all of us need to get ahead in this challenging times" are: "the ability to work as part of a team, ... the ability to communicate, ... the ability to use a computer, ... the ability to do basic math."

   Nuala Beck in her book (1992) on the new economy writes: "Artificial intelligence and fuzzy logic systems, already in use experimentally in insurance and banking and defense, will find their way indo education ...." "Each era has its *winners* and *losers*. It's not too early to predict that the losers of tomorrow will include many of winners of today. If a successful company starts believing it has all the answers—or that its tree will grow to the sky—it is already heading down the wrong track. If a Microsoft, for example, doesn't go beyond software and make the leap into artificial intelligence and commercialize fuzzy logic on a massive scale, then its star will inevitably fall."

2. The idea for Case Study 6 comes from Novák (1989).

3. The specific data concerning job selection by Mary (Case Study 8) are modification of data given by Klir and Folger (1988).

4. Case Study 9 is based on material in the book by Li and Yen (1995).

5. Some of the requirements (rules) concerning pricing of new products (Section 4.3) are based on Cox (1995); the linguistic values in his book are described by bell-shaped fuzzy numbers.

6. Grant (1993) in the chapter on assessing profit prospects in his book writes: "To survive and prosper in the face of price competition requires that the firm establishes a low-cost position."

7. One of the five deadly business sins according to Drucker (Managing in a Time of Great Change, 1995) is "cost-driven pricing." Further he writes: "The only thing that works is price-driven costing. Most American and practically all European companies arrive at their prices by adding up costs and putting a profit margin on top .... Their argument? We have to recover our costs and make a profit. This is true but irrelevant: customers do not see it as their job to ensure manufacturers a profit ... Cost-driven pricing is the reason there is no American consumer-electronics industry anymore. It had the technology and the products. But it operated on cost-led pricing—and the Japanese practiced price-led costing."

8. Case studies 14 and 15 in Section 4.5 deal with individual planning policy wihch depends on falling or rising prime interest rates. This reflects only one facet of the problem. The experts also should relay on data concerning the state of the stock market, the trade balance, unemployment rate, level of inventory stockage, etc. In that connection, and to stress the complexity of that type of problems in business and finance where many factors are involved and interrelated, and also to focus on a moral issue, we make a quote from the article "Wanted, Economic Vision That Focuses on Working People" by B. Herbert (*International Herald Tribune*, July 10, 1996). "Last Friday, a kernel of good news on the employment front caused a panic on Wall Street. The consensus: The Fed will have to raise interest rates to ensure that any improvement do not get out of hand."

Chapter 5

Fuzzy Logic Control for Business, Finance, and Management

Fuzzy logic control methodology has been developed mainly for the needs of industrial engineering. This chapter introduces the basic architecture of fuzzy logic control for the needs of business, finance, and management. It will show how decisions can be made by using and aggregating *if ... then* inferential rules. Instead of trying to build conventional mathematical models, a task almost impossible when complex phenomena are under study, the presented methodology creats fuzzy logic models reflecting a given situation in reality and provides solution leading to suggestion for action. Application is made to a client financial risk tolerance ability model.

5.1   Introduction

Complex systems involve various types of fuzziness and undoubtedly represent an enormous challenge to the modelers.

The classical control methodologies developed mainly for engineering are usually based on mathematical models of the objects to be controlled. Mathematical models simplify and conceptualize events in nature and human activities by employing various types of equations which must be solved. However, the use of mathematical models gives rise to the question how accurate they reflect reality. In complicated cases the construction of such models might be impossible. This is especially true for business, financial, and managerial systems which involve a great number of interacting factors, some of socio-psychological nature.

Fuzzy logic models employ fuzzy sets to handle and describe imprecise and complex phenomena and uses logic operations to arrive to conclusion.

Fuzzy sets (in particular fuzzy numbers) and fuzzy logic applied to control problems form a field of knowledge called *fuzzy logic control* (FLC).[1] It deals with control problems in an environment of uncertainty and imprecision; it is very effective when high precision is not required and the control object has variables available for measurement or estimation.

Imitating human judgment in common sense reasoning FLC uses linguistic values framed in *if ... then* rules. For instance: *if client's annual income is low and total networth is high, then client's risk tolerance is moderate.* Here the linguistic variables *annual income* and *total networth* are *inputs*; the linguistic variable *risk tolerance* is *output*; *low*, *high*, and *moderate* are *values* (*terms* or *labels*) of linguistic variables.

The implementation of FLC requires the development of a *knowledge base* which would make possible the stipulation of *if ... then* rules by using fuzzy sets. Important role here plays the experience and knowledge of human experts. They should be able to state the objective of the system to be controlled.

The goal of control in engineering is action. In business, finance, and management we expand the meaning of control and give broader interpretation of action; it might be also advise, suggestion, instruction, conclusion, evaluation, forecasting.

This chapter introduces the basic architecture of FLC. It shows how control problems can be solved by *if ... then* inferential rules without using conventional mathematical models. The presented methodology of heuristic nature can be easily applied to numerous control problems in industry, business, finance, and management. FLC is effective when a good solution is sought; it cannot be used to find the optimal (best) solution. However in the real world it is difficult to determine what is meant by the best.

A block diagram for control processes is depicted in Fig. 5.1. The meaning of each block is explained in the sections in this chapter.

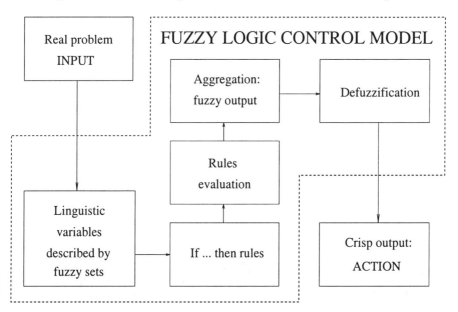

Fig. 5.1. Block diagram for fuzzy logic control process.

The FLC process will be illustrated step by step on a simplified *client financial risk tolerance model.*

5.2 Modeling the Control Variables

Control problems have *inputs* and *outputs* considered to be *linguistic variables.*

Here we explain the FLC technique on a system with two inputs $\mathcal{A}, \mathcal{B}$ and one output $\mathcal{C}$. The same technique can be extended and applied to problems with more inputs and outputs. It can be applied also in the case when the problem has only one input and one output.

Linguistic variables are modeled by sets $\mathcal{A}, \mathcal{B}, \mathcal{C}$ (see Section 2.4) containing certain number of terms $\mathcal{A}_i, \mathcal{B}_j, \mathcal{C}_k$:

$$
\begin{aligned}
\mathcal{A} &= \{\mathcal{A}_1, \ldots, \mathcal{A}_i, \mathcal{A}_{i+1}, \ldots, \mathcal{A}_n\}, \\
\mathcal{B} &= \{\mathcal{B}_1, \ldots, \mathcal{B}_j, \mathcal{B}_{j+1}, \ldots, \mathcal{B}_m\}, \\
\mathcal{C} &= \{\mathcal{C}_1, \ldots, \mathcal{C}_k, \mathcal{C}_{k+1}, \ldots, \mathcal{C}_l\}.
\end{aligned}
\tag{5.1}
$$

The terms $\mathcal{A}_i, \mathcal{B}_j$, and $\mathcal{C}_k$ are fuzzy sets defined as

$$
\begin{aligned}
\mathcal{A}_i &= \{(x, \mu_{\mathcal{A}_i}(x)) | x \in A_i \subset U_1\}, \quad i = 1, \ldots, n, \\
\mathcal{B}_j &= \{(y, \mu_{\mathcal{B}_j}(y)) | y \in B_j \subset U_2\}, \quad j = 1, \ldots, m, \\
\mathcal{C}_k &= \{(z, \mu_{\mathcal{C}_k}(z)) | z \in C_k \subset U_3\}, \quad k = 1, \ldots, l.
\end{aligned}
\tag{5.2}
$$

The design of the sets (5.2) requires:

(i) Determination of the universal sets U_1, U_2, U_3 (or operating domains) of the base variables x, y, z for the linguistic variables described by $\mathcal{A}, \mathcal{B}, \mathcal{C}$ (see Section 2.4).

(ii) Selection of shapes, peaks, and flats of the membership functions of $\mathcal{A}_i, \mathcal{B}_j, \mathcal{C}_k$ (the terms). Most often triangular, trapezoidal, or bell-shaped types of membership functions are used (or part of these), hence then (5.2) are fuzzy numbers.

(iii) Specifying the number of terms in (5.1), i.e. the numbers n, m, and l. Usually these numbers are between 2 and 7.

(iv) Specifying the supporting intervals (domains) for the terms $\mathcal{A}_i, \mathcal{B}_j, \mathcal{C}_k$.

Case Study 17 (Part 1) *A Client Financial Risk Tolerance Model*

Financial service institutions face a difficult task in evaluating clients risk tolerance. It is a major component for the design of an investment policy and understanding the implication of possible investment options in terms of safety and suitability.

Here we present a simple model of client's *risk tolerance ability* which depends on his/hers *annual income* (*AI*) and *total networth* (*TNW*).

The control objective of the client financial risk tolerance policy model is for any given pair of input variables (*annual income, total networth*) to find a corresponding output, a *risk tolerance* (*RT*) level.

Suppose the financial experts agree to describe the input variables *annual income* and total *networth* and the output variable *risk tolerance* by the sets (particular case of (5.1)):

$$Annual\ invcome \stackrel{\triangle}{=} \mathcal{A} = \{\mathcal{A}_1, \mathcal{A}_2, \mathcal{A}_3\} = \{\mathbf{L}, \mathbf{M}, \mathbf{H}\},$$

$$Total\ networth \stackrel{\triangle}{=} \mathcal{B} = \{\mathcal{B}_1, \mathcal{B}_2, \mathcal{B}_3\} = \{\mathbf{L}, \mathbf{M}, \mathbf{H}\},$$

$$Risk\ tolerance \stackrel{\triangle}{=} \mathcal{C} = \{\mathcal{C}_1, \mathcal{C}_2, \mathcal{C}_3\} = \{\mathbf{L}, \mathbf{MO}, \mathbf{H}\},$$

hence the number of terms in each term set is $n = m = l = 3$. The terms have the following meaning: $\mathbf{L} \stackrel{\triangle}{=} low, \mathbf{M} \stackrel{\triangle}{=} medium, \mathbf{H} \stackrel{\triangle}{=} high$, and $\mathbf{MO} \stackrel{\triangle}{=} moderate$. They are fuzzy numbers whose supporting intervals belong to the universal sets $U_1 = \{x \times 10^3 | 0 \le x \le 100\}, U_2 = \{y \times 10^4 | 0 \le y \le 100\}, U_3 = \{z | 0 \le z \le 100\}$ (see Figs. 5.2–5.4). The real numbers x and y represent dollars in thousands and hundred of thousands, correspondingly, while z takes values on a psychometric scale from 0 to 100 measuring risk tolerance. The numbers on that scale have specified meaning for the financial experts.

The terms of the linguistic variables *annual income, total networth,* and *risk tolerance* described by triangular and part of trapezoidal numbers formally have the same membership functions presented analytically below (see (1.13) and (1.15)):

$$\mu_L(v) = \begin{cases} 1 & \text{for } 0 \le v \le 20, \\ \frac{50-v}{30} & \text{for } 20 \le v \le 50, \end{cases}$$

$$\mu_M(v) = \begin{cases} \frac{v-20}{30} & \text{for } 20 \le v \le 50, \\ \frac{80-v}{30} & \text{for } 50 \le v \le 80, \end{cases} \tag{5.3}$$

$$\mu_H(v) = \begin{cases} \frac{v-50}{30} & \text{for } 50 \le v \le 80, \\ 1 & \text{for } 80 \le v \le 100. \end{cases}$$

Here v stands for x, y, and z, meaning x substituted for v in (5.3) gives the equations of the terms in Fig. 5.2, y substituted for v produces the equations of terms in Fig. 5.3, and z substituted for v gives the equations of the terms in Fig. 5.4 (the second term $\mu_M(v)$ should read $\mu_{MO}(z)$).

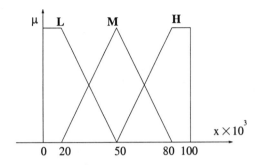

Fig. 5.2. Terms of the input *annual income*.

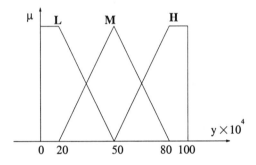

Fig. 5.3. Terms of the input *total networth*.

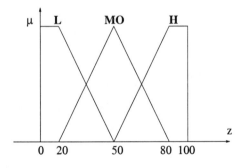

Fig. 5.4. Terms of the output *risk tolerance*.

5.3 If ... and ... then Rules

Next step is setting the *if ... and ... then* rules of inference called also *control rules* or *production rules*.

The number of the rules is nm, the product of the number of terms in each input linguistic variable $\mathcal{A}$ and $\mathcal{B}$ (see (5.1)).[2] The rules are designed to produce or have as a conclusion or consequence $l < nm$ different outputs (l is the number of terms in the output variable $\mathcal{C}$).

The rules with the possible fuzzy outputs labeled $\mathcal{C}_{ij}$ are presented symbolically on the rectangular $n \times m$ (n rows and m columns) Table 5.1 called decision table where $\mathcal{C}_{ij}, i = 1, \ldots, n, \quad j = 1, \ldots, m$, are renamed elements of the set $\{\mathcal{C}_1, \ldots, \mathcal{C}_l\}$.

Table 5.1. Decision table: *if ... and ... then* rules.

	$\mathcal{B}_1$	$\cdots$	$\mathcal{B}_j$	$\mathcal{B}_{j+1}$	$\cdots$	$\mathcal{B}_m$
$\mathcal{A}_1$	$\mathcal{C}_{11}$	$\cdots$	$\mathcal{C}_{1j}$	$\mathcal{C}_{1,j+1}$	$\cdots$	$\mathcal{C}_{1,m}$
$\vdots$	$\vdots$		$\vdots$	$\vdots$		$\vdots$
$\mathcal{A}_i$	$\mathcal{C}_{i1}$	$\cdots$	$\mathcal{C}_{ij}$	$\mathcal{C}_{i,j+1}$	$\cdots$	$\mathcal{C}_{i,m}$
$\mathcal{A}_{i+1}$	$\mathcal{C}_{i+1,1}$	$\cdots$	$\mathcal{C}_{i+1,j}$	$\mathcal{C}_{i+1,j+1}$	$\cdots$	$\mathcal{C}_{i+1,m}$
$\vdots$	$\vdots$		$\vdots$	$\vdots$		$\vdots$
$\mathcal{A}_n$	$\mathcal{C}_{n1}$	$\cdots$	$\mathcal{C}_{nj}$	$\mathcal{C}_{n,j+1}$	$\cdots$	$\mathcal{C}_{nm}$

The actual meaning of the *if ... and ... then* rules is

$$\text{If } x \text{ is } \mathcal{A}_i \text{ and } y \text{ is } \mathcal{B}_j \quad \text{then } z \text{ is } \mathcal{C}_k. \tag{5.4}$$

On Table 5.1, $\mathcal{C}_k$ renamed $\mathcal{C}_{ij}$ is located in the cell at the intersection of ith row and jth column. Denoting

$$p_i \overset{\triangle}{=} x \text{ is } \mathcal{A}_i, \quad q_j \overset{\triangle}{=} y \text{ is } \mathcal{B}_j, \quad r_k \overset{\triangle}{=} z \text{ is } \mathcal{C}_k, \tag{5.5}$$

we can write (5.4) as

$$\text{If } p_i \text{ and } q_j \text{ then } r_k, \ r_k = r_{ij}. \tag{5.6}$$

The *and* part in (5.4) and (5.6), called *precondition*,

$$x \text{ is } \mathcal{A}_i \text{ and } y \text{ is } \mathcal{B}_j, \text{ i.e. } p_i \text{ and } q_j, \tag{5.7}$$

is defined to be *composition conjunction* (2.10). It is a fuzzy relation in $A \times B \subseteq U_1 \times U_2$ with membership function

$$p_i \wedge q_j = \min(\mu_{\mathcal{A}_i}(x), \mu_{\mathcal{B}_j}(y)), \quad (x, y) \in A \times B \subset U_1 \times U_2. \quad (5.8)$$

The *if ... then* rule of inference (5.6) is implication. It expresses the truth of the precondition. There are several ways to define this rule. Here following Mamdani (1975) we define the *rule of inference* as a *conjunction-based* rule expressed by operation $\wedge$(min); r_k is called *conclusion* or *consequent*. Hence (5.6) can be presented in the form

$$p_i \wedge q_j \wedge r_k = \min(\mu_{\mathcal{A}_i}(x), \mu_{\mathcal{B}_j}(y), \mu_{\mathcal{C}_{ij}}(z)), \quad r_k = r_{ij}, \quad (5.9)$$

$i = 1, \ldots, n; j = 1, \ldots, m; k = 1, \ldots, l$; and $(x, y, z) \in A \times B \times C \subseteq U_1 \times U_2 \times U_3$.

This presentation gives the truth value of the rule which is the result of the min operation on the membership functions of the fuzzy sets $\mathcal{A}, \mathcal{B}$, and $\mathcal{C}$.

Case Study 17 (Part 2) *A Client Financial Risk Tolerance Model*

For the client financial risk tolerance model in Case Study 17 (Part 1), $n = m = l = 3$. Hence the number of *if ... then* rules is 9 and the number of different outputs is 3. Assume that the financial experts selected the rules presented on the decision Table 5.2.

Table 5.2. *If ... and ... then* rules for the client financial risk tolerance model.

Total networth $\mathcal{B} \longrightarrow$

		L	M	H
Annual income $\mathcal{A} \downarrow$	L	L	L	MO
	M	L	MO	H
	H	MO	H	H

The rules have as a conclusion the terms in the output $\mathcal{C}$ (see 5.3). They read:

Rule 1: *If client's annual income (CAI) is low (**L**) and client's total networth (CTN) is low (**L**), then client's risk tolerance (CRT) is low (**L**);*

Rule 2: *If CAI is* **L** *and CTN is medium* (**M**), *then CRT is* **L**;

Rule 3: *If CAI is* **L** *and CTN is high* (**H**), *then CRT is moderate* (**MO**);

Rule 4: *If CAI is* **M** *and CTN is* **L**, *then CRT is* **L**;

Rule 5: *If CAI is* **M** *and CTN is* **M**, *then CRT is* **MO**;

Rule 6: *If CAI is* **M** *and CTN is* **H**, *then CRT is* **H**;

Rule 7: *If CAI is* **H** *and CTN is* **L**, *then CRT is* **MO**;

Rule 8: *If CAI is* **H** *and CTN is* **M**, *then CRT is* **H**;

Rule 9: *If CAI is* **H** *and CTN is* **H**, *then CRT is* **H**.

Using the notations (5.5)–(5.8) the above rules can be presented in the form (5.9):

$$
\begin{aligned}
\text{Rule 1:} \quad & p_1 \wedge q_1 \wedge r_{11} = \min(\mu_{\mathbf{L}}(x), \mu_{\mathbf{L}}(y), \mu_{\mathbf{L}}(z)), \\
\text{Rule 2:} \quad & p_1 \wedge q_2 \wedge r_{12} = \min(\mu_{\mathbf{L}}(x), \mu_{\mathbf{M}}(y), \mu_{\mathbf{L}}(z)), \\
\text{Rule 3:} \quad & p_1 \wedge q_3 \wedge r_{13} = \min(\mu_{\mathbf{L}}(x), \mu_{\mathbf{H}}(y), \mu_{\mathbf{MO}}(z)), \\
\text{Rule 4:} \quad & p_2 \wedge q_1 \wedge r_{21} = \min(\mu_{\mathbf{M}}(x), \mu_{\mathbf{L}}(y), \mu_{\mathbf{L}}(z)), \\
\text{Rule 5:} \quad & p_2 \wedge q_2 \wedge r_{23} = \min(\mu_{\mathbf{M}}(x), \mu_{\mathbf{M}}(y), \mu_{\mathbf{MO}}(z)), \\
\text{Rule 6:} \quad & p_2 \wedge q_3 \wedge r_{23} = \min(\mu_{\mathbf{M}}(x), \mu_{\mathbf{H}}(y), \mu_{\mathbf{H}}(z)), \\
\text{Rule 7:} \quad & p_3 \wedge q_1 \wedge r_{31} = \min(\mu_{\mathbf{H}}(x), \mu_{\mathbf{L}}(y), \mu_{\mathbf{MO}}(z)), \\
\text{Rule 8:} \quad & p_3 \wedge q_2 \wedge r_{32} = \min(\mu_{\mathbf{H}}(x), \mu_{\mathbf{M}}(y), \mu_{\mathbf{H}}(z)), \\
\text{Rule 9:} \quad & p_3 \wedge q_3 \wedge r_{33} = \min(\mu_{\mathbf{H}}(x), \mu_{\mathbf{M}}(y), \mu_{\mathbf{H}}(z)).
\end{aligned}
$$

These rules stem from everyday life. It is quite natural for a person with low income and low networth to undertake a low risk and a person with high annual income and high networth to afford high risk. However, for various reasons a client may not want to tolerate high risk or on the contrary, may be willing to accept it regardless of income and networth. The experts, following a discussion with the client eventually have to redesign the rules. For instance, in the first case when the client prefers not to take a high risk, the conclusion part of the rules could be changed: in rules 3, 5, and 7, **MO** could be substituted by **L**; in rules 6 and 8, **H** could be substituted by **MO**. That will ensure a lower risk tolerance for the client which will lead to a more conservative investment policy.

□

5.4   Rule Evaluation

If the inputs to the FLC model are $x = x_0$ and $y = y_0$, then we have to find a corresponding value of the output z. The real numbers x_0 and y_0 are called readings; they can be obtained by measurement, observation, estimation, etc. To enter the FLC model, x_0 and y_0 have to be translated to proper terms of the corresponding linguistic variables.

A reading has to be matched against the appropriate membership functions representing terms of the linguistic variable. The matching is necessary because of the overlapping of terms (see Figs. 5.2, 5.3); it is called *coding the inputs*.

This is illustrated in Fig. 5.5 where to the reading $x_0 \in U_1$ there correspond two constant values, $\mu_{\mathcal{A}_i}(x_0)$ and $\mu_{\mathcal{A}_{i+1}}(x_0)$ called *fuzzy reading inputs*. They can be interpreted as the truth values of x_0 related to $\mathcal{A}_i$ and to $\mathcal{A}_{i+1}$, correspondingly.

In the same way we can obtain the *fuzzy reading inputs* corresponding to the reading $y_0 \in U_2$ (Fig. 5.6). In both figures only several terms of the fuzzy sets $\mathcal{A}$ and $\mathcal{B}$ (see (5.1)) are presented.

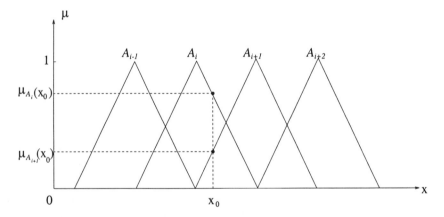

Fig. 5.5. Fuzzy reading inputs corresponding to reading x_0.

The straight line passing through x_0 parallel to μ axis intersects only the terms $\mathcal{A}_i$ and $\mathcal{A}_{i+1}$ of $\mathcal{A}$ in (5.1) thus reducing the fuzzy terms to crisp values (singletons) denoted $\mu_{\mathcal{A}_i}(x_0), \mu_{\mathcal{A}_{i+1}}(x_0)$. The line $x = x_0$ does not intersect the rest of the terms, hence we may say that the intersection is empty set with membership function 0. Similarly the line passing through y_0 intersects only the terms $\mathcal{B}_j$ and $\mathcal{B}_{j+1}$ of $\mathcal{B}$ in (5.1) which gives the crisp values (singletons) $\mu_{B_j}(y_0), \mu_{B_{j+1}}(y_0)$.

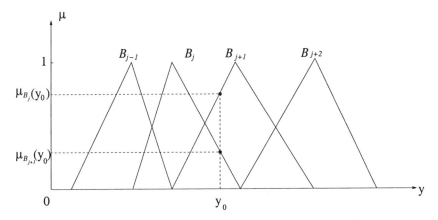

Fig. 5.6. Fuzzy reading inputs corresponding to reading y_0.

The decision Table 5.1 with $x = x_0$ and $y = y_0$, and the terms substituted by their corresponding membership functions, reduces to Table 5.3 which we call *induced decision table*.

Table 5.3. Induced decision table and active cells.

	0	$\cdots$	$\mu_{B_j}(y_0)$	$\mu_{B_{j+1}}(y_0)$	$\cdots$	0
0	0	$\cdots$	0	0	$\cdots$	0
$\vdots$	$\vdots$		$\vdots$	$\vdots$		$\vdots$
$\mu_{A_i}(x_0)$	0	$\cdots$	$\mu_{C_{ij}}(z)$	$\mu_{C_{i,j+1}}(z)$	$\cdots$	0
$\mu_{A_{i+1}}(x_0$	0	$\cdots$	$\mu_{C_{i+1,j}}(z)$	$\mu_{C_{i+1,j+1}}(z)$	$\cdots$	0
$\vdots$	$\vdots$		$\vdots$	$\vdots$		$\vdots$
0	0	$\cdots$	0	0	$\cdots$	0

Only four cells contain nonzero terms. Let us call these cells *active*. This can be seen from rules (5.8); if for $x = x_0$ and $y = y_0$ at least one of the membership functions is zero, the min operator produces 0.

5.5   Aggregation (Conflict Resolution)

The *application of a control rule* is also called *firing*. *Aggregation* or *conflict resolution* is the methodology which is used in deciding what control action should be taken as a result of the firing of several rules.

Table 5.3 shows that only four rules have to be fired. The rest will not produce any results.

We will illustrate the process of conflict resolution by using those four rules numbered for convenience from one to four; they form a subset of (5.4):

Rule 1: *If x is $\mathcal{A}_i^{(0)}$ and y is $\mathcal{B}_j^{(0)}$ then z is $\mathcal{C}_{ij}$,*

Rule 2: *If x is $\mathcal{A}_i^{(0)}$ and y is $\mathcal{B}_{j+1}^{(0)}$ then z is $\mathcal{C}_{i,j+1}$,*

Rule 3: *If x is $\mathcal{A}_{i+1}^{(0)}$ and y is $\mathcal{B}_j^{(0)}$ then z is $\mathcal{C}_{i+1,j}$,*

Rule 4: *If x is $\mathcal{A}_{i+1}^{(0)}$ and y is $\mathcal{B}_{j+1}^{(0)}$ then z is $\mathcal{C}_{i+1,j+1}$,*

The *and* part of each rule, i.e. the *precondition*, called here *strength of the rule* or *level of firing* is denoted by

$$
\begin{aligned}
\alpha_{ij} &= \mu_{\mathcal{A}_i}(x_0) \wedge \mu_{\mathcal{B}_j}(y_0) = \min(\mu_{\mathcal{A}_i}(x_0), \mu_{\mathcal{B}_j}(y_0)), \\
\alpha_{i,j+1} &= \mu_{\mathcal{A}_i}(x_0) \wedge \mu_{\mathcal{B}_{j+1}}(y_0) = \min(\mu_{\mathcal{A}_i}(x_0), \mu_{\mathcal{B}_{j+1}}(y_0)), \\
\alpha_{i+1,j} &= \mu_{\mathcal{A}_{i+1}}(x_0) \wedge \mu_{\mathcal{B}_j}(y_0) = \min(\mu_{\mathcal{A}_{i+1}}(x_0), \mu_{\mathcal{B}_j}(y_0)), \\
\alpha_{i+1,j+1} &= \mu_{\mathcal{A}_{i+1}}(x_0) \wedge \mu_{\mathcal{B}_{j+1}}(y_0) = \min(\mu_{\mathcal{A}_{i+1}}(x_0), \mu_{\mathcal{B}_{j+1}}(y_0)).
\end{aligned}
\tag{5.10}
$$

The equalities (5.10) can be obtained from (5.8) for $x = x_0$ and $y = y_0$. The real numbers $\alpha_{ij}, \alpha_{i,j+1}, \alpha_{i+1,j}$, and $\alpha_{i+1,j+1}$ are placed in the Table 5.4 called here *rules strength table*.

Table 5.4. Rules strength table.

	0	$\cdots$	$\mu_{\mathcal{B}_j}(y_0)$	$\mu_{\mathcal{B}_{j+1}}(y_0)$	$\cdots$	0
0	0	$\cdots$	0	0	$\cdots$	0
$\vdots$	$\vdots$		$\vdots$	$\vdots$		$\vdots$
$\mu_{\mathcal{A}_i}(x_0)$	0	$\cdots$	α_{ij}	$\alpha_{i,j+1}$	$\cdots$	0
$\mu_{\mathcal{A}_{i+1}}(x_0$	0	$\cdots$	$\alpha_{i+1,j}$	$\alpha_{i+1,j+1}$	$\cdots$	0
$\vdots$	$\vdots$		$\vdots$	$\vdots$		$\vdots$
0	0	$\cdots$	0	0	$\cdots$	0

Table 5.4 is very similar to Table 5.3 with the difference that the active cells in Table 5.4 are occupied by the members expressing the strength of the rules while the same cells in Table 5.3 are occupied by fuzzy sets (outputs). We use the elements in the four active cells in both tables to introduce the notion *control output*.

Control output (CO) of each rule is defined by operation conjunction applied on its *strength* and *conclusion* as follows:

CO of rule 1 : $\alpha_{ij} \wedge \mu_{C_{ij}}(z) = \min(\alpha_{ij}, \mu_{C_{ij}}(z))$,

CO of rule 2 : $\alpha_{i,j+1} \wedge \mu_{C_{i,j+1}}(z) = \min(\alpha_{i,j+1}, \mu_{C_{i,j+1}}(z))$,

CO of rule 3 : $\alpha_{i+1,j} \wedge \mu_{C_{i+1,j}}(z) = \min(\alpha_{i+1,j}, \mu_{C_{i+1,j}}(z))$,   (5.11)

CO of rule 4 : $\alpha_{i+1,j+1} \wedge \mu_{C_{i+1,j+1}}(z) = \min(\alpha_{i+1,j+1}, \mu_{C_{i+1,j+1}}(z))$.

These control outputs can be obtained from (5.9) for $x = x_0, y = y_0$. This is equivalent to performing operation conjunction or min on the corresponding elements in the active cells in Table 5.4 and Table 5.3 as shown below

Table 5.5. Control outputs of rules 1–4.

$\cdots$	$\cdots$	$\cdots$	$\cdots$
$\cdots$	$\alpha_{ij} \wedge \mu_{C_{ij}}(z)$	$\alpha_{i,j+1} \wedge \mu_{C_{i,j+1}}(z)$	$\cdots$
$\cdots$	$\alpha_{i+1,j} \wedge \mu_{C_{i+1,j}}(z)$	$\alpha_{i+1,j+1} \wedge \mu_{C_{i+1,j+1}}(z)$	$\cdots$
$\cdots$	$\cdots$	$\cdots$	$\cdots$

The nonactive cells have elements zero; they are not presented in Table 5.5.

The outputs of the four rules (5.11) located in the active cells (Table 5.5) now have to be *combined* or *aggregated* in order to produce one control output with membership function $\mu_{agg}(z)$. It is natural to use for aggregation the operator $\vee$ (*or*) expressed by max:

$$
\begin{aligned}
\mu_{agg}(z) &= (\alpha_{ij} \wedge \mu_{C_{ij}}(z)) \vee (\alpha_{i,j+1} \wedge \mu_{C_{i,j+1}}(z)) \\
&\quad \vee (\alpha_{i+1,j} \wedge \mu_{C_{i+1,j}}(z)) \vee (\alpha_{i+1,j+1} \wedge \mu_{C_{i+1,j+1}}(z)) \\
&= \max\{(\alpha_{ij} \wedge \mu_{C_{ij}}(z)), (\alpha_{i,j+1} \wedge \mu_{C_{i,j+1}}(z)), \\
&\quad (\alpha_{i+1,j} \wedge \mu_{C_{i+1,j}}(z)), (\alpha_{i+1,j+1} \wedge \mu_{C_{i+1,j+1}}(z))\}. \quad (5.12)
\end{aligned}
$$

Note that in (5.11) and (5.12) operation $\wedge$ (min) is performed on a number and a membership function of a fuzzy set. Previously we have been using operation min on two numbers, two crisp sets, and two fuzzy sets, hence now some clarification is needed. Suppose we have the real number α and the fuzzy set C with membership function $\mu_C(z)$. Then we define

$$\mu_{\alpha \wedge \mu_C}(z) = \alpha \wedge \mu_C(z) = \min(\mu_\alpha(z) = \alpha, \mu_C(z)) \qquad (5.13)$$

where $\mu_\alpha(z) = \alpha$ is a straight line parallel to z-axis; geometrically this is a truncation of the shape of $\mu_C(z)$.

The membership function (5.13) is shown in Fig. 5.7 for the two most often used shapes of $\mu_C(z)$, triangular and trapezoidal; it represents a clipped fuzzy number (a nonnormalized fuzzy set).

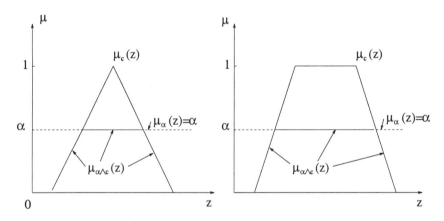

Fig. 5.7. Clipped triangular and trapezoidal numbers.

The aggregated membership function (5.12) also represents a non-normalized fuzzy set consisting of parts of clipped membership functions (5.13) of the type shown on Fig. 5.7 (or similar). In order to obtain a crisp control output action, decision, or command we have to defuzzify $\mu_{agg}(z)$; this is the subject of the next section.

Case Study 17 (Part 3) *A Client Financial Risk Tolerance Model*

Consider Case Study 17 (Parts 1 and 2) assuming readings: $x_0 = 40$ in thousands (annual income) and $y_0 = 25$ in ten of thousands (total networth). They are matched against the appropriate terms in Fig. 5.8 (for the terms see Figs. 5.2 and 5.3). The fuzzy inputs are calculated from (5.3). Note that $x = 40$ and $y = 25$ are substituted for v instead of 40,000 and 250,000 since x and y are measured in thousands and ten of thousands. The result is

$$\mu_L(40) = \frac{1}{3}, \quad \mu_M(40) = \frac{2}{3}, \quad \mu_L(25) = \frac{5}{6}, \quad \mu_M(25) = \frac{1}{6}.$$

For $x = x_0 = 40$ and $y = y_0 = 25$ the decision Table 5.2 (a particular case of Table 5.1) reduces to the induced Table 5.6 (a particular case of Table 5.3).

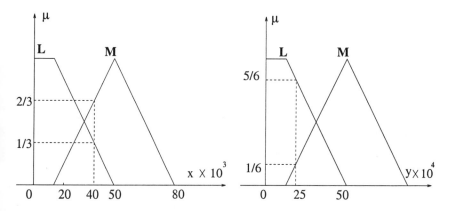

Fig. 5.8. Fuzzy reading inputs for the clients financial risk tolerance model. Readings: $x_0 = 40$ and $y_0 = 25$.

Table 5.6. Induced decision table for the clients financial risk tolerance model.

	$\mu_L(25) = \frac{5}{6}$	$\mu_M(25) = \frac{1}{6}$	0
$\mu_L(40) = \frac{1}{3}$	$\mu_L(z)$	$\mu_L(z)$	0
$\mu_M(40) = \frac{2}{3}$	$\mu_L(z)$	$\mu_{MO}(z)$	0
0	0	0	0

There are four active rules, 1,2,4,5 given in Case Study 17 (Part 2).

The strength of these rules (the *and* part) according to (5.10) is calculated as follows:

$$\alpha_{11} = \mu_L(40) \wedge \mu_L(25) = \min(\tfrac{1}{3}, \tfrac{5}{6}) = \tfrac{1}{3},$$
$$\alpha_{12} = \mu_L(40) \wedge \mu_M(25) = \min(\tfrac{1}{3}, \tfrac{1}{6}) = \tfrac{1}{6},$$
$$\alpha_{21} = \mu_M(40) \wedge \mu_L(25) = \min(\tfrac{2}{3}, \tfrac{5}{6}) = \tfrac{2}{3},$$
$$\alpha_{22} = \mu_M(40) \wedge \mu_M(25) = \min(\tfrac{2}{3}, \tfrac{1}{6}) = \tfrac{1}{6}. \tag{5.14}$$

These results are presented in the rules strength Table 5.7, a particular case of Table 5.4.

Table 5.7. Rules strength table for the clients financial risk tolerance model.

	$\mu_L(25) = \tfrac{5}{6}$	$\mu_M(25) = \tfrac{1}{6}$	0
$\mu_L(40) = \tfrac{1}{3}$	$\tfrac{1}{3}$	$\tfrac{1}{6}$	0
$\mu_M(40) = \tfrac{2}{3}$	$\tfrac{2}{3}$	$\tfrac{1}{6}$	0
0	0	0	0

For the control outputs (CO) of the rules we obtain from (5.11) with (5.14)

$$\text{CO of rule } 1 : \alpha_{11} \wedge \mu_L(z) = \min(\tfrac{1}{3}, \mu_L(z)),$$
$$\text{CO of rule } 2 : \alpha_{12} \wedge \mu_L(z) = \min(\tfrac{1}{6}, \mu_L(z)),$$
$$\text{CO of rule } 3 : \alpha_{21} \wedge \mu_L(z) = \min(\tfrac{2}{3}, \mu_L(z)),$$
$$\text{CO of rule } 4 : \alpha_{22} \wedge \mu_{MO}(z) = \min(\tfrac{1}{6}, \mu_{MO}(z)), \tag{5.15}$$

which is equivalent to performing operation min on the corresponding cells in Table 5.7 and Table 5.6. The result concerning only the active cells (a particular case of Table 5.5) is given on Table 5.8.

Table 5.8. Control outputs for the client financial risk tolerance model.

...	...	...	...
...	$\tfrac{1}{3} \wedge \mu_L(z)$	$\tfrac{1}{6} \wedge \mu_L(z)$	...
...	$\tfrac{2}{3} \wedge \mu_L(z)$	$\tfrac{1}{6} \wedge \mu_{MO}(z)$	...
...	...	...	...

The procedure for obtaining Table 5.8 can be summarized on the scheme in Fig. 5.9 which consists of 12 triangular and trapezoidal fuzzy numbers located in 4 rows and 3 columns.

The min operations in (5.14) between the fuzzy inputs located in the first two columns (Fig. 5.9) produce correspondingly the strength of the rules $\frac{1}{3}, \frac{1}{6}, \frac{2}{3}, \frac{1}{6}$ which give the level of firing shown by dashed horizontal arrows in the second column in the direction to the triangles and trapezoidals in the third column.

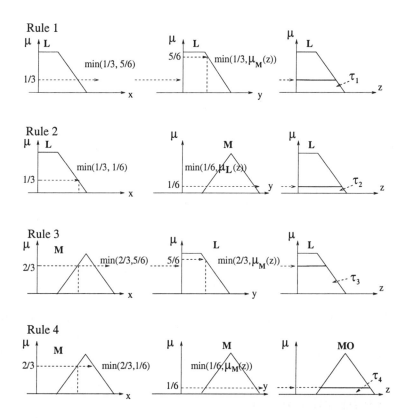

Fig. 5.9. Firing of rules for the client financial risk tolerance model.

The min operations in (5.15) in the sense of (5.13) and Fig. 5.7 result in the sliced triangular and trapezoidal numbers by the arrows (Fig. 5.9) thus producing the trapezoids T_1, T_2, T_3, and T_4.

To aggregate the control outputs (5.15) presented also on Table 5.8 we use (5.12). Geometrically this means that we have to superimpose trapezoids on top of one another in the same coordinate system (z, μ). However, the outputs of rule 1 and rule 2 are included in the output of rule 3 which has the largest strength $\frac{2}{3}$. This is shown in Fig. 5.9; the trapezoids T_1 and T_2 are contained in T_3. Hence we may only consider aggregation of rule 3 and rule 4.

The aggregated output

$$\mu_{agg}(z) = \max\{\min(\frac{2}{3}, \mu_{\text{L}}(z)), \min(\frac{1}{6}, \mu_{\text{MO}}(z))\} \tag{5.16}$$

is geometrically presented in Fig. 5.10. The trapezoids T_3 and T_4 in Fig. 5.9 are superimposed a top one another.

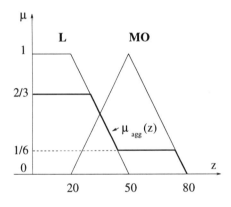

Fig. 5.10.   Aggregated output for the client financial risk tolerance model.

□

5.6   Defuzzification

Defuzzification for average triangular and trapezoidal numbers was presented in Chapter 3, Section 3.3 and for a fuzzy set representing decision in Chapter 4, Section 4.1. Here we deal with a more complicated type of defuzzification.

Defuzzification or decoding the outputs is operation that produces a nonfuzzy control action, a single value $\hat{z}$, that adequately represents the membership function $\mu_{agg}(z)$ of an aggregated fuzzy control action. There is no unique way to perform the operation defuzzification. The several existing methods for defuzzification[3] take into consideration the shape of the clipped fuzzy numbers, namely length of supporting intervals, height of the clipped triangles and trapezoids, closeness to central triangular numbers, and also complexity of computations. We describe here three methods for defuzzification.

Center of area method (CAM)

Suppose the aggregated control rules result in a membership function $\mu_{agg}(z), z \in [z_0, z_q]$, shown in Fig. 5.11.

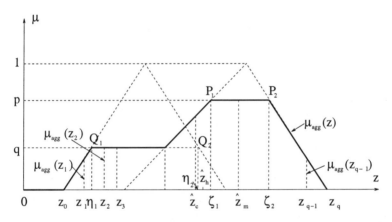

Fig. 5.11. Defuzzification by the center of area method (CAM).

Let us subdivide the interval $[z_0, z_q]$ into q equal (or almost equal) subintervals by the points $z_1, z_2, \ldots, z_{q-1}$.

The crisp value $\hat{z}_c$ according to this method is the weighted average of the numbers z_k (see (3.2) where now $r_k = z_k$ and $\lambda_k = \mu_{agg}(z_k)$),

$$\hat{z}_c = \frac{\sum_{k=1}^{q-1} z_k \mu_{agg}(z_k)}{\sum_{k=1}^{q-1} \mu_{agg}(z_k)}. \tag{5.17}$$

The geometric interpretation of $\hat{z}_c$ is that it is the first coordinate (abscissa) of the center $(\hat{z}_c, \mu_C)$ of the area under the curve $\mu_{agg}(z)$

bounded below by the z-axis. The physical interpretation is that if this area is cut off from a thin piece of metal or wood, the center of the area will be the center of gravity. That is why CAM is called also *center of gravity method.*

This method for defuzzification, perhaps the most popular, is quite natural from point of view of common sense. However, the required computations are sometimes complex.

Mean of maximum method (MMM)

Consider the same membership function $\mu_{agg}(z)$ as in the center of area method (Fig. 5.11). The function has two flat segments (parallel to z axis). The projection of the flat segment P_1P_2 with maximum height on z axis is the interval $[\zeta_1, \zeta_2]$ (see Fig. 5.11). Then neglecting the contribution of the clipped triangular number with flat segment Q_1Q_2 we define $\hat{z}_m$ to be the midpoint of the interval $[\zeta_1, \zeta_2]$, i.e.

$$\hat{z}_m = \frac{\zeta_1 + \zeta_2}{2}. \tag{5.18}$$

This is a simple formula but not very accurate.

Height defuzzification method (HDM)

This is a generalization of mean of maximum method. It uses all clipped flat segments obtained as result of firing rules (see Fig. 5.11). Besides the segment P_1P_2 with height p there is another flat segment Q_1Q_2 with lower height q. The midpoint of the interval $[\eta_1, \eta_2]$, the projection of Q_1Q_2 on z, is $\frac{\eta_1+\eta_2}{2}$. Then the HDM produces $\hat{z}_h$:

$$\hat{z}_h = \frac{p\frac{\zeta_1+\zeta_2}{2} + q\frac{\eta_1+\eta_2}{2}}{p+q} = w_1\frac{\zeta_1+\zeta_2}{2} + w_2\frac{\eta_1+\eta_2}{2}, \tag{5.19}$$

i.e. $\hat{z}_h$ is the weighted average (3.2) of the midpoints of $[\zeta_1, \zeta_2]$ and $[\eta_1, \eta_2]$ with weights $w_1 = \frac{p}{p+q}, w_2 = \frac{q}{p+q}$, where p and q are the heights of the flat segments.

If there are more than two segments, formula (5.19) can be extended accordingly.

HDM could be considered as both a simplified version of CAM and a generalized version of MMM.

Case Study 17 (Part 4) *A Client Financial Risk Tolerance Model*

Let us defuzzify the aggregated output for the client financial risk tolerance model (Case Study 17 (Part 3)) by the three methods.

First we express analytically the aggregated control output with membership function $\mu_{agg}(z)$ shown on Fig. 5.12 (see also (5.10)). It consists of the four segments P_1P_2, P_2Q, QQ_2, and Q_2Q_3 located on the straight lines $\mu = \frac{2}{3}$, $\mu = \frac{50-z}{30}$, $\mu = \frac{1}{6}$, and $\mu = \frac{80-z}{30}$, correspondingly. Solving together the appropriate equations gives the projections of P_2, Q, Q_2 on z axis, namely 30, 45, 75 (Fig. 5.12). They are used to specify the domains of the segments forming $\mu_{agg}(z)$. Hence

$$\mu_{agg}(z) = \begin{cases} \frac{2}{3} & \text{for } 0 \le z \le 30, \\ \frac{50-z}{30} & \text{for } 30 \le z < 45, \\ \frac{1}{6} & \text{for } 45 \le z < 75, \\ \frac{-z+80}{30} & \text{for } 75 \le z \le 80. \end{cases}$$

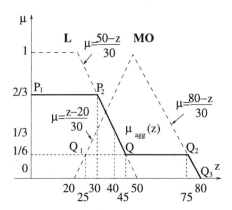

Fig. 5.12. Defuzzification: client financial risk tolerance model.

Center of area method

It is convenient to subdivide the interval $[0,80]$ (Fig. 5.12) into eight equal parts each with length 10.

The substitution of $z_k = 10, 20, \ldots, 70$ into $\mu_{agg}(z)$ gives

z_k	10	20	30	40	50	60	70
$\mu_{agg}(z_k)$	$\frac{2}{3}$	$\frac{2}{3}$	$\frac{2}{3}$	$\frac{1}{3}$	$\frac{1}{6}$	$\frac{1}{6}$	$\frac{1}{6}$

According to (5.17) we find,

$$
\hat{z}_c = \frac{10(\frac{2}{3}) + 20(\frac{2}{3}) + 30(\frac{2}{3}) + 40(\frac{1}{3}) + 50(\frac{1}{6}) + 60(\frac{1}{6}) + 70(\frac{1}{6})}{\frac{2}{3} + \frac{2}{3} + \frac{2}{3} + \frac{1}{3} + \frac{1}{6} + \frac{1}{6} + \frac{1}{6}}
$$
$$
= 29.41 .
$$

Mean of maximum method

The points P_1, P_2 form the highest flat segment, $\zeta_1 = 0$ and $\zeta_2 = 30$.
Then (5.18) gives

$$
\hat{z}_m = \frac{0 + 30}{2} = 15.
$$

Height defuzzification method

Substituting $\mu = \frac{1}{6}$ into $\mu = \frac{z-20}{30}$ gives the number 25, the projection of
the point Q_1. Hence the flat segments $P_1 P_2$ and $Q_1 Q_2$ in Fig. 5.12 have
projections [0,30] and [25, 75], and heights $\frac{2}{3}$ and $\frac{1}{6}$, correspondingly,
i.e. $\zeta_1 = 0, \zeta_2 = 30, \eta_1 = 25, \eta_2 = 75, p = \frac{2}{3}, q = \frac{1}{6}$. The result of
substituting these values in (5.19) is

$$
\hat{z}_h = \frac{\frac{2}{3}\frac{0+30}{2} + \frac{1}{6}\frac{25+75}{2}}{\frac{2}{3} + \frac{1}{6}} = 22 .
$$

The defuzzification results $\hat{z}_c = 29.41 \approx 29, \hat{z}_m = 15$, and $\hat{z}_h = 22$
obtained by the three methods are close. MMM is very easy to apply but
produces here an underestimated result since it neglects the contribution
of rule 4 whose firing level $\frac{1}{6}$ intersects the output **MO**; $\hat{z}_m$ lies in the
middle of the supporting interval of output **L**. CAM requires some
calculations but takes into consideration the contributions of both rules,
3 and 4. The value $\hat{z}_c$ looks more realistic than $\hat{z}_m$. The HDM results
in a value $\hat{z}_h = 22$; it is easy to apply and similarly to CAM reflects the
contributions of rules 3 and 4.

The financial experts could estimate the clients financial risk tolerance given that his/her annual income is 40,000 and total networth is
250,000 to be 22 on a scale from 0 to 100 if they adopt the HDM (29 if
they adopt CAM). Accordingly they could suggest a conservative risk
investment strategy.

□

5.7   Use of Singletons to Model Outputs

A segment or interval $[0, h], h \leq 1$ is its height, parallel to the vertical axis μ is considered as a fuzzy singleton (see Section 1.2).

Aggregation procedure and defuzzification calculations can be carried out more easily in comparison to those introduced in Sections 5.5 and 5.6 if singletons with height one are chosen to represent the terms C_k (see 5.2) of the output C (see 5.1).

This is illustrated on the client financial risk tolerance model (Case Study 17 (Parts 1–4)).

Case Study 18 *Use of Singletons for a Client Financial Risk Tolerance Model*

Assume that the financial experts use singletons to model the output risk tolerance (see Fig. 5.13(a)) while the inputs are defined as in Case Study 17 (Part 1). Hence instead of the three fuzzy numbers in Fig. 5.4 now there are three singletons in Fig. 5.13(a).

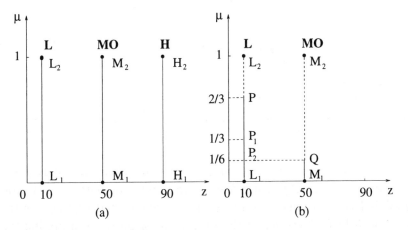

Fig. 5.13. (a) Terms of the output *risk tolerance* presented by singletons. (b) Firing of rules and defuzzification.

Consider the same *if... and ... then* rules given in Table 5.2. Now **L, MO,** and **H** are singletons, not triangular and trapezoidal numbers. Also adopt the same readings as in Case Study 17 (Part 3) shown on Fig. 5.8. Then formula (5.14) expressing the strength of the rules is valid. The control outputs (5.15) are valid but now $\mu_L(z)$ and $\mu_{MO}(z)$ are substituted by the singletons **L** and **MO** shown in Fig. 5.13 (a).

The firing of the rules follows the procedure schematically presented in Fig. 5.9. The first two columns of figures remain without change. There is a difference only in the third column—the terms **L**, **L**, **L**, and **MO** are substituted by the corresponding singletons.

The min operations (5.15) expressing the control outputs now result in sliced singletons presented in one figure (Fig. 5.13 (b))—not in four as in Fig. 5.9. The firing of rules 1 and 2 cut the segments L_1P_1 and L_1P_2 out from the singleton **L**. The firing of rule 3 cut the segment L_1P out from the singleton **L**; it includes the segments L_1P_1 and L_1P_2. The firing of rule 4 cut the segment M_1Q out from the singleton **MO**. Hence only two segments, L_1P and M_1Q form the aggregated output (Fig. 5.13 (b)).

Operation defuzzification is performed by calculating the weighted average (see (3.2)) of the points L_1 and M_1 representing 10 and 50:

$$\hat{z} = \frac{\frac{2}{3}(10) + \frac{1}{6}(50)}{\frac{1}{6} + \frac{2}{3}} = 18.$$

Essentially this is a particular case of formula (5.17), CAM, and also particular case of (5.19), HDM.

The resulting number 18 is more conservative than 29 and 22 produced correspondingly by CAM and HDM when the terms of the output C were described not by singletons but by fuzzy numbers (see Case Study 17 (Part 4)).

$\Box$

When using singletons, we can expect results close (or equal) to those which we could get by using fuzzy terms, but not better. Advantage: simplified calculations. Disadvantage: disconnected segment outputs (see Fig. 5.13 (b)) weakened the protection of partly overlapping fuzzy outputs against a model which might be good to lesser degree.

5.8   Tuning of Fuzzy Logic Control Models

In Section 5.2 four steps for designing the terms A_i, B_j, and C_k (see (5.2)) have been presented. In Section 5.3 *if ... then* rules involving these terms (see (5.4)) have been formally constructed. That, together with the readings, predetermines the final result obtained by applying FLC. However in some situations the experts may find the results to be somewhat not very satisfactory from common-sense point of view and this may raise doubt in their own judgement. Then the experts have the option to improve the FLC model by modification and revision of the shapes and number of terms, location of peaks, flats, supporting intervals. Also they may reconsider and redesign the control rules. This revision is called *tuning* or *refinement*. Unfortunately there is no unique method for such tuning. There are some suggestions in the engineering literature but this is out of the scope of the book. The experts who designed the FLC model using their good knowledge and experience would simply have to do more work and thinking to improve the model if they feel that this may bring better results.

As an illustration again we use the model in Case Study 17 (Parts 1–4).

Case Study 19 *Tuning of a Client Financial Risk Tolerance Model*

Assume the experts consider the conclusion of the FLC model, namely the crisp value 22(HDM) measuring the risk tolerance on the scale from 0 to 100 to be too small for a person with annual income 40,000 and total networth 250,000. Hence they decide to tune the model making slight change to the terms of output *C-risk tolerance*. The modified terms are shown on Fig. 5.14.

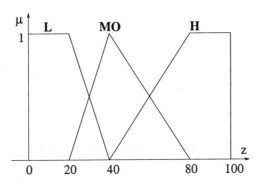

Fig. 5.14. Modified terms of the output *risk tolerance*.

In comparison to Fig. 5.4 there are several changes: (1) The new terms **L** and **H** have new supporting intervals $[0, 40]$ instead of $[0, 50]$ and $[40, 100]$ instead of $[50, 100]$, correspondingly; (2) the new term **MO** has its peak shifted to the left by 10 units; it is still a triangular number but not in central form.

Assuming everything else in the model in Case Study 17 (Parts 1–4) stays without change, firing of the same rules produces here the aggregated output given in Fig. 5.15.

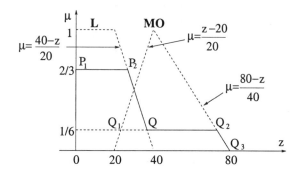

Fig. 5.15. Aggregated outputs and defuzzification for the tuned client financial risk tolerance model.

Solving together $\mu = \frac{2}{3}$ and $\mu = \frac{40-z}{20}$, $\mu = \frac{1}{6}$ and $\mu = \frac{z-20}{20}$, $\mu = \frac{1}{6}$ and $\mu = \frac{80-z}{40}$ we find that the projections of $P_1 P_2$ and $Q_1 Q_2$ are $[0, \frac{80}{3}]$ and $[\frac{70}{3}, \frac{220}{3}]$.

The HDM (formula (5.19)) gives the nonfuzzy control output

$$\hat{z}_h^t = \frac{\frac{2}{3} \frac{0 + \frac{80}{3}}{2} + \frac{1}{6} \frac{\frac{70}{3} + \frac{220}{3}}{3}}{\frac{2}{3} + \frac{1}{6}} = 30.$$

This value is larger than 22 of the initial model obtained by HDM. It suggests a quite moderate financial risk tolerance.

□

5.9   One-Input–One-Output Control Model

It was noted in the beginning of Section 5.2 that the control methodology can be applied to the simple case of one-input–one-output.

Let us consider as an illustration one input $\mathcal{A}$ and one output $\mathcal{C}$ each consisting of four terms of triangular shape (see Figs. 5.16 and 5.17).

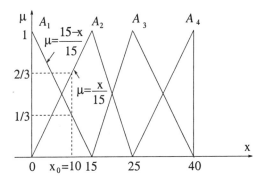

Fig. 5.16. Input $\mathcal{A}$; terms of $\mathcal{A}$. Reading x_0 and fuzzy reading inputs.

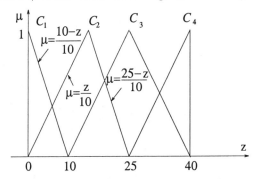

Fig. 5.17. Output $\mathcal{C}$; terms of $\mathcal{C}$.

The number of the *if ... then* rules is four – that is the number of terms in the input $\mathcal{A}$. Since there is no second input, the rules do not contain the *and* connective; they are of the type (5.4) but *and* and $\mathcal{B}_j$ are missing.

Assume the rules are

Rule 1: *If x is $\mathcal{A}_1$ then $\mathcal{C}_1$,*
Rule 2: *If x is $\mathcal{A}_2$ then $\mathcal{C}_2$,*
Rule 3: *If x is $\mathcal{A}_3$ then $\mathcal{C}_3$,*
Rule 4: *If x is $\mathcal{A}_4$ then $\mathcal{C}_4$,*

It is not necessary for $\mathcal{C}_i$ to take part in rule $i, i = 1, \ldots, 4$. That depends on the meaning of $\mathcal{A}_i$ and $\mathcal{C}_i$ in a particular situation.

Assume reading $x_0 = 10$. Then substituting 10 for x into $\mu = \frac{15-x}{15}$ and $\mu = \frac{x}{15}$ gives the fuzzy reading inputs $\frac{1}{3}$ and $\frac{2}{3}$ (see Fig. 5.16).

Since there is only one input, the strengths or the rules or levels of firing (5.10) reduce to $\alpha_1 = \frac{1}{3}$ and $\alpha_2 = \frac{2}{3}$, hence two rules are to be fired.

The control output (CO) of each rule (see 5.11) is

CO of rule 1: $\alpha_1 \wedge \mu_{C_1}(z) = \min(\frac{1}{3}, \mu_{C_1}(z))$,

CO of rule 2: $\alpha_2 \wedge \mu_{C_2}(z) = \min(\frac{2}{3}, \mu_{C_1}(z))$.

The firing of these rules produces independently two clipped triangular numbers. The operation is presented in one figure (Fig. 5.18).

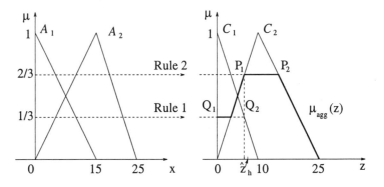

Fig. 5.18. Firing of two rules. Aggregated output $\mu_{agg}(z)$.

The sliced triangular numbers C_1 and C_2 give two trapezoids whose aggregated output is $\mu_{agg}(z)$ shown on Fig. 5.18 with tick lines,

$$\mu_{agg}(z) = \max(\min(\frac{1}{3}, \mu_{C_1}(z)), \min(\frac{2}{3}, \mu_{C_2}(z));$$

it is a particular case of (5.12).

For defuzzification we apply the HDM. Substituting $\mu = \frac{1}{3}$ into $\mu = \frac{10-z}{10}$ and $\mu = \frac{2}{3}$ into $\mu = \frac{z}{10}$ and into $\mu = \frac{25-z}{15}$ gives the numbers $\frac{20}{3}, \frac{20}{3}, 15$, hence the projections of $P_1 P_2$ and $Q_1 Q_2$ are $[\frac{20}{3}, 15]$ and $[0, \frac{20}{3}]$.

Using formula (5.19) we obtain

$$\hat{z}_h = \frac{\frac{2}{3} \frac{\frac{20}{3}+15}{2} + \frac{1}{3} \frac{0+\frac{20}{3}}{2}}{\frac{2}{3} + \frac{1}{3}} = 8.33.$$

5.10 Notes

1. The conceptual base for fuzzy logic control was established by Zadeh (1973) in the paper *Outline of a New Approach to the Analysis of Complex Systems and Decision Processes*. Zadeh's paper inspired Mamdani to introduce a specific fuzzy control methodology (Mamdani and Assilian (1975)) which was later developed further, extended, and applied by many researchers to different industrial engineering problems. A modern monograph book on fuzzy modeling and control has been written by Yager and Filev (1994).

2. Consider more than two inputs (but one output), say three having correspondingly n, m, and p terms. Then the inference rules will be of the type *if ... and ... and ... then* involving two logical connectives *and*. The number of the rules is determined by the product $n \times m \times p$. Accordingly this can be generalized for more inputs. For instance, if $n = m = p = 3$, the number of rules is $3 \times 3 \times 3 = 3^3 = 27$. If another (fourth) input also with three terms is added, the number of rules becomes $27 \times 3 = 3^4 = 81$, etc. Naturally more than two inputs will cause difficulties and they will increase faster than the increase of the number of inputs. The use of computer programs helps. In Chapter 6, Section 6.4, a simplified FLC technique is used in a case with three inputs. Also it is possible to have models with more than one output. The number of outputs requires the same number of decision tables. A two-input–three-output FLC models is presented in Chapter 6, Section 6.1.

3. Six defuzzification methods are described and analyzed by Hellendoorn and Thomas (1993).

Chapter 6

Applications of Fuzzy Logic Control

This chapter demonstrates the usefulness and capability of the fuzzy logic control (FLC) methodology presented in Chapter 5. It is applied to a variety of real life problems: investment advisory models, pest management, inventory control models, problem analysis, and potential problem analysis.[1]

6.1 Investment Advisory Models

Financial service organizations have developed various advisory investment models for clients based on age and risk tolerance. The objective is to advice clients how to allocate portions of their investments across the three main asset types: savings, income, and growth (asset allocation).

The concepts age and risk tolerance are measured on suitable scales. Age is partitioned into three groups, for instance young (≤ 30 years), middle age (between 30 and 60 years), and old (≥ 60 years). The risk tolerance is partitioned on a psychometric scale from 0 to 100 into low (≤ 30), moderate (between 30 and 70), and high (≥ 70). A questionary filled by the client help financial experts to determine his/her risk tolerance group (low, moderate, or high). Knowing the client's age and risk tolerance group and using results from previous studies presented in tables and charts, the financial experts are in a position to advise a client how to allocate money into savings, income, and growth.

A deficiency in this model is that a person 31 years old is middle age as well as a person who is 45 years old. All ages in the interval [31, 59] have the same status; they equally qualify to be middle age; there is no gradation level of belonging to the interval. The same is valid for those who are young and old. Similar difficulty arises with the notion of risk tolerance.

Classical (crisp) models of this type can be improved by using FLC methodology. This is illustrated in the following case study.

Case Study 20 *Client Asset Allocation Model*

The inputs (linguistic variables) in the fuzzy logic client asset allocation model are *age* and *risk tolerance* (*risk*). The *risk* can be estimated as in Case Study 17, Parts 1–4, Chapter 5. It is important to observe that here, in comparison to Case Study 17, there are three outputs (linguistic variables), *savings, income,* and *equity.* Hence this is a two-input–three-output model. Nevertheless the technique in Chapter 5 can be applied but that requires the design of three decision tables (see Notes, 2, Chapter 5).

The control objective is for any given pair (*age, risk*) which reflects the state of a client to find how to allocate the asset to *savings, income,* and *growth.*

Assume that the financial experts describe the two input and three output variables by the terms of triangular and trapezoidal shape as follows:

$$Age \triangleq \{\mathbf{Y}(young), \mathbf{MI}(middle\ age), \mathbf{OL}(old)\},$$

$$Risk \triangleq \{\mathbf{L}(low), \mathbf{MO}(moderate), \mathbf{H}(high)\},$$

$$Saving \triangleq \{\mathbf{L}(low), \mathbf{M}(medium), \mathbf{H}(high)\},$$

$$Income \triangleq \{\mathbf{L}(low), \mathbf{M}(medium), \mathbf{H}(high)\},$$

$$Growth \triangleq \{\mathbf{L}(low), \mathbf{M}(medium), \mathbf{H}(high)\}.$$

They are shown on Figs. 6.1–6.3.

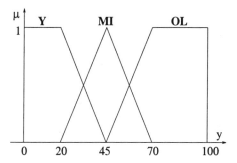

Fig. 6.1. Terms of the input *age*.

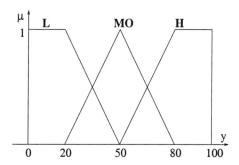

Fig. 6.2. Terms of the input *risk tolerance*.

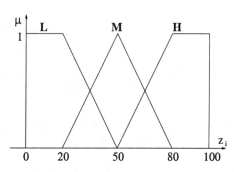

Fig. 6.3. Terms of the output variables *savings, income, growth*.

The universal sets (operating domains) of the input and output variables are $U_1 = \{x|0 \leq x \leq 100\}$ where the base variable x represents years, $U_2 = \{y|0 \leq y \leq 100\}$ with base variable y measured on a pschychometric scale, $U_3 = \{z_i|0 \leq z_i \leq 100, i = 1, 2, 3\}$ where the base variables z_i take values on scale from 0 to 100.

The terms of linguistic variables *risk, savings, income,* and *growth* are described by the same membership functions as the linguistic variables in Case Study 17 (see (5.3)). The variable *age* (Fig. 6.1) differs slightly from the other variables; the membership functions of its terms are

$$
\begin{aligned}
\mu_{\mathbf{Y}}(x) &= \begin{cases} 1 & \text{for } x \le 20, \\ \frac{45-x}{25} & \text{for } 20 \le x \le 45, \end{cases} \\
\mu_{\mathbf{MI}}(x) &= \begin{cases} \frac{x-20}{25} & \text{for } 20 \le x \le 45, \\ \frac{70-x}{25} & \text{for } 45 \le x \le 70, \end{cases} \\
\mu_{\mathbf{OL}}(x) &= \begin{cases} \frac{x-45}{25} & \text{for } 45 \le x \le 70, \\ 1 & \text{for } 70 \le x. \end{cases}
\end{aligned}
\tag{6.1}
$$

There are nine *if ... and ... then* rules like in Case Study 17 but each inference rule produces three (not one) conclusions, one for *savings,* one for *income,* and one for *growth.* Consequently the financial experts have to design three decision tables. Assume that these are the tables presented below.

Table 6.1. Decision table for the output *savings.*

Risk tolerance →

Age ↓		Low	Moderate	High
	Young	M	L	L
	Middle	M	L	L
	Old	H	M	M

Table 6.2. Decision table for the output *income.*

Risk tolerance →

Age ↓		Low	Moderate	High
	Young	M	M	L
	Middle	H	H	M
	Old	H	H	M

Table 6.3. Decision table for the output *growth*.
Risk tolerance →

		Low	Moderate	High
Age	Young	M	H	H
↓	Middle	L	M	H
	Old	L	L	M

For instance the first two *if ... then* rules read:

If client's age is young and client's risk tolerance is low, then asset allocation is: medium in savings, medium in income, medium in growth.

If client's age is young and client's risk tolerance is moderate, then asset allocation is: low in savings, medium in income, high in growth.

Consider a client whose age is $x_0 = 25$ and risk tolerance level is $y_0 = 45$. Matching the readings 25 and 45 against the appropriate terms in Figs. 6.1 and 6.2 and using Eqs. (5.3) and (6.1) gives the fuzzy reading inputs

$$\mu_{\mathbf{Y}}(25) = \frac{4}{5}, \quad \mu_{\mathbf{MI}}(25) = \frac{1}{5}, \quad \mu_{\mathbf{L}}(45) = \frac{1}{6}, \quad \mu_{\mathbf{MO}}(45) = \frac{5}{6}.$$

The strength of the rules calculated using (5.10) are:

$$\alpha_{11} = \mu_{\mathbf{Y}}(25) \wedge \mu_{\mathbf{L}}(45) = \min(\frac{4}{5}, \frac{1}{6}) = \frac{1}{6},$$

$$\alpha_{12} = \mu_{\mathbf{Y}}(25) \wedge \mu_{\mathbf{MO}}(45) = \min(\frac{4}{5}, \frac{5}{6}) = \frac{4}{5},$$

$$\alpha_{21} = \mu_{\mathbf{MI}}(25) \wedge \mu_{\mathbf{L}}(45) = \min(\frac{1}{5}, \frac{1}{6}) = \frac{1}{6},$$

$$\alpha_{22} = \mu_{\mathbf{MI}}(25) \wedge \mu_{\mathbf{MO}}(45) = \min(\frac{1}{5}, \frac{5}{6}) = \frac{1}{5}.$$

The control outputs of the rules are presented in the active cells in three decision tables (a particular case of Table 5.5).

Table 6.4. Control output *savings*.

	Low	Moderate
Young	$\frac{1}{6} \wedge \mu_{\mathbf{M}}(z_1)$	$\frac{4}{5} \wedge \mu_{\mathbf{L}}(z_1)$
Middle	$\frac{1}{6} \wedge \mu_{\mathbf{M}}(z_1)$	$\frac{1}{5} \wedge \mu_{\mathbf{L}}(z_1)$

Table 6.5. Control output *income*.

	Low	*Moderate*
Young	$\frac{1}{6} \wedge \mu_{\mathrm{M}}(z_2)$	$\frac{4}{5} \wedge \mu_{\mathrm{M}}(z_2)$
Middle	$\frac{1}{6} \wedge \mu_{\mathrm{H}}(z_2)$	$\frac{1}{5} \wedge \mu_{\mathrm{H}}(z_2)$

Table 6.6. Control output *growth*.

	Low	*Moderate*
Young	$\frac{1}{6} \wedge \mu_{\mathrm{M}}(z_3)$	$\frac{4}{5} \wedge \mu_{\mathrm{H}}(z_3)$
Middle	$\frac{1}{6} \wedge \mu_{\mathrm{L}}(z_3)$	$\frac{1}{5} \wedge \mu_{\mathrm{M}}(z_3)$

The outputs in the four active cells in Tables 6.4–6.6 have to be aggregated separately. The results (see Figs. 6.4–6.6) obtained by following Case Study 17 (Part 3) are:

$$\mu_{agg}(z_1) = \max\{\min(\frac{1}{6}, \mu_{\mathrm{M}}(z_1)), \min(\frac{4}{5}, \mu_{\mathrm{L}}(z_1))\};$$

$$\mu_{agg}(z_2) = \max\{\min(\frac{4}{5}, \mu_{\mathrm{M}}(z_2)), \min(\frac{1}{5}, \mu_{\mathrm{H}}(z_2))\};$$

$$\mu_{agg}(z_3) = \max\{\min(\frac{1}{5}, \mu_{\mathrm{M}}(z_3)), \min(\frac{4}{5}, \mu_{\mathrm{H}}(z_3)), \min(\frac{1}{6}, \mu_{\mathrm{L}}(z_3))\}.$$

The aggregated outputs shown on Figs. 6.4–6.6 are defuzzified by using HDM. The results are given in the same figures.

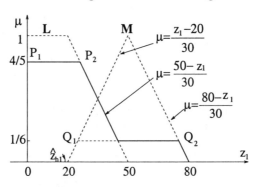

Fig. 6.4. Aggregated output *savings*. Defuzzification.

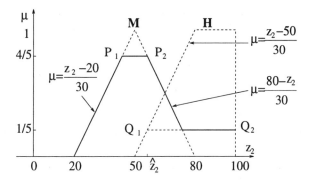

Fig. 6.5. Aggregated output *income*. Defuzzification.

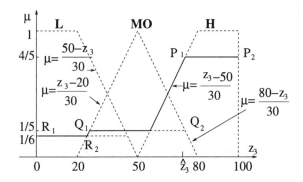

Fig. 6.6. Aggregated output *growth*. Defuzzification.

The projections of the flat segments can be easily found using their height and the relevant equations of inclined segments indicated in the figures. For instance, consider Fig. 6.4. Substituting $\frac{4}{5}$ for μ in $\mu = \frac{50-z_1}{30}$ gives the projection of P_2 to be 26. Substituting $\frac{1}{6}$ for μ in $\mu = \frac{z_1-20}{30}$ and $\mu = \frac{80-z_1}{30}$ gives the projections of Q_1 and Q_2 to be 25 and 75. Similarly one can find that the projections of P_1P_2 and Q_1Q_2 in Fig. 6.5 are the intervals [44,56] and [56, 100]. There are three flat segments P_1P_2, Q_1Q_2, and R_1R_2 in Fig. 6.6. Their projections are [74,100], [26, 74], and [0, 45].

Then using the defuzzification formula (5.19) we find

$$\hat{z}_{h1} = \frac{\frac{4}{5}\frac{0+26}{2} + \frac{1}{6}\frac{25+75}{2}}{\frac{4}{5} + \frac{1}{6}} = 19.38(saving),$$

$$\hat{z}_{h2} = \frac{\frac{4}{5}\frac{44+56}{2} + \frac{1}{5}\frac{56+100}{2}}{\frac{4}{5} + \frac{1}{5}} = 55.60(income),$$

$$\hat{z}_{h3} = \frac{\frac{4}{5}\frac{74+100}{2} + \frac{1}{5}\frac{26+74}{2} + \frac{1}{6}\frac{0+45}{2}}{\frac{4}{5} + \frac{1}{5} + \frac{1}{6}} = 71.44(growth).$$

The sum $\hat{z}_{h1} + \hat{z}_{h2} + \hat{z}_{h3} = 146.42$ represents the total asset (100%). To convert each $\hat{z}_{hi}, i = 1, 2, 3$, into percentage we use the formula

$$\frac{100\hat{z}_{hi}}{\hat{z}_{h1} + \hat{z}_{h2} + \hat{z}_{h3}} = \frac{100}{146.42}\hat{z}_{hi} = 0.68\hat{z}_{hi}, \quad i = 1, 2, 3.$$

This gives the following asset allocation of the client whose age is 25 and risk tolerance 45:

$$Savings : \ 0.68(19.38)\% = 13.18\%,$$
$$Income : \ 0.68(55.60)\% = 37.81\%,$$
$$Growth : \ 0.68(71.44)\% = 48.58\%.$$

Rounding off gives savings 13%, income 38%, and growth 49%.

These numbers can be used by financial experts as a base for making an asset allocation recommendation suitable for a person whose age is 25 and risk tolerance is 45 (on a scale from 0 to 100). □

6.2 Fuzzy Logic Control for Pest Management

There is no definite knowledge in science to tell us how to model in a unique way processes in nature, and in particular population behavior. Ecological and bio-economical systems involve various types of uncertainties and vague phenomena which makes their study extremely complicated. The better understanding of these complex systems will create conditions for better and more rational resource management and efficient control policies for restriction of undesirable growth.

In this section the fuzzy logic control (FLC) methodology is applied to population dynamics, in particular to a predator–prey system. The same methodology can be applied with some modifications to other types of interactions, for instance competition between two populations. Also it can be applied to more than two interacting populations.

Consider the prey to be a pest which serves as a host for the predator, a parasite. The pest population has size (density) x and the parasite population has size (density) y. It is assumed that the system is observable, hence the population sizes can be counted or estimated.

The predator–prey interaction takes place in a fuzzy environment due to climate conditions, diseases, harvesting, migration, interaction with other species not accounted in the system, etc. Age, sex, and genotype differences are presented in the system, and the changes in density of the populations are not only instantaneous but may depend on the past history (time-lag).

No mathematical model can describe satisfactory such a complex system. The theoretical modelers who want to derive behavior rules of general nature about the interacting populations are bound to make simplifying assumptions. They may present interesting results and elegant theorems. Unfortunately often the relation between theorems and reality is not close. Hence it is natural to look for alternative methodologies.

The control objective of the resource management is to design a growth restriction policy for the pest population (eventually extinction) by using as a control output the change (increase) in the size of the parasite; in other words to release (stock) predators in order to control pests.

We will illustrate the FLC on a case study.

Case Study 21 *Control of a Parasite–Pest System*

The number of both pests and parasites in a certain environment is assumed to vary between 0 and 16,000.

The following selections are made: inputs—*pest population size* and *parasite population size*; output—*increase of size of parasites*. They are modeled by sets of the type (5.1) each containing six terms of triangular shape. The labels of the terms are indicated in Figs. 6.7–6.9. The base variables x and y for the inputs and the base variable $\triangle y$ for the output represent numbers measuring the population sizes x and y, and the increase $\triangle y$ of the size of parasites in thousands. Equations of the segments which will be used are given in Figs. 6.7–6.8.

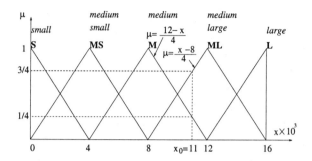

Fig. 6.7. Terms of the input *pest population size*.

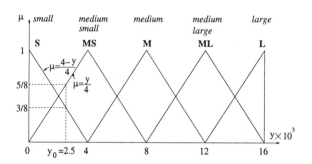

Fig. 6.8. Terms of the input *parasite population size*.

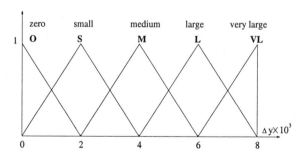

Fig. 6.9. Terms of the output *increase of parasite population size*.

The selected rules by the resource management are presented in the decision Table 6.7.

Table 6.7. *If ... and ... then* rules for parasite–pest system.
Parasite population size →

	y	S	MS	M	ML	L
Pest population size ↓	x					
	S	0	0	0	0	0
	MS	S	0	0	0	0
	M	M $\sqrt{}$	S $\sqrt{}$	0	0	0
	ML	L $\sqrt{}$	M $\sqrt{}$	S	0	0
	L	VL	L	M	S	0

There are 25 rules. We present only those which will be used later.

(a) *If pest population is medium and parasite population is small then exert medium increase of parasite population size.*

(b) *If pest population is medium and parasite population is medium small then exert small increase of parasite population.*

(c) *If pest population is medium large and parasite population is small then exert large increase of parasite population size.*

(d) *If pest population is medium large and parasite population is medium small then exert medium increase of parasite population size.*

Assume that at a certain time t_0 the number of pest population is estimated by resource management experts to be 11,000 or $x_0 = 11$ in thousands and the number of parasite population is estimated to be 2,500 or $y_0 = 2.5$ in thousands. The matching against appropriate terms of the input variables is shown in Figs. 6.7 and 6.8.

Using the membership function of the triangular numbers in Figs. 6.7 and 6.8 we calculate the fuzzy readings as follows. The value $x_0 = 11$ is consequently substituted for x into equations $\mu = \frac{12-x}{4}$ and $\mu = \frac{x-8}{4}$ which gives $\frac{1}{4}$ and $\frac{3}{4}$. Similarly $y_0 = 2.5$ substituted for y into equations $\mu = \frac{4-y}{4}$ and $\mu = \frac{y}{4}$ produces $\frac{3}{8}$ and $\frac{5}{8}$, correspondingly. Hence

$$\mu_M(x_0) = \frac{1}{4}, \quad \mu_{ML}(x_0) = \frac{3}{4}, \quad \mu_S(y_0) = \frac{3}{8}, \quad \mu_{MS}(y_0) = \frac{5}{8}.$$

Then the induced decision Table 5.3 reduces to the marked cells in Table 6.7 (the rest of the cells are nonactive).

The four rules to be fired are (a)–(d) induced by the marked cells in Table 6.7.

To find the levels of firing (strength of the rules) according to Section 5.5 we use formulas (5.10) which give

$$\alpha_1 = \mu_M(x_0) \wedge \mu_S(y_0) = \min(\frac{1}{4}, \frac{3}{8}) = \frac{1}{4},$$

$$\alpha_2 = \mu_M(x_0) \wedge \mu_{MS}(y_0) = \min(\frac{1}{4}, \frac{5}{8}) = \frac{1}{4},$$

$$\alpha_3 = \mu_{ML}(x_0) \wedge \mu_S(y_0) = \min(\frac{3}{4}, \frac{3}{8}) = \frac{3}{8},$$

$$\alpha_4 = \mu_{ML}(x_0) \wedge \mu_{MS}(y_0) = \min(\frac{3}{4}, \frac{5}{8}) = \frac{5}{8}.$$

The control outputs of the rules (see (5.11)) are

(a) $\alpha_1 \wedge \mu_M(\triangle y) = \min(\frac{1}{4}, \mu_M(\triangle y))$,

(b) $\alpha_2 \wedge \mu_S(\triangle y) = \min(\frac{1}{4}, \mu_S(\triangle y))$,

(c) $\alpha_3 \wedge \mu_L(\triangle y) = \min(\frac{3}{8}, \mu_L(\triangle y))$,

(d) $\alpha_4 \wedge \mu_M(\triangle y) = \min(\frac{5}{8}, \mu_M(\triangle y))$.

Noticing that the output of rule (a) is included into rule (d), the aggregation of the control outputs of rules (b)–(d) according to formula (5.12) produces

$$\mu_{agg}(\triangle y) = \max\{\min(\frac{1}{4}, \mu_S(\triangle y)), \min(\frac{3}{8}, \mu_L(\triangle y)), \min(\frac{5}{8}, \mu_M(\triangle y))\}.$$

This is a union of the three triangular fuzzy numbers **S, M, L**, presented in Fig. 6.9, sliced correspondingly with the straight lines $\mu = \frac{1}{4}, \mu = \frac{3}{8}, \mu = \frac{5}{8}$, and placed on top one other. The result is shown in Fig. 6.10 (the thick segments).

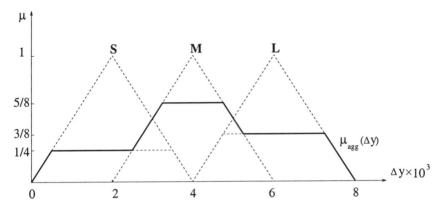

Fig. 6.10. Aggregated output for the parasite–pest system.

The mean of maximum method (MMM) is very suitable to be applied for defuzzification since precision is not important in the complex parasite–pest system under consideration. The crisp output is $\triangle \hat{y}_m = 4$ (**M** is a central triangular fuzzy number, Section 1.5.).

Hence the control action which the management should undertake is to increase the parasite population by $4 \times 10^3 = 4000$ members.

The MMM reflects only the firing of rule (d). However, the neglected rules (b) and (c) produce clipped triangulars on both sides of **M** which almost balance each another. Actually the clipped **L** (level of firing $\frac{3}{8}$) is a little bit stronger that the clipped **S** (level of firing $\frac{1}{4}$), hence MMM in this case gives a slightly conservative value which is justified from the biological point of view.

In order to make comparison, let us apply the HDM. Note that the midpoints of the flat segments of the clipped triangular numbers **S**, **M**, and **L** are 2, 4, and 6, correspondingly. Then the extended formula (5.19) (Section 5.6) gives $\triangle \hat{y}_h = 4.2$, which is close to $\triangle \hat{y}_m = 4$.

Later at a properly selected time t_1, the numbers of the prey and predator populations are to be counted or estimated. Assume they are x_1 and y_1 correspondingly. Then the whole process is to be repeated using x_1 for x_0 and y_1 for y_0. The new calculated crisp values $\triangle \hat{y}_{m1}$ will indicate what control action is needed (increase of parasite population size) to keep the pest population below 16×10^3. Again and again the same process is to be repeated.

□

6.3   Inventory Control Models

Storage cost is a major concern of production. Classical inventory models have been constructed to deal with minimizing storage cost. Their aim is to maintain enough quantities of needed parts to produce a product without incurring excessive storage cost. The product is supposed to satisfy the demand on the market. The basic inventory management problem is to decide when new parts should be ordered (order point) and in what quantities to minimize the storage cost. This is a complicated optimization problem (see for instance Fogarty and Hoffmann (1983)). Unfortunately the existing classical mathematical methods may produce a solution quite different from the real situation.

A good alternative to those methods is the FLC methodology. Its purpose is not to minimize cost directly but to maintain a proper inventory level reflecting the demand at a given time. The experience and knowledge of the managers in charge is of great importance in constructing an inventory FLC model.

The fuzzy inventory models discussed here have two input variables: *demand value* $\mathcal{D}$ for a product and *quantity-on-hand parts* (in stock) QOH needed to build the product (see Cox (1995)). There is one output variable—the *inventory action IA* which suggests reordering of parts, reducing the number of the already existing, or no action at that time.

The reduction of number of parts can be done in various ways depending on a specific situation, for instance returning parts to supplier at some nominal loss, sending parts to a sister company, etc. If this options are not available or the management decides not to use them, then the parts can be kept with anticipation demand to improve.

Inventory model 1—parts reduction possible

Following Cox (1995) we model the inputs by sets containing five terms and the output by a set containing seven terms (while Cox uses bell–shaped fuzzy numbers, we employ triangular and trapezoidal numbers):

$$Demand(\mathcal{D}) \triangleq \{\mathbf{F}, \mathbf{D}, \mathbf{S}, \mathbf{I}, \mathbf{R}\},$$

where $\mathbf{F} \triangleq falling$, $\mathbf{D} \triangleq decreased$, $\mathbf{S} \triangleq steady$, $\mathbf{I} \triangleq increased$, $\mathbf{R} \triangleq rising$;

$$Quantity\text{-}on\text{-}hand(QOH) \triangleq \{\mathbf{M}, \mathbf{L}, \mathbf{A}, \mathbf{H}, \mathbf{E}\},$$

where $\mathbf{M} \triangleq$ *minimal*, $\mathbf{L} \triangleq$ *low*, $\mathbf{A} \triangleq$ *adequate*, $\mathbf{H} \triangleq$ *high*, $\mathbf{E} \triangleq$ *excessive*;

$$Inventory\ action\ (\ IA\ ) \triangleq \{\mathbf{NL}, \mathbf{NM}, \mathbf{NS}, \mathbf{O}, \mathbf{PS}, \mathbf{PM}, \mathbf{PL}\},$$

where $\mathbf{NL} \triangleq$ *negative large*, $\mathbf{NM} \triangleq$ *negative moderate*, $\mathbf{NS} \triangleq$ *negative small*, $\mathbf{O} \triangleq$ *zero*, $\mathbf{PS} \triangleq$ *positive small*, $\mathbf{PM} \triangleq$ *positive moderate*, $\mathbf{PL} \triangleq$ *positive large*. The terms of *Inventory action* mean corresponding change to quantity-on-hand; negative stands for reduction of number of parts, positive for ordering, and zero for no action.

According to Section 5.3 the number of rules to be design is 25. They must have as a conclusion the terms of the output. Assume the management constructs the decision Table 6.8.

Table 6.8. *If ... and ... then* rules for the inventory control model.

	Quantity–on–hand →				
	Minimal	*Low*	*Adequate*	*High*	*Excessive*
Demand	**M**	**L**	**A**	**H**	**E**
↓ *Falling* **F**	O	O	NS	NM	NL
Decreased **D**	PS	O	NS	NM	NM
Steady **S**	PM	PS	O	NS	NM
Increased **I**	PM	PM	PS	O	O
Rising **R**	PL	PL	PM	PS	O

The rules leading to inventory action are listed below.

Rule 1: *If D is falling and QOH is minimal, then do nothing;*

Rule 2: *If D is falling and QOH is low, then do nothing;*

Rule 3: *If D is falling and QOH is adequate, then reduce action is negative small;*

Rule 4: *If D is falling and QOH is high, then reduce action is negative moderate;*

Rule 5: *If D is falling and QOH is excessive, then reduce action is negative large;*

Rule 6: *If $\mathcal{D}$ is decreased and QOH is minimal, then order action is positive small;*

Rule 7: *If $\mathcal{D}$ is decreased and QOH is low, then do nothing;*

Rule 8: *If $\mathcal{D}$ is decreased and QOH is adequate, then reduce action is negative small;*

Rule 9: *If $\mathcal{D}$ is decreased and QOH is high, then reduce action is negative moderate;*

Rule 10: *If $\mathcal{D}$ is decreased and QOH is excessive, then reduce action is negative large;*

Rule 11: *If $\mathcal{D}$ is steady and QOH is minimal, then order action is positive moderate;*

Rule 12: *If $\mathcal{D}$ is steady and QOH is low, then order action is positive small;*

Rule 13: *If $\mathcal{D}$ is steady and QOH is adequate, then do nothing;*

Rule 14: *If $\mathcal{D}$ is steady and QOH is high, then reduce action is negative small;*

Rule 15: *If $\mathcal{D}$ is steady and QOH is excessive, then reduce action is negative moderate;*

Rule 16: *If $\mathcal{D}$ is increased and QOH is minimal, then order action is positive moderate;*

Rule 17: *If $\mathcal{D}$ is increased and QOH is low, then order action is positive moderate;*

Rule 18: *If $\mathcal{D}$ is increased and QOH is adequate, then order action is positive small;*

Rule 19: *If $\mathcal{D}$ is increased and QOH is high, then do nothing;*

Rule 20: *If $\mathcal{D}$ is increased and QOH is excessive, then do nothing;*

Rule 21: *If $\mathcal{D}$ is rising and QOH is minimal, then order action is positive large;*

Rule 22: *If $\mathcal{D}$ is rising and QOH is low, then order action is positive large;*

Rule 23: *If $\mathcal{D}$ is rising and QOH is adequate, then order action is positive moderate;*

Rule 24: *If $\mathcal{D}$ is rising and QOH is high, then order action is positive small;*

Rule 25: *If $\mathcal{D}$ is rising and QOH is excessive, then do nothing.*

Inventory model 2—parts reduction not possible

The input variables $\mathcal{D}$ and QOH are the same introduced in Inventory model 1. Since now reduce action is not available, the output *inventory action* is partition into four terms instead of seven,

$$\text{Inventory action } (IA) \triangleq \{\mathbf{O}, \mathbf{PS}, \mathbf{PM}, \mathbf{PL}\},$$

where $\mathbf{O}, \mathbf{PS}, \mathbf{PM}$, and $\mathbf{PL}$ have the same meaning as in Inventory model 1.

The decision table is Table 6.8 with terms $\mathbf{O}$ above the major diagonal.

Table 6.9. *If ... and ... then* rules for Inventory model 2.

Quantity-on-hand →

		M	L	A	H	E
	F	O	O	O	O	O
Demand	D	PS	O	O	O	O
↓	S	PM	PS	O	O	O
	I	PM	PM	PS	O	O
	R	PL	PL	PM	PS	O

The rules producing the inventory action (the *if ... and ... then* rules) can be obtained from those for Inventory model 1 if in rules 3, 4, 5, 8, 9, 10, 14, and 15 the *then* part (conclusion) is substituted with *do nothing*; the rest of the rules remain unchanged.

The control actions discussed in this section are of qualitative nature. In order to produce a crisp action initial data (readings) are needed. This is illustrated in the following case study.

Case Study 22 *An Inventory Model with Order and Reduction Control Action.*

Assume that the input *demand* ($\mathcal{D}$) is defined on the interval $[-50, 50]$ (universal set) (Fig. 6.11) and the input *quantity-on-hand* (QOH) is defined on the interval $[100, 200]$ (Fig. 6.12).

While the scale x (base variable) on which the terms of *demand* are defined is predetermined, the scale y depends on the type and number of QOH parts in a real situation.

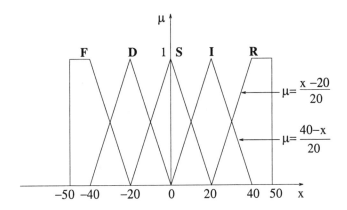

Fig. 6.11. Terms of the input variable *demand* $\mathcal{D}$.

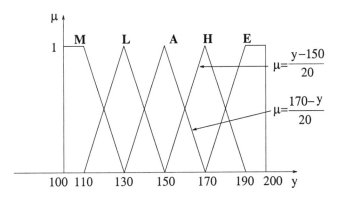

Fig. 6.12. Terms of the input variable *quantity-on-hands* (*QOH*).

Assume also that the output *inventory action (IA)* is defined on the interval $[-50, 50]$ (Fig. 6.13). It is a percentage scale z (base variable) whose selection depends on an estimate of the maximum number (in percentage) by which the number of inventory parts could be increased or decreased.

The terms of the inputs and the output are triangular and parts of trapezoidal numbers whose membership functions can be easily written (see Sections 1.5 and 1.6). Those to be used later (depending on the readings) are given in the figures.

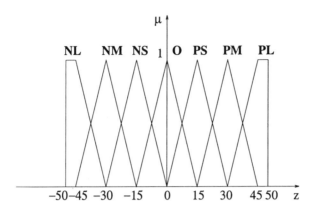

Fig. 6.13. Terms of the output variable *inventory action* (IA).

Assume that at time t_0 the demand (it has to be estimated using for instance the technique in Chapter 3, Section 4, or by other means) is $x_0 = 32$ and quantity-on-hand is $y_0 = 165$. These readings have to be matched against appropriate terms in Fig. 6.11 and Fig. 6.12. Substituting x_0 into $\mu = \frac{40-x}{20}$ and $\mu = \frac{x-20}{20}$, and y_0 into $\mu = \frac{170-y}{20}$ and $\mu = \frac{y-150}{20}$ gives

$$\mu_I(32) = \frac{2}{5}, \quad \mu_R(32) = \frac{3}{5}, \quad \mu_A(165) = \frac{1}{4}, \quad \mu_H(165) = \frac{3}{4}.$$

The induced decision Table 5.3 reduces to Table 6.10 where only the active cells are shown.

Table 6.10. Induce decision table for the inventory model.

	$\mu_A(165) = \frac{1}{4}$	$\mu_H(165) = \frac{3}{4}$
$\mu_I(32) = \frac{2}{5}$	$\mu_{PS}(z)$	$\mu_O(z)$
$\mu_R(32) = \frac{3}{5}$	$\mu_{PM}(z)$	$\mu_{PS}(z)$

The four rules to be fired are 18, 19, 23, 24.
The strengths of these rules are (see (5.10)):

$$\alpha_1 = \mu_I(32) \wedge \mu_A(165) = \min(\frac{2}{5}, \frac{1}{4}) = \frac{1}{4},$$

$$\alpha_2 = \mu_I(32) \wedge \mu_H(165) = \min(\frac{2}{5}, \frac{3}{4}) = \frac{2}{5},$$

$$\alpha_3 = \mu_R(32) \wedge \mu_A(165) = \min(\frac{3}{5}, \frac{1}{4}) = \frac{1}{4},$$

$$\alpha_4 = \mu_R(32) \wedge \mu_H(165) = \min(\frac{3}{5}, \frac{3}{4}) = \frac{3}{5}.$$

The control outputs (CO) of the rules are (see (5.11)):
   CO of rule 18: $\alpha_1 \wedge \mu_{PS}(z) = \min(\frac{1}{4}, \mu_{PS}(z))$,
   CO of rule 19: $\alpha_2 \wedge \mu_O(z) = \min(\frac{2}{5}, \mu_O(z))$,
   CO of rule 23: $\alpha_3 \wedge \mu_{PM}(z) = \min(\frac{1}{4}, \mu_{PM}(z))$,
   CO of rule 24: $\alpha_4 \wedge \mu_{PS}(z) = \min(\frac{3}{5}, \mu_{PS}(z))$.
The output of the rule 18 is included into that of rule 24. Hence the
aggregation of the control outputs (see (5.12)) gives (Fig. 6.14):

$$\mu_{agg}(z) = \max\{\min(\frac{2}{5}, \mu_O(z)), \min(\frac{1}{4}, \mu_{PM}(z)), \min(\frac{3}{5}, \mu_{PS}(z))\}.$$

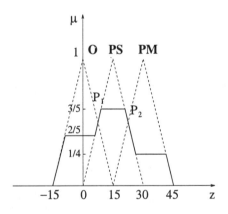

Fig. 6.14. Aggregated output for the inventory model. Defuzzification.

Similar to Case Study 21 (see Fig. 6.10), we can use for defuzzification MMM which gives $\hat{z}_m = 15$ (**PS** is triangular number in central
form). Since rule 19 has level of firing $\frac{2}{5}$ which is stronger than $\frac{1}{4}$, that
of the rule 23, $\hat{z}_m = 15$ is a little bit optimistic value meaning that
ordering of parts is not on the conservative side. Of course the HDM,
which will produce a smaller value than 15, could be easily applied (see
Case Studies 20 and 21).

Now we have to translate $\hat{z}_m = 15$ (in percentage) into a corresponding inventory action. If the QOH at the time t_0 of the study ($x_0 = 32, y_0 = 165$) denoted $(QOH)_{current}$ is considered as unit 1 (or 100%), then it has to be increased by 15 %. This gives $1 + \frac{15}{100} = 1.15$ called *adjustment factor* (AF). The control action leads to a new QOH denoted $(QOH)_{new}$ which is $(QOH)_{current}$ multiplied by (AF), i.e. $165 \times 1.15 = 188.75 \approx 199$. The difference $199 - 165 = 34$ suggests that 34 new parts are to be ordered.

The following general formula can be used:

$$(QOH)_{new} = (QOH)_{current} \times AF,$$

where

$$AF = 1 + \frac{\hat{z}}{100};$$

$\hat{z}$ is a defuzzified value obtained by one of the available methods.

If $\hat{z} > 0$ like in the case discussed, the control action is ordering of new parts; if $\hat{z} < 0$, the control action is reduction.

$\square$

6.4 Problem Analysis

Problem analysis or *deviation performance analysis* deals with problems created when there are undesirable deviations from some expected standard performance. The cause of such deviations is an unplanned and unanticipated change (see Kepner and Tregoe (1965) and Simon (1960)).

The manager or a managerial body in charge of certain areas of operation must recognize an undesirable deviation if such has developed or occurred. Also several deviations may occur concurrently. The manager must find what is wrong and what is the cause for it in order to do the necessary correction. A good knowledge of the expected performance standards in each area of operation will help the manager to identify deviations from such performance. Some deviations are permissible within certain limits established by the manager or a governing body. They have to be watched; no correction at that time is needed.

Once the manager has made sure that the deviations are identified, they have to be ranked according to their importance.

Kepner and Tregoe (1965) who contributed to classical problem analysis suggest that several important questions have to be addressed by
the manager:
(1) How urgent is the deviation?
(2) How serious is the deviation?
(3) What is the deviation growth potential?
(4) What is the priority of the deviation?
The answer to these questions requires experience and skills from the
manager. Valuable instructions and examples are provided by Kepner
and Tregoe (1965).

Our approach in dealing with the above questions is different. We
use the tools of fuzzy logic control (FLC) to quantify more realistically
the classical problem analysis and arrive to conclusion.

Urgent, serious, and *growth potential* are considered here as linguistic variables; they are the inputs. The output variable is *priority of
deviation.* Since high precision is not needed, we model each variable
by three terms (using triangular and trapezoidal numbers):

$$Urgent(U) \triangleq \{\mathbf{N}, \mathbf{S}, \mathbf{V}\},$$

$$Serious(S) \triangleq \{\mathbf{N}, \mathbf{S}, \mathbf{V}\},$$

$$Growth\ potential(GP) \triangleq \{\mathbf{L}, \mathbf{M}, \mathbf{H}\},$$

$$Priority\ of\ deviation(POD) \triangleq \{\mathbf{L}, \mathbf{M}, \mathbf{H}\},$$

where $\mathbf{N} \triangleq not$, $\mathbf{S} \triangleq somewhat$, $\mathbf{V} \triangleq very$, $\mathbf{H} \triangleq high$, $\mathbf{L} \triangleq low$,
$\mathbf{M} \triangleq medium$.

Since we are dealing with three inputs according to Chapter 5
(Notes,2) we have to design $3 \times 3 \times 3 = 27$ rules of the type *if ...
and ... and ... then.* For instance, *if deviation (D) is somewhat urgent
and D is very serious and D growth potential is medium then priority
of deviation is high.*

From these rules eight have to be fired hence the aggregated conclusion will consists of eighth (or less) superimposed clipped fuzzy numbers.
This can be done but is complicated.

In order to simplify the control procedure we consider as in Chapter 5, Section 5.9, the input variables to be independent of each other

meaning that the rules will be of the type *if . . . then* without using *and* (*precondition*) part. This approach reduces the number of rules from 27 to 9. They are listed below in three groups concerning *urgent* (U), *serious* (S), and *growth potential* (*GP*); in each group there is one input and one output.

$$
\begin{aligned}
&\text{Rule 1:} && \text{\it If D is NU then POD is L,} \\
&\text{Rule 2:} && \text{\it If D is SU then POD is M,} \\
&\text{Rule 3:} && \text{\it If D is VU then POD is H,}
\end{aligned}
\quad\Bigg\} \quad (6.2)
$$

$$
\begin{aligned}
&\text{Rule 4:} && \text{\it If D is NS then POD is L,} \\
&\text{Rule 5:} && \text{\it If D is SS then POD is M,} \\
&\text{Rule 6:} && \text{\it If D is VS then POD is H,}
\end{aligned}
\quad\Bigg\} \quad (6.3)
$$

$$
\begin{aligned}
&\text{Rule 7:} && \text{\it If D is with LGP then POD is L,} \\
&\text{Rule 8:} && \text{\it If D is with MGP then POD is M,} \\
&\text{Rule 9:} && \text{\it If D is with HGP then POD is H.}
\end{aligned}
\quad\Bigg\} \quad (6.4)
$$

For instance, the first rule reads: *if deviation is not urgent then priority of deviation is low.*

The FLC is applied separately for each group of rules and the obtained conclusions are aggregated. In practice this means that we have to apply the simplified procedure in Section 5.9 three times for one-input–one-output control model and then to aggregate the three outputs.

Details are presented in the following case study.

Case Study 23 *Fuzzy Logic Control for Problem Analysis*

Let us assume that the three input variables and the output variable are defined on a psychometric scale $[0, 100]$ as shown in Figs. 6.15–6.18.

Assume that the manager detects a deviation performance and gives the assessments (readings) $x_0 = 40, y_0 = 20, z_0 = 75$ of the base variables x, y, and z measuring how urgent is the deviation, how serious is it, and what is its growth potential on the scale $[0, 100]$.

The fuzzy reading inputs generated by x_0, y_0, and z_0 are shown in Figs. 6.15–6.17. They are actually the strength of the rules (the levels of firing).

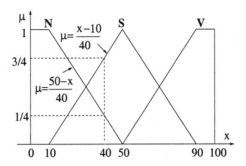

Fig. 6.15. Terms of the input variable *urgent*.

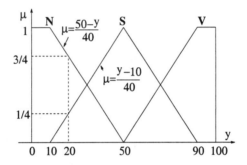

Fig. 6.16. Terms of the input variable *serious*.

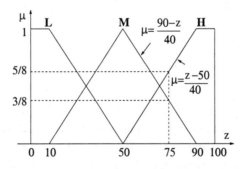

Fig. 6.17. Terms of the output variable *growth potential*.

Now the technique in Case Study 18 has to be applied three times since the three inputs U, S, and GP are considered as independent which is reflected in the three groups of rules (6.1)–(6.3). For each group the FLC requires that two rules are to be fired at specified levels. When combined they produce three independent control outputs $\mu_x(v), \mu_y(v)$, and $\mu_z(v)$ whose aggregation will give the membership function $\mu_{agg}(v)$ of the final conclusion concerning priority of deviation (POD).

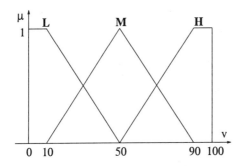

Fig. 6.18. Terms of the output variable *priority of deviation*.

The procedure is performed in Fig. 6.19. Only the relevant terms are presented.

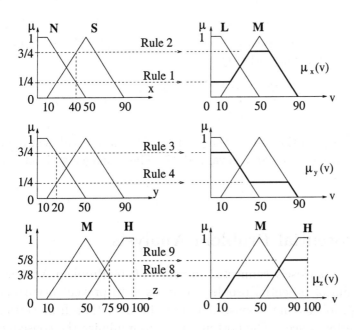

Fig. 6.19. Firing of rules for three independent inputs.

The aggregation of $\mu_x(v), \mu_y(v)$, and $\mu_z(v)$ using operation max gives the output

$$\mu_{agg}(v) = \max(\mu_x(v), \mu_y(v), \mu_z(v))$$

geometrically presented in Fig. 6.20. It is obtained by superimposing $\mu_x(v), \mu_y(v)$, and $\mu_z(v)$ a top one other (see Section 5.5).

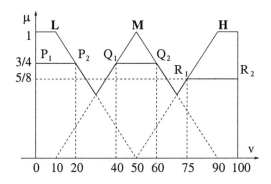

Fig. 6.20. Aggregation of the independent inputs. Defuzzification.

To defuzzify $\mu_{agg}(v)$ we use the HDM. Since the projections of the flat segments P_1P_2, Q_1Q_2, and R_1R_2 are $[0,20]$, $[40, 60]$, and $[75, 100]$, the extended formula (5.19) gives

$$\hat{v}_h = \frac{\frac{3}{4}\frac{0+20}{2} + \frac{3}{4}\frac{40+60}{2} + \frac{5}{8}\frac{75+100}{2}}{\frac{3}{4} + \frac{3}{4} + \frac{5}{8}} = 46.91 \approx 47.$$

The interpretation is that the priority of deviation is almost medium; on a scale from 0 to 100 it is ranked 47. The manager will act accordingly.

□

6.5   Potential Problem Analysis

This section is closely connected to Section 6.4—Problem Analysis.

The aim of potential problem analysis is to prevent occurrence of possible problems (in the sense of undesirable deviations from certain expected performance). The bottom line is to minimize the consequences of potential problems if they do occur (see Kepner and Tregoe (1965)).

Here we use FLC methodology to model some aspects of classical problem analysis considered by Kepner and Tregoe (1965).[2]

A manager in charge of a project may find several potential problems with various degrees of risk for the project. The manager has to concentrate to those that are more dangerous on the project. The following questions are important and deserve consideration:

(1) How serious will be for the project if a potential problem (deviation) occurs?

(2) How possible is that a potential problem might occur?

(3) In what degree (magnitude) a potential problem might happen?

(4) Which are the potential problems that require attention or response?

Serious (concerning consequence of occurence of potential problem), *possible* (concerning occurence of potential problem), and *degree* (extent, magnitude, concerning partial occurence of a potential problem) are inputs; *response* is the output. They are described by fuzzy sets containing three terms.

$$Serious\ (S) \triangleq \{\mathbf{A}, \mathbf{HU}, \mathbf{F}\},$$

$$Possible\ (P) \triangleq \{\mathbf{N}, \mathbf{S}, \mathbf{V}\},$$

$$Degree\ (D) \triangleq \{\mathbf{L}, \mathbf{M}, \mathbf{H}\},$$

$$Response\ (R) \triangleq \{\mathbf{I}, \mathbf{WP}, \mathbf{MP}\},$$

where $\mathbf{A} \triangleq$ *annoying*, $\mathbf{HU} \triangleq$ *hurt*, $\mathbf{F} \triangleq$ *fatal*, $\mathbf{N} \triangleq$ *not*, $\mathbf{S} \triangleq$ *somewhat*, $\mathbf{V} \triangleq$ *very*, $\mathbf{L} \triangleq$ *low*, $\mathbf{M} \triangleq$ *medium*, $\mathbf{H} \triangleq$ *high*, $\mathbf{I} \triangleq$ *ignore*, $\mathbf{WP} \triangleq$ *want to prevent* (or minimize effects), $\mathbf{MP} \triangleq$ *must prevent*.

Similarly to Section 6.4 (Problem Analysis) we can apply the simplified FLC technique considering the input variables as independent. Then the rules are reduced to 9; they are of the type (6.2)–(6.4). Denoting *potential problem* or *potential deviation* by *PD*, the selected rules are:

Rule 1: If PD is **A**S then R is **I**,
Rule 2: If PD is **HU**S then R is **WP**,   (6.5)
Rule 3: If PD is **F**S then R is **MP**,

Rule 4: If PD is **N**P then R is **I**,
Rule 5: If PD is **S**P then R is **WP**,   (6.6)
Rule 6: If PD is **V**P then R is **MP**,

Rule 7: If PD is **L**D then R is **I**,
Rule 8: If PD is **M**D then R is **WP**,   (6.7)
Rule 9: If PD is **H**D then R is **MP**.

The first rule for instance reads: *if potential deviation is annoyingly serious then response is ignore.*

Case Study 24 *Fuzzy Logic Control for Potential Problem Analysis*

We will specify the inputs S, P, D, and the output R introduced above similarly to the variables in Case Study 23. However to avoid repetition we can define the variables under consideration using those in Case Study 23 as follows.

Urgent (U) (Fig. 6.15) is substituted by *Serious* (S),

Serious (S) (Fig. 6.16) is substituted by *Possible* (P),

Growth potential (GP) (Fig. 6.17) is substituted by *Degree* (D),

Priority of deviation (POD) (Fig. 6.18) is substituted by *Response* (R).

Also the terms of the variables U, S, GP, and POD in Case Study 23 are substituted by the terms of S, P, D, and R in this case study, correspondingly.

Then the rules (6.2)–(6.4) are substituted by the rules (6.5)–(6.7), respectively.

To make a full use of the calculations in Case Study 23 here we assume the same readings: $x_0 = 40, y_0 = 20, z_0 = 75$ on a scale $[0,100]$ but now the base variables have different meaning; x stands for seriousness, y for possibility, and z for degree.

The firing of the rules (Fig. 6.19), the aggregation (Fig. 6.20), and the defuzzified value $\hat{v}_h \approx 47$ remain valid.

The manager, in response to the potential deviation evaluated to be 47 on a scale from 0 to 100, wants to prevent it and he/she will work to do this. The project will be hurt in case of no action.

□

6.6 Notes

1. Graham and Jones (1988) outlined financial applications where fuzzy methods were employed (some concern *if ... then* rules). They listed various computer products, suppliers, and areas of use. Cox's book (1995) contains interesting applications in business and finance; it includes two discs and provides the C^{++} code listings for programs, demonstrations, and algorithms used in the book.

2. Kepner and Tregoe wrote in 1965 (it is still of interest today):

   "The systematic analysis of potential problem is still rare. Yet it is not difficult to show that skill in analyzing and preventing or minimizing potential problems can provide the most returns for the effort and time expended by a manager. The point is so well-known that it has become an axiom: an ounce of prevention is worth a pound of cure. So few managers apply the axiom, however, that it is reasonable to assume there are major obstacles preventing them from doing so. One obstacle is that managers are generally far more concerned with correcting today's problems than with preventing or minimizing tomorrow's. This is not surprising, of course, since the major rewards in money and promotion so often go to those who show the best records of solving current problems in management, and there is rarely a direct reward for those whose foresight keeps problems from occurring. There are also other reasons why so few managers analyze and deal with potential problems. There is the common tendency to overlook the critical consequences of an action. Such consequences may be missed because they seem too disagreeable or unpalatable to face, or the consequence may be literally invisible."

Chapter 7

Fuzzy Queries from Databases: Applications

Database is an organized structure designed with the help of computer science to store, relate, and retrieve data. Standard databases contain crisp data which can be retrieved by formulating crisp queries. The concept of standard database has been generalized by the means of fuzzy sets and fuzzy logic in order to include and handle vague, incomplete, and contradictory data. In this chapter we concentrate on formulating queries of fuzzy nature to the database for instance "which funds have a big asset increase and high return." These types of fuzzy queries can be used as a decision aid in various business, finance, and management activities. Applications involve small companies, stocks, and mutual funds.

7.1   Standard Relational Databases

There are many types of standard databases with crisp data called also classical databases. We review briefly only *relational databases*[1]; they provide the foundation for the *fuzzy databases*.[2]

A standard relational database consists of a group of relations expressed as tables made of columns and rows. The names of the columns are called *attributes*. The cells in a column form the *domain* of the attribute. The rows called *tuples* contain records or entries each occupying a cell. Several tables having common domains connected together represent a *relational database*.

Example 7.1

Typical inventory records contain whatever data are relevant such as part number, part name, standard cost, quantity, specification, size, color, weight, supplier, etc. Table 7.1 formed by three connected tables represent a simplified inventory relational database of a small aircraft component manufacturing company.

Table 7.1. Inventory relational database of a small aircraft component manufacturing company.

PART

P#	P NAME	SPECIFICATION	SIZE	CITY
P1	Solid rod	QA 225/6	144 in	Pico Rivera (CA)
P2	Plate	MS 516-02	6912 si	Los Angeles (CA)
P3	Sheet	QA 250/5	45 sf	Los Angeles (CA)
P4	Rubber	MS 2221	96 in	Tukwilla (WA)

SUPPLIER

S#	S NAME	CITY
S1	Aero-Space Metals	Pico Rivera
S2	Ruber and Metal	Tukwilla
S3	Metal Products	Los Angeles

SHIPPING

S#	P#	QUANTITY
S1	P1	30
S2	P1	20
S2	P4	120
S3	P3	15
S3	P4	55

This relational database above is made of three related tables: PART, SUPPLIER, and SHIPPING. For instance in the table labeled PART the first row or tuple starting with $P1$ is usually represented as

$< P_1,$ Solid rod, QA225/6, 144in, Pico Rivera (CA) $>$. The attributes in PART are P#, P NAME, SPECIFICATION, SIZE, CITY; the domain of the attribute P NAME consists of solid rod, plate, sheet, rubber. The framework of the database can be written as

PART (P#, P NAME, SPECIFICATION, SIZE, CITY),

SUPPLIER (S#, S NAME, CITY),

SHIPPING (S#, P#, QUANTITY).

□

Searching and finding data of interest out of a database is a process called *retrieval of data*. For the retrieval of data from a standard database a query language call SEQUEL (Structured English Query Language) was design (see Chamberlin and Boyce (1974)).

Access to the data is made by the SELECT command followed by clarifications FROM and WHERE (or WITH). SELECT command means to select attributes FROM one or more specified tables. WHERE means to select in the query process rows from a table that meet certain specified condition. The attributes are considered to be crisp objects; the query is called *standard query*.

Example 7.2

Consider the standard query from the relational database in Table 7.1 (Example 7.1):

SELECT NAME

FROM PART

WHERE QUANTITY < 100

The outcome of the query is given in Table 7.2.

Table 7.2. Parts whose quantity is smaller than 100.

S#	P#	QUANTITY
S1	P1	30
S2	P2	20
S3	P3	15

□

7.2   Fuzzy Queries

The query language SEQUEL has been used also to retrieve data when the query is of fuzzy nature (Tahani (1977)). By this we mean that the attributes of the database are considered to be linguistic variables.

The difference between standard and fuzzy query is outlined in the following case study.

Case Study 25 (Part 1) *Retrieval from a Small Company Employee Database*

Consider an employee database of a small company shown in Table 7.3. The employees are labeled by $E_i, i = 1, \ldots, 16$.

Table 7.3. Employee database of a small company.

NAME	AGE	SALARY
E_1	30	28,000
E_2	25	24,000
E_3	30	35,000
E_4	34	38,000
E_5	20	24,000
E_6	55	76,000
E_7	25	30,000
E_8	40	80,000
E_9	36	42,000
E_{10}	54	65,000
E_{11}	38	40,000
E_{12}	28	34,000
E_{13}	46	50,000
E_{14}	50	110,000
E_{15}	63	40,000
E_{16}	42	72,000

1. Standard retrieval of data

A simple standard query from the database in Table 7.3 involving only two attributes, name and age, can be presented in the form

SELECT NAME

FROM EMPLOYEE

WHERE $35 \leq AGE \leq 45$

The intent of the query is to select middle age employees where middle is defined by the interval $[35, 45]$ on a scale measured in years. Table 7.4 shows the result of the query.

Table 7.4. Standard query where age is between 35 and 45.

NAME	AGE
E_8	40
E_9	36
E_{11}	38
E_{16}	42

Employee E_8, whose age is 40—in the middle of the interval $[35, 45]$—fits best the intent of the query. Then follow employees E_{11} and E_{16}, and employee E_9 who, although close to the lower boarder 35, is still inside the interval.

From Talbel 7.3 we see that employee E_4 (age 34) lacks one year to be considered as middle age and employee E_{13} (age 46) is one year older than the upper boarder 45; they do not qualify for inclusion in Table 7.4. However, they could be included with a note that they are close to the boundaries (cut-off points) of the interval $[35, 45]$. Another option is to change the boundaries of the interval describing middle age. Assume the new interval is $[30, 50]$. Then five more employees, E_1, E_3, E_4, E_{13}, and E_{14} are to be added to Table 7.4. But then employees E_1 (age 30), E_3 (age 30), and E_{14} (age 50) who are borderline cases qualify equally to be on the list middle age as employee E_8 (age 40). In other words, there is no graduation concerning age between the employees.

A further extension of the interval to $[25, 55]$ will include employees E_2 (age 25), E_7 (age 25), and E_{10} (age 54) into Table 7.4. But who will accept a person of 25 years to be characterized as being middle age.

We encounter similar difficulty with a query from the database on Table 7.3 when dealing with the attributes name and salary:

SELECT NAME

FROM EMPLOYEE

WHERE SALARY $\geq$ 80,000

The intent of the query is to select employees with high salary defined as 80,000 or greater. The search produces Table 7.5 with only two employees.

Table 7.5. Standard query where salary $\geq$ 80,000.

NAME	SALARY
E_8	80,000
E_{14}	110,000

Employee E_6 (salary 76,000) does not qualify to be in the table. Moving the boundary down, from 80,000 to 75,000 will include E_6, but not E_{16} (salary 72,000). Also there is no gradation between 80,000 and 110,000.

From the standard queries considered here arise the questions: does the definitions of middle age and high salary lacking any gradation reflect the intention of the query? If we start changing the boundaries of the defining intervals, where we have to stop?

The problem is rooted in the words *middle age* and *high salary*. They are linguistic values and can be defined better by recognizing their fuzzy nature.

2. Fuzzy retrieval of data

The attribute name on Table 7.3 is crisp but the attributes *age* and *salary* are fuzzy. They are linguistic variables (see Section 2.4). For instance in Example 2.4 (Section 2.4) *age* is described by five terms while in Case Study 20 (Section 6.1) it is described by three terms. That depends on the context in which *age* is seen, say by a medical doctor, financial expert, or a personnel officer.

Suppose that for the present study the financial experts find it relevant to partition *age* and *salary* into the following terms (linguistic values):

$$Age = \{young, middle, old\},$$
$$Salary = \{low, medium, high\}$$

shown in Fig. 7.1 and Fig. 7.2.

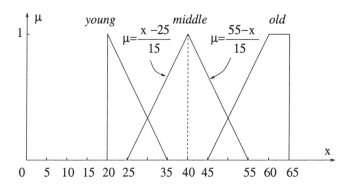

Fig. 7.1. Terms of the linguistic variable *age* in a Small Company Employee Database.

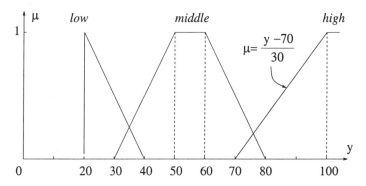

Fig. 7.2. Terms of the linguistic variable *salary* in a Small Company Employee Database.

The base variables x and y represent age in years and salary in thousands of dollars, correspondingly.

The membership functions of the terms in Fig. 7.1 and Fig. 7.2 overlap partially on the universal sets years and dollars. In Fig. 7.1 there is no overlapping on the intervals [15, 25], [35, 45], and [55, 65]; in Fig. 7.2 there is no overlapping on the intervals [20, 30], [40, 70], and [80, 100]. In most cases the terms are design to overlap entirely on the universal set, but this is not a mandatory requirement. It depends on the opinion of the experts dealing with a particular situation. Note that the terms of *age* in Fig. 7.1 have different supporting intervals from those of *age* in Case Study 20.

Now we make two simple fuzzy queries involving only one fuzzy attribute.

Query 1. Of employee database of a small company (Table 7.3) select employees who are *middle age*:

SELECT NAME

FROM EMPLOYEE

WHERE AGE IS MIDDLE

We have to match (Section 5.4) each entry in the second column (attribute AGE) (Table 7.3) with the term *middle* (Fig. 7.1) meaning to calculate the corresponding degree of membership. The term *middle* is represented by a triangular number on the supporting interval $[25, 55]$. The entries in the domain of AGE which fall in this interval substituted for x in $\mu = \frac{x-25}{15}$ for $25 < x < 40$ and $\mu = \frac{55-x}{15}$ for $40 < x < 55$ produce the ranked data in Table 7.6.

Table 7.6. Fuzzy query from a Small Company Employee Database: employee whose *age* is *middle*.

NAME	AGE MIDDLE	MEMBERSHIP DEGREE
E_8	40	1.00
E_{11}	38	0.87
E_{18}	42	0.87
E_9	36	0.73
E_4	34	0.60
E_{13}	46	0.60
E_1	30	0.33
E_3	30	0.33
E_{14}	50	0.33
E_{12}	28	0.20
E_{10}	54	0.07

Employee E_{10} has a very small membership grade 0.07, i.e. belongs little to the term *middle age*. The experts may decide to exclude E_{10} from the table if they establish a threshold value (see Section 1.3, pp. 14–15) for the membership grades, say 0.1. Then any grade below 0.1 is practically reduced to zero. Usually the threshold value is specified at the beginning of the query.

Employee E_8 is full member of the fuzzy set (term) *middle age* (membership degree 1), E_{11} and E_{16} are almost full members (degree 0.87), E_9 is close to full member (degree 0.73). In contrast, when classical query was used (Table 7.4), those employees had equal status as being of middle age. In the case of extended interval [30, 50] (classical query), employees E_3 and E_{14} who had the same status as E_8, now when the query is fuzzy belong to middle age only to degree 0.33.

Query 2. Of all employee in Table 7.3 select those with high salaries, i.e.

SELECT NAME

FROM EMPLOYEE

WHERE SALARY IS HIGH

The term *high salary* has a zero degree membership value below (including) 70,000 (see Fig. 7.2). Salaries above 70,000 qualify as high to various degrees. The entries 76,000, 80,000, 110,000, and 72,000 into the attribute salary in Table 7.3 have to be substituted for y in $\mu = \frac{y-70}{30}$ for $70 \leq y < 100$; for $y \geq 100$ the degree is one. The query produces the ranked Table 7.7.

Table 7.7. Fuzzy query from a Small Company Employee Database: employee with *high salary*.

NAME	SALARY HIGH	MEMBERSHIP DEGREE
E_{14}	110,000	1.00
E_8	80,000	0.33
E_6	76,000	0.20
E_{16}	72,000	0.07

Now let us compare Table 7.7 to Table 7.5 (classical query). Employee E_{14} (Table 7.7) is full member of the term *high salary*, E_8 has degree of membership 0.33, i.e. has a salary that is a little high. According to the classical query, both, E_{14} adn E_8 have high salary, i.e. have equal membership in the classical set salary $\geq$ 80,000. Employees E_6 and E_{16} are included in Table 7.7 but not in Table 7.5. Actually E_{16} whose membership degree is very low, only 0.07—below a threshold value 0.1, may be excluded from the list. While the standard query has to specify a rigid salary (80,000) as a lower boundary below which salaries do not qualify as high, the fuzzy query using grades of the term *high* (Fig. 7.2) can include for consideration salaries close to 80,000 from below.

□

7.3   Fuzzy Complex Queries

Queries based on logical connectives

Most often a fuzzy SEQUEL query involves two or more fuzzy attributes in the WHERE predicate. They are joined by the logical connectives *conjunction* (*and*) and *disjunction* (*or*) defined by min and max in Section 2.1 formulas (2.2) and (2.3), correspondingly. The truth values of p and q in (2.2) and (2.3) are expressed by membership grades.

The asking of fuzzy complex queries is illustrated in a case study (continuation of Case Study 25 (Part 1)).

Case Study 25 (Part 2) *Fuzzy Complex Query from a Small Company Employee Database by Logical Connectives*

Query 3. Of all employee in Table 7.3 select those whose *age* is *middle* and *salary* is *high*:

SELECT NAME
FROM EMPLOYEE
WHERE AGE IS MIDDLE
AND SALARY IS HIGH

In this query there are three attributes; name is a crisp one, *age* and *salary* are fuzzy (connected by *and*).

To facilitate the complex query we combine Table 7.3 with Table 7.6 and 7.7 into one containing the degree of membership of *high salary* and *middle age* (first five columns in Table 7.8).

The following abrievations are introduced in Table 7.8: A=AGE, N=NAME, DM=DEGREE MIDDLE, SAL=SALARY, DH=DEGREE HIGH, AVE=AVERAGE.

The task is to establish a list of employees who satisfy to various degrees the query.

Table 7.8. Fuzzy complex queries from a Small Company Employee Database.

N	A	DM	SAL	DH	AND	OR	AVE
E_1	30	0.33	28,000	0	0	0.33	0.17
E_2	25	0	24,000	0	0	0	0
E_3	30	0.33	35,000	0	0	0.33	0.17
E_4	34	0.60	38,000	0	0	0.6	0.3
E_5	20	0	24,000	0	0	0	0
E_6	55	0	76,000	0.2	0	0.20	0.10
E_7	25	0	30,000	0	0	0	0
E_8	40	1.00	80,000	0.33	0.33	1.0	0.67
E_9	36	0.73	42,000	0	0	0.73	0.37
E_{10}	54	0.07	65,000	0	0	0.07	0.04
E_{11}	38	0.87	40,000	0	0	0.87	0.44
E_{12}	28	0.20	34,000	0	0	0.20	0.10
E_{13}	46	0.60	50,000	0	0	0.60	0.30
E_{14}	50	0.33	110,000	1.00	0.33	1.00	0.67
E_{15}	63	0	40,000	0	0	0	0
E_{16}	42	0.87	72,000	0.07	0.07	0.87	0.44

For instance, for the first tuple in Table 7.3, $< E_1, 30, 28,000 >, E_1$ has the membership values $\mu_{middle}(30) = 0.33$ and $\mu_{high}(28) = 0$ in the terms *middle age* and *high salary* (see Table 7.8). The degree to which employee E_1 satisfies the query according to (2.2) is $\min(0.33, 0) = 0$. Hence E_1 is not included in the list. This is true for the employees who have at least one membership value equal to zero. Only the employees in the 8th,14th, and 16th tuples qualify to be in the list. For $E_8, \min(1.00, 0.33) = 0.33$; for $E_{14}, \min(0.33, 1.00) = 0.33$, and for $E_{16}, \min(0.87, 0.07) = 0.07$ (below threshold value 0.1). These results are registered in Table 7.8 in the 6th column labeled AND. We can say that they reflect the *degree of membership* of each employee *in the conclusion* in the query.

The fact that the degree of membership in the conclusion cannot be stronger (greater) than the weakest (smallest) individual grade is a conservative requirement. In some cases it can be a severe restriction on the query. For instance if a grade in one term is zero no matter what is the value of the grade in the other terms, the degree of membership in the conclusion is also zero. That is why in Table 7.8, column AND, only three grades are different from zero. An alternative approach based on averaging is discussed at the end of this section.

Query 4. Of all employee in Table 7.3 select those whose *age* is *middle* or *salary* is *high*:

> SELECT NAME
> FROM EMPLOYEE
> WHERE AGE IS MIDDLE
> OR SALARY IS HIGH

In this query the two fuzzy attributes *age* and *salary* are connected by *or* (max), hence formula (2.3) applies. The employees who are either in Table 7.6 or in Table 7.7, or in both, qualify to be in the list. For instance, for employee $E_1, \max(0.33, 0) = 0.33$, for $E_2, \max(0, 0) = 0$, for $E_3, \max(0.33, 0) = 0.33$, for $E_4, \max(0.60, 0) = 0.60, \ldots$, for $E_{16}, \max(0.87, 0.07) = 0.87$. The results are presented in Table 7.8, 7th column labeled OR.

In conclusion, the numbers in the AND and OR columns indicate to what degree an employee satisfies the corresponding query. The degree is also interpreted as truth value for the query concerning each employee. □

Queries based on averaging

The joining of attributes in the WHERE predicate by the logical connective *and* can be replaced by the average (see (3.1), Section 3.1) of the individual degrees of membership. This technique ensures that each individual membership grade contributes to the degree of membership in the conclusion.

Case Study 25 (Part 3) *Fuzzy Complex Query from a Small Company Employee Database by using Averaging*

Consider again *Query 3* but instead of the connective *and* (min) let us use the average. From 3th and 5th columns of Table 7.8 we calculate: for $E_1, \frac{0.33+0}{2} = 0.17, \ldots$, for $E_6, \frac{0+0.20}{2} = 0.10, \ldots$, for $E_8, \frac{1+0.33}{2} = 0.67$, etc. The results are presented in Table 7.8 in the last column labeled

AVE. There are 12 employees in the list produced by the query while there were only three when then the connective *and* (min) was used.

□

7.4 Fuzzy Queries for Small Manufacturing Companies

Cox (1995) used a database consisting of small companies to show the advantage fuzzy queries have against standard queries. Here we present a case study which is typical of small manufacturing companies. The database is a modification of that considered by Cox. Also we model the attributes by triangular and trapezoidal numbers while in Cox they are described by bell-shaped fuzzy numbers.

Case Study 26 *Fuzzy Complex Queries of Database of Small Manufacturing Companies*

The database consists of 12 small companies labeled $C_i, i = 1, \ldots, 12$, listed in Table 7.9, ranked in 1996 according to their age measured in years.

Table 7.9. Database of small manufacturing companies in 1996.

CN	AGE	AR	PC	EC	PR	EPS
C_1	44	52	2	81	0.8	0.5
C_2	42	38	2	30	1.0	1.6
C_3	34	105	12	120	3.2	3.0
C_4	26	34	1	18	-0.3	0.3
C_5	24	47	6	64	1.4	2.5
C_6	23	92	8	70	2.6	2.2
C_7	17	68	5	48	0	0.2
C_8	16	65	6	44	2.0	5.0
C_9	12	90	4	50	1.0	2.4
C_{10}	8	70	3	109	-0.8	0
C_{11}	3	59	7	72	1.7	1.7
C_{12}	2	84	9	91	2.1	3.2

In this table only the first attribute—company—is crisp. The other six are considered to be fuzzy attributes (linguistic variables).

In Table 7.9 we use the notations: CN=COMPANY NAME, AR=ANNUAL REVENUE (in millions), PC=PRODUCT COUNT, EC=EMPLOYEE COUNT, PR=PROFIT (in millions), EPS = EARNING PER SHARE (in dollars).

To be able to make fuzzy queries we model the attributes by fuzzy sets (terms) shown below. The equations of the segments to be used later are given in the figures.

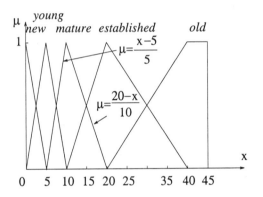

Fig. 7.3. Terms of company *age*.

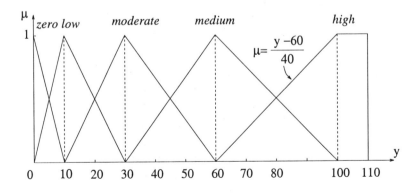

Fig. 7.4. Terms of *annual revenues*.

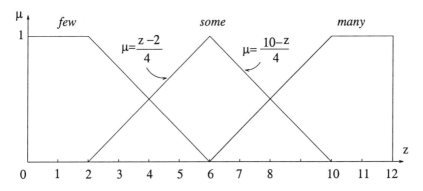

Fig. 7.5. Terms of *product count*.

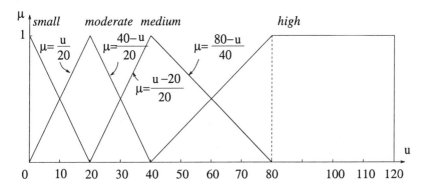

Fig. 7.6. Terms of *employee count*.

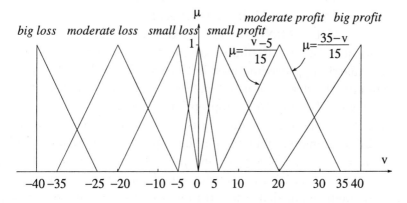

Fig. 7.7. Terms of *profit*; negative profit is *loss*.

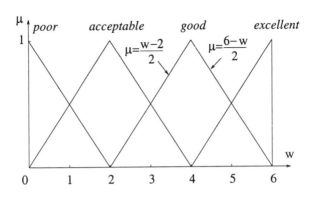

Fig. 7.8. Terms of *earnings per share*.

The base variables defined on the universal sets are measured as follows: x in years, y and v in millions of dollars, w in dollars, z and u are integer numbers.

We will use the database in Table 7.9 to make four complex queries.

Query 1 Consider the companies in Table 7.9.

SELECT NAME

FROM COMPANY

WHERE AGE IS MATURE

    AND ANNUAL REVENUE IS HIGH

    AND PRODUCT COUNT IS SOME

    AND EMPLOYEE COUNT IS MODERATE

    AND PROFIT IS MODERATE

    AND EARNING PER SHARE IS GOOD

In this query all six attributes are involved. We have to repeat six times the matching procedure used in Case Study 25 (Part 1), Query 1. This will give the degree of membership of each entry in every term in the query which belongs to an appropriate attribute.

For instance the term *mature* in the attribute *age* (Fig. 7.3) is described by a triangular number on the supporting interval [5, 20] as follows: $\mu = \frac{x-5}{5}$ for $5 \le x \le 10$ and $\mu = \frac{20-x}{10}$ for $10 \le x \le 20$. The values (entries) 8, 12, 16, 20 of the domain of *age* which belong to [5, 20] have to be matched against the term *mature*. Substituting 8 (row C_{10}) into the first equation, 12 (row C_9), 16 (row C_8), and 17 (row C_7) into the second equation gives μ the values 0.6, 0.8, 0.4, 0.3 correspondingly. The other entries of the domain of *age* are not in [5, 20]; they have zero degree of membership in the term *mature*. These results are recorded in Table 7.10, the second column—*age* is *mature*.

The same procedure is applied to the other five terms, *high*, *some*, *moderate*, *moderate*, *good* shown in Figs. 7.4–7.8, correspondingly. The membership degrees obtained are recorded in Table 7.10, third to seventh columns. The following short notations are used in Table 7.10: CN=COMPANY NAME, DMA=DEGREE MATURE, H=HIGH, S=SOME, DMOE=DEGREE MODERATE (concerning employee count), DMOP = DEGREE MODERATE PROFIT, DG = DEGREE GOOD.

The attributes in the query are connected by *and* (min). Most of the companies (excluding C_8 and C_9) have at least one entry 0, hence the outcome of the min operation is also 0 (column AND in Table 7.10). For instance, for company C_3, $\min(0, 1, 0, 0, 0.2, 0.5) = 0$; for C_8 we calculate $\min(0.4, 0.125, 1, 0.9, 1, 0.5) = 0.125$ and for C_9, $\min(0.8, 0.75, 0.5, 0.75, 0.33, 0.2) = 0.2$.

Table 7.10. Fuzzy complex Querie 1 from the database of small manufacturing companies.

CN	DMA	H	S	DMOE	DMOP	DG	AND	AVE
C_1	0	0	0	0	0.2	0	0	0.03
C_2	0	0	0	0.5	0.33	0	0	0.14
C_3	0	1	0	0	0.2	0.5	0	0.28
C_4	0	0	0	0	0	0	0	0
C_5	0	0	1	0.4	0.6	0.25	0	0.38
C_6	0	0.8	0.5	0.25	0.6	0.1	0	0.38
C_7	0.3	0.2	0.75	0.8	0	0	0	0.34
C_8	0.4	0.125	1	0.9	1	0.5	0.125	0.65
C_9	0.8	0.75	0.5	0.75	0.33	0.2	0.2	0.56
C_{10}	0.6	0.25	0.25	0	0	0	0	0.18
C_{11}	0	0	0.75	0.2	0.8	0	0	0.29
C_{12}	0	0.6	0.25	0	0.93	0.6	0	0.40

One can observe that as the number of *and* connections in the WHERE predicate increases the likelihood is that the membership grade in the conclusion (AND) decreases. The contrary is true when the connection is *or* (see Query 2 which follows).

Let us use averaging instead of *and* (min) to connect the attributes (see Queries based on averaging, in Section 7.3). The results are recorded in the last column AVE in Table 7.10. For instance, for company C_3 we get the membership degree in the conclusion by adding the six entries in the same row and dividing the sum by 6, i.e. $\frac{0+1+0+0+0.2+0.5}{6} = 0.28$. Similarly for company C_8 we calculate $\frac{0.4+0.125+1+0.9+1+0.5}{6} = 0.65$.

Query 2.

SELECT NAME
FROM COMPANY
WHERE AGE IS MATURE
    OR ANNUAL REVENUES ARE HIGH
    OR PRODUCT COUNT IS SOME
    OR EMPLOYEE COUNT IS MODERATE
    OR PROFIT IS MODERATE
    OR EARNING PERSHARE IS GOOD

This query formally can be obtained from Query 1 by changing AND by OR. Hence now the attributes are connected by *or* (max). For company C_3 (Table 7.10) for instance we get $\max(0, 1, 0, 0, 0.2, 0.5) = 0.5$; for C_8, $\max(0.4, 0.125, 1, 0.9, 1, 0.5) = 1$. The results for all companies are given in the second column OR in Table 7.11.

Query 3.

SELECT NAME
FROM COMPANY
WHERE AGE IS MATURE
    AND ANNUAL REVENUES ARE HIGH
    AND EARNING PER SHARE IS GOOD

This query does not involve all attributes in the database. We use from Table 7.10 only the columns labeled DMA, H, and DG to find the membership degree in the conclusion AND (see Table 7.11).

Table 7.11. Fuzzy complex Queries 2, 3, 4 from the database of small manufacturing companies.

CN	Query 2 OR	Query 3 AND	Query 4 AND/OR
C_1	0.2	0	0
C_2	0.5	0	0
C_3	0.5	0	0
C_4	0	0	0
C_5	1	0	0.25
C_6	0.8	0	0.1
C_7	0.8	0	0.2
C_8	1	0.125	0.5
C_9	0.8	0.2	0.75
C_{10}	0.6	0	0.25
C_{11}	0.8	0	0
C_{12}	0.93	0	0

Query 4

SELECT NAME
FROM COMPANY
WHERE AGE IS MATURE
    AND ANNUAL REVENUES ARE HIGH
    OR EMPLOYEE COUNT IS MODERATE
    AND EARNING PER SHARE IS GOOD

Four attributes take part in the WHERE predicate. They are joined by both connectives *and* and *or*. The membership grades for each tuple can be calculated from the schematically presented formula

[MATURE *and* HIGH] *or* [MODERATE *and* GOOD]

which can be written as

$$\max[\min(\text{MATURE, HIGH}), \min(\text{MODERATE, GOOD})], \quad (7.1)$$

where the terms are substituted by the appropriate entries in the tuples.

We use the entries forming the domains of DMA, H, DMOE, and DG in Table 7.10. For instance for company C_8 formula (7.1) gives

$$[\max[\min(0.4, 0.125), \min(1, 0.5)]] = \max[0.125, 0.5] = 0.5$$

Similarly the rest of the membership grades are calculated and presented in the column AND/OR in Table 7.11.

□

7.5   Fuzzy Queries for Stocks and Funds Databases

Common stocks represent one of the most complex and varied fields of investment. The stock market is an arena in which success measured in profit depends not only on combination of skills, information, and knowledge, but also on unforeseen events of political and social character, drastic changes in nature, and on the subjectivity of investors expectations and confidence. There are thousand of stocks in the world that are traded in hundreds of stock exchanges. For a common investor to play on the stock market is both risky and time consuming. Stock markets go up and down generally along an increasing saw-line curve but also on rare occasions catastrophes called crashes happened. For instance the largest decline in one day in the history of the stock market, "Black Monday," occured on Monday, October 19, 1987. Then the Dow Jones Industrial Average in U.S.A. declined by 23 %; other countries also had a fast and large decline in their stock market. The worst stock market crash occured on 29 October, 1929. The consequences for millions of people were devastating.

Mutual funds are financial vehicles that offer portfolio diversification and professional management. One advantage is a great deal of time saved for the investor, but funds, in general less risky than stocks, are not risk-free. There are thousands of funds managed by financial corporations, companies, banks, and trusts. They are in fierce competition trying to perform better and attract more costumers. Fund managers are presenting their investment strategy and recommendations in various reports and letters. Buy and sell decisions usually reflect the consensus of several managers in charge of funds in a group.

Since the 1960s the stock markets have experienced fast changes. One major factor for that has been the advances in computer technology.

Computer selected stocks

Of particular interest is using computers to select stocks or funds in order to outperform the market. While there are activities in this area not much can be found in the literature.[4]

One such case was reported on a single page by Mandelman (1979). All U.S.A. stocks were screened with a computer. Aim: to select those that met five requirements:

"Low debt in the underlying company's capital structure.

A high return on equity.

A high dividend yield on the stock.

A very low PE ratio.

A low stock price."

Here PE means price–earnings ratio; it is a tool for comparing the relative merit of different stocks. For instance if a company A produces a product that has estimated year-end earnings of $2 per share and the trading at the moment is $12 per share, the PE ratio is $\frac{12}{2} = 6$. Another company B produces similar product with the same earnings of $2 per share but the trading is $16 per share, hence the PE ratio is $\frac{16}{2} = 8$. Then normally one could expect that company A is more attractive.

It is not explained how the border lines for "low debt," "high return," "high dividend," "very low PE ratio," and "low stock price" were determined. This might be a difficult task since the words "low debt" and "low stock price" require analysis and clarifications; "high dividend" is easier to define, say above $4.50. Only nine stocks were selected and bought on March 12, 1979. On Oct. 16, after seven months, the gain was 15.7% (28.4% if annualized). This is considered in the report as a good gain under the specific circumstances at that time: "New York market was drifting sideways for much of the summer, and that we've taken the prices of the stocks on October 16—well after the big slump that began October 8." The author concludes "Our experiment confirms our belief that a computer can be a worthwhile tool in selecting stocks."

Essentially this is a standard retrieval from a large database—all stocks in U.S.A.

Fuzzy logic approach

The fuzzy logic methodology can produce better results. Each requirement stated by Mandelman (1979) has to be characterized by the linguistic variables: *debt, return, dividend yield, PE ratio*, and *stock price. Low, very low*, and *high* are terms of appropriate linguistic variables. The financial experts should be able to describe the above variables (see Chapter 5, Section 5.2) and initiate a fuzzy complex query using computers:

SELECT NAME
FROM STOCKS
WHERE DEBT IS LOW
    AND RETURN IS HIGH
    AND DIVIDEND YIELDS IS HIGH
    AND PE RATIO IS VERY LOW
    AND STOCK PRICE IS LOW

There are financial institutions in various countries using fuzzy logic for portfalio management, but it is very difficult to obtain information about their activities.[3] In a short note, Schwartz (1990) reports: "Fuzzy information processing takes place every day at Yamaichi Securities, the first securities-trading company to offer a fund with purchases based on fuzzy-system decisions. Currently, the system monitors over 1100 stocks, but makes only a few trades each day. Employing fuzzy reasoning, expert system technology, and conventional number crunching, the system is tuned daily by Yamaichi trading experts. The fund has been operating for approximately nine months and claims to be sporting a 40-percent annual return for investors.[4]"

We illustrate the fuzzy logic approach on a small database containing funds.

Case Study 27 *Fuzzy Query from the 20 Biggest Mutual Funds in Canada*

Consider the database presented in Table 7.12.

Table 7.12. The 20 biggest mutual funds in Canada ranked by total assets at 31 Dec. 1995; in billions of dollors.

FN	TOTAL ASSET		CH %	RETURN %		
	31/12/95	31/03/94		1 Y	3 Y	5 Y
F_1	4.08	2.31	76.6	14.1	17.3	19.4
F_2	3.19	1.57	103.2	14.2	18.2	21.7
F_3	3.03	3.59	−15.6	11.5	6.6	8.0
F_4	2.61	1.86	40.3	18.8	9.8	10.8
F_5	2.45	2.58	−5.3	10.3	8.3	9.1
F_6	2.44	1.81	34.8	9.9	14.3	13.6
F_7	2.36	2.43	−3.0	6.3	5.2	6.4
F_8	2.13	0.64	232.8	11.7	14.6	n/a
F_9	2.10	1.31	60.3	10.6	13.3	12.2
F_{10}	2.04	2.79	−26.9	12.9	7.8	9.8
F_{11}	2.00	1.70	17.6	14.8	19.6	24.6
F_{12}	1.98	1.60	23.8	11.9	12.9	9.6
F_{13}	1.94	2.03	−4.4	6.1	4.9	n/a
F_{14}	1.92	2.22	−13.5	14.3	11.0	11.3
F_{15}	1.88	1.46	28.8	15.3	18.2	17.6
F_{16}	1.81	1.16	56.0	16.7	20.8	23.9
F_{17}	1.79	0.97	84.5	15.0	14.1	13.4
F_{18}	1.64	1.72	−4.7	19.3	9.2	10.8
F_{19}	1.59	1.68	−5.4	19.9	23.0	n/a
F_{20}	1.44	1.20	20.0	10.7	15.9	15.8

We use the abrivations: FN=FUND NAME, CH=CHANGE, 1 Y=1 YEAR, 3 Y=3 YEAR, and 5 Y=5 YEAR. Table 7.12 is taken from "The Mutual Fund Advisory" written and edited by C. Tidd (February 1996). We do not give the real names of the funds; here they are labeled $F_i, i = 1, \ldots, 20$.

The author reminds "that the single purpose of this particular exercise is to determine shifts into (and out of) the country's 20 largest Mutual Funds" and also makes a short analysis based on the data covering 21 months (31 March 1994 to 31 December 1995).

Our aim is to use the real data in Table 7.12 for making fuzzy queries.

We consider *change* and *return* as linguistic variables. They are partitioned into terms (linguistic values) presented in Fig. 7.9 (*change*) and Fig. 7.10 (one-, two-, and three-year *return*).

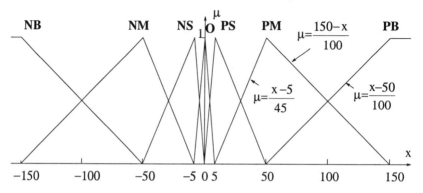

Fig. 7.9. Terms of *change* for the 20 biggest mutual funds in Canada.

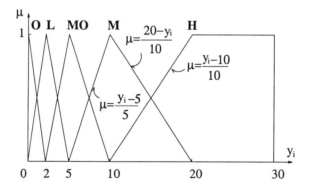

Fig. 7.10. Terms of *one-,three-,five-year return* for the 20 biggest mutual funds in Canada; $y_i = 1, 3, 5$.

The terms of *change* are defined as follows: **NB** $\stackrel{\triangle}{=}$ *negative big*, **NM** $\stackrel{\triangle}{=}$ *negative medium*, **NS** $\stackrel{\triangle}{=}$ *negative small*, **O** $\stackrel{\triangle}{=}$ *zero*, **PS** $\stackrel{\triangle}{=}$ *positive small*, **PM** $\stackrel{\triangle}{=}$ *positive medium*, **PB** $\stackrel{\triangle}{=}$ *positive big*. The base variable x is measured in percentage.

The terms of *return* (1, 3, and 5 year) are defined by **O** $\stackrel{\triangle}{=}$ *zero*, **L** $\stackrel{\triangle}{=}$ *low*, **MO** $\stackrel{\triangle}{=}$ *moderate*, **M** $\stackrel{\triangle}{=}$ *medium*, **H** $\stackrel{\triangle}{=}$ *high*. The base variable $y_i, i = 1, 3, 5$, is expressed in percentage; y_i is positive since the return for all funds (Table 7.12) is gain. In situations with negative return (loss) Fig. 7.10 has to be extended to the left symmetrically about the μ-axis.

Now we consider three queries.

Query 1

SELECT FUND
FROM TABLE 7.12
WHERE CHANGE IS POSSITIVE BIG
  AND 1 YEAR RETRUN IS HIGH
  AND 3 YEAR RETRUN IS HIGH
  AND 5 YEAR RETRUN IS HIGH

The aim of this query is to identify funds picking up huge amount of money (meaning more business) while producing consistently high returns.

Following the procedure for calculating the membership values in this chapter we obtain the results in Table 7.13. (second to fifth columns), where CHPB= CHANGE POSITIVE BIG and 1,3,5 YH $= 1$, 3, 5 YEAR HIGH. We present the calculations only for fund F_1. Substituting 76.6 from Table 7.12 for x into equation $\mu = \frac{x-50}{100}$ (see Fig. 7.9) gives 0.27. Substituting 14.1 for y_1, 17.3 for y_3, and 19.4 for y_5 from the same table correspondingly into equation $\mu = \frac{y_i-10}{10}$, $i = 1, 3, 5$, gives 0.41, 0.73, and 0.94.

The aggregation by *and* is given in the sixth column labeled AND and that by *averaging* in the seventh column labeled AVE. For the fund F_1 aggregation by *and* gives $\min(0.27, 0.41, 0.73, 0.94) = 0.27$ and aggregation by averaging produces $\frac{0.27+0.41+0.73+0.94}{4} = 0.59$. For the fund F_8 5 year return is not available (n/a); the fund is younger than 5 years. The aggregation for F_8 is based on the presented data, i.e. for operation *and*, $\min(1, 0.17, 0.46) = 0.17$, for average, $\frac{1+0.17+0.43}{3} = 0.54$.

We can use the membership values in the conclusions AND and AVE in Table 7.13 to rank the funds which satisfy the query. Also we can use a threshold value $\alpha = 0.2$, which means that the funds with membership values below 0.2 are to be dropped. The results are presented in Table 7.14.

Table 7.13. Membership grades for Query 1 from 20 biggest mutual funds in Canada (31 March 1994 to 31 December 1995).

FN	CHPB	1 YH	3 YH	5 YH	AND	AVE
F_1	0.27	0.41	0.73	0.94	0.27	0.59
F_2	0.53	0..42	0.82	1.00	0.42	0.69
F_3	0	0.15	0	0	0	0.04
F_4	0	0.88	0	0.08	0	0.24
F_5	0	0.03	0	0	0	0.01
F_6	0	0	0.43	0.36	0	0.20
F_7	0	0	0	0	0	0
F_8	1	0.17	0.46	n/a	0.17	0.54
F_9	0.10	0.06	0.33	0.22	0.06	0.18
F_{10}	0	0.29	0	0	0	0.07
F_{11}	0	0.48	0.96	1.00	0	0.61
F_{12}	0	0.19	0.29	0	0	0.12
F_{13}	0	0	0	n/a	0	0
F_{14}	0	0.43	0.10	0.13	0	0.17
F_{15}	0	0.53	0.82	0.76	0	0.53
F_{16}	0.04	0.67	1.00	1.00	0.04	0.68
F_{17}	0.35	0.50	0.41	0.34	0.34	0.40
F_{18}	0	0.93	0	0.08	0	0.25
F_{19}	0	0.99	1.00	n/a	0	0.66
F_{20}	0	0.07	0.59	0.58	0	0.31

If a threshold value $\alpha = 0.1$ is addopted, then more funds have to be included in the ranked tables (Table 7.14) as follows. The fund F_8 goes to the first table (AND) and the funds F_9 and F_{14} join the second table (AVE).

Both aggragation procedures, *and* and *average*, rank fund F_2 at first place but after that there is considerable difference. It was already indicated that *and* procedure is quite conservative (Section 7.3). In this case it emphasizes too much the linguistic variable *change*: namely funds whose *positive change* is below 50% do not qualify. On the other hand side, fund F_8 with the biggest increase of 232.8% is not included for ranking since one-year return of 11.7% has a low membership value 0.17. The fund managers may decide to tune the model representation of the linguistic variables *change* and *return* (see Section 5.8) shifting to the left the lower boundaries 50 of **PB** and 10 of **H**. Actually for Query 1 only the terms **PB** (Fig. 7.9) and **H** (Fig. 7.10) are needed. Having the other terms allows the making of various queries.

Table 7.14. Ranking the biggest mutual funds in Canada produced by Query 1.

RANK	FN	AVE
1	F_2	0.69
2	F_{16}	0.68
3	F_{19}	0.66
4	F_{11}	0.61
5	F_1	0.59
6	F_8	0.54
7	F_{15}	0.53
8	F_{17}	0.40
9	F_{20}	0.31
10	F_{18}	0.25
11	F_3	0.24
12	F_6	0.20

RANK	FN	AND
1	F_2	0.42
2	F_{17}	0.34
3	F_1	0.27

Query 2

SELECT FUND
FROM TABLE 7.13
WHERE CHANGE IS POSITIVE MEDIUM
    AND 1 YEAR RETURN HIGH
    AND 3 YEAR RETURN IS HIGH
    AND 5 YEAR RETURN IS MEDIUM

This query is focused on funds which are expanding their business and producing high returns in the last three years thus improving their performance.

The final results are presented in Table 7.15 where CHPM=CHANGE POSITIVE MEDIUM and 5YM=5 YEAR MEDIUM. The attributes 1 YH and 3 YH have the same domain as those in Table 7.13.

Table 7.15. Membership grades for Query 2 from 20 biggest mutual funds in Canada (31 March 1994 to 31 December 1995).

FN	CH PM	1 YH	3 YH	5 YM	AND	AVE
F1	0.73	0.41	0.73	0.06	0.06	0.48
F2	0.47	0.42	0.82	0	0	0.43
F3	0	0.15	0	0.60	0	0.19
F4	0.64	0.88	0	0.92	0	0.61
F5	0	0.33	0	0.82	0	0.29
F6	0.54	0	0.43	0.57	0	0.39
F7	0	0	0	0.14	0	0.04
F8	0	0.17	0.46	n/a	0	0.21
F9	0.90	0.06	0.33	0.78	0.06	0.52
F10	0	0.29	0	0.96	0	0.31
F11	0.23	0.48	0.96	0	0	0.42
F12	0.34	0.19	0.29	0.92	0.19	0.44
F13	0	0	0	n/a	0	0
F14	0	0.43	0.10	0.87	0	0.35
F15	0.43	0.53	0.82	0.24	0.24	0.51
F16	0.94	0.67	1.00	0	0	0.65
F17	0.66	0.50	0.41	0.66	0.41	0.56
F18	0	0.93	0	0.92	0	0.46
F19	0	0.99	1.00	n/a	0	0.66
F20	0.27	0.07	0.59	0.42	0.07	0.34

Query 3

SELECT FUND
FROM TABLE 7.13
WHERE CHANGE IS NEGATIVE SMALL
    AND 1 YEAR RETURN IS MODERATE
    AND 3 YEAR RETRUN IS MODERATE
    OR LOW

The query wants to depict funds that are lossing business (the worst case is −26.9%) and also having an unimpressive return during the last three years in comparison to their competitors. In the one-year performance there is no fund with low return while in the three-year there is one such fund. This explains the introduction of *or* connective into the WHERE predicate concerning the attribute 3 YEAR in Table 7.12.

The calculations are similar to those in the previous queries discussed in this chapter. We have to construct a table similar to Table 7.13 and 7.15 having top row

FN	CNNS	1YMO	3YMO	3YL	AND/OR

where CNNS=CHANGE NEGATIVE SMALL, 1YMO=1 YEAR MODERATE, 3YMO=3 YEAR MODERATE, and 3YL=3 YEAR LOW.

The membership grades for each tuple can be calculated according to the formula

$$\text{CNNS } and \text{ 1YMO } and \text{ (3YMO } or \text{ 3YL)}$$

which can be expressed by min and max in the form

$$\min(\text{CNNS, 1YMO}, \max(\text{3YMO, 3YL})).$$

Here CNNS, 1YMO, 3YMO, and 3YL have to be substituted by the appropriate entries in the tuples. Note that here the connective *or* (max) appears in a different place than *or* (max) in Case Study 26, Query 4.

□

7.6 Notes

1. Research on database began with a paper on a relational data model by Codd (1960), a researcher at the IBM Santa Terresa in San Jose, California.

2. According to Terano, Asai, and Sugeno (1987), the term fuzzy database was first used by Kunii (1976). Fuzzy databases are briefly considered by Klir and Folger (1988).

3. Graham and Jones (1988) made the comment "One major difficulty in surveying financial applications is the secrecy and even paranoia which surrounds successful ones. Because one of their

chief benefits is the competitive edge they provide this is hardly surprising, but as with the defence sector a certain amount of knowledge is in the public domain. Although this is manifest it is also possible that some of the secrecy could have arisen from the vested interests of the developers, who are concerned not to expose their infant and struggling applications to the glare of publicity until they are proved to be robust."

4. Management Intelligenter Technologien GmbH, Promenade 9, 52076 Aachen, Germany, advertises a software tool based on fuzzy logic and neural networks for analyzing complex tasks that was successfully used for the forecasting of the Standard & Poor's 500 Index.

References

Aristotle (1966) *The Metaphysics* (H. G. Apostle, trans.), Indiana University Press, Bloomington.

Baldwin, J. F. (1979) *A New Approach to Approximate Reasoning Using a Fuzzy Logic*, FSS **2**, pp. 309–325.

Beck, N. (1992) *Shifting Gears*, Harper Collins Publishers Ltd., Toronto.

Beck, N. (1995) *Excelerate: Growing in the New Economy*, Harper Collins Publishers Ltd., Toronto.

Bellman, R. E. and Zadeh, L. A. (1970) *Decision Making in a Fuzzy Enviroment*, Management Science, **17:4**, pp. 141–164; also in *Fuzzy Sets and Applications: Selected Papers by L. A. Zadeh*, John Wiley & Sons, New York, pp. 53–79 (1987).

Black, M. (1937) *Vagueness: An Exercise in Logical Analysis*, Philosophy of Science, **4**, pp. 472–455.

Bojadziev, G. and Bojadziev, M. (1995) *Fuzzy Sets, Fuzzy Logic, Applications*, World Scientific, Singapore.

Chamberlin, D. D. and Boyce, R. F. (1974) *SEQUEL: A Structured English Query Language*, Proceedings of ACM–SIGFIDET Workshop, Ann Arbor (May 1974).

Codd, E. F. (1970) *A Relational Model for Large Shared Data Banks*, Communications of the ACM, **13**, pp. 377–387.

Cox, D. E. (1995) *Fuzzy Logic for Business and Industry*, Charles River Media, Inc., Rockland, Massachusetts.

Drucker, P. F. (1995) *Managing in a Time of Great Change*, Truman Talley Books/Dutton, New York.

Dubois, D. and Prade, H. (1978) *Operations on Fuzzy Numbers*, Int. Journal System Sciences, **9**(6), pp. 613–626.

Dubois, D. and Prade, H. (1980) *Fuzzy Sets and Systems: Theory and Applicaitons*, Academic Press, New York.

Earl, E. (1995) *Microeconomics for Business and Marketing*, Edward Elgar Publishing Ltd., England.

Fogarty, D. W. and Hoffmann, T. R. (1983) *Production and Inventory Management*, South-Western Publishing Co., Cincinnati.

Frege, G. (1879) *Begriffsschrift, eine der Arithmetischen Nachgebildete Formelsprache des reinen Denkens*, Halle.

Graham, I. G. and Jones, P. L. (1988) *Expert Systems: Knowledge, Uncertainty and Decision*, Chapman and Hall, London.

Grant, R.M. (1993) *Contemporary Strategy Analysis*, Blackwell Publishers, Cambridge, Massachussetts.

Hellendoorn, H. and Thomas, C. (1993) *Defuzzification Fuzzy Controllers*, Journal of Intelligent and Fuzzy Systems, **1**, pp. 109–123, John Wiley and Sons, Inc.

Herbert, B. (1996, July 10) *Wanted, Economic Vision that Focuses on Working People*, International Herald Tribune, published with New York Times & Washington Post, Frankfurt.

Kandel, A. (1986) *Fuzzy Mathematical Techniques with Applications*, Addison-Wesley Publishing Company, Reading, Massachutts.

Kaufmann, A. (1975) *Introduction to the Theory of Fuzzy Subsets*, Academic Press, New York.

Kaufmann, A. and Gupta, M. M. (1985) *Introduction to Fuzzy Arithmetic: Theory and Applications*, Van Nostrand Reinhold, New York.

Kaufmann, A. and Gupta, M. M. (1988) *Fuzzy Mathematical Models in Engineering and Management Science*, North-Holland, Amsterdam.

Kepner, C. H. and Tregoe, B. B. (1976) *The Rational Manager*, Kepner-Tregoe Inc., Princeton.

Klir, G. J. and Folger, T. A. (1988) *Fuzzy Sets, Uncertainty, and Information*, Prentice Hall, Englewood Cliffs, New Jersey.

Kosko, B. (1993) *Fuzzy Thinking*, Hyperion, New York.

Kunii, T. L. (1976) DATA PLAN: *An Interface Generator for Database Semantics*, Information Sciences, **10**, pp. 279–298.

Li, H. X. and Yen, V. C. (1995) *Fuzzy Sets and Fuzzy Decision Making*, CPC Press, Boca Raton, Florida.

Łukasiewicz, J. (1920) *On 3-valued logic*, Ruch Filozoficzny, **5**, pp. 169–171 (in Polish).

Makridakis, S. (1990) *Forecasting, Planning, and Strategy for the 21st Century*, Free Press, New York.

Mamdani, E. H. and Assilian, S. (1975) *An Experiment in Linguistic Synthesis with a Fuzzy Logic Controller*, Int. Journal Man–Machine Studies **7**, pp. 1–13.

Mandelman, A. (1979, Nov.12) *Computer Select Stocks Outperform the Market*, The Money Letter, **3** (29), Publisher Ron Hume, Willowdale, Ontario.

Mintzberg, H. (1994) *The Rise and Fall of Strategic Planning*, Free Press, New York.

McNeill, D. and Freiberger, P. (1993) *Fuzzy Logic: The Discovery- and how it is Changing our World*, Simon & Schuster, New York.

Mizumoto, M. (1985) *Extended Fuzzy Reasoning*, in Approximate

Reasoning in Expert Systems, eds. M. Gupta *et al*, North-Holland, Amsterdam, pp. 71–85.

Nahmias, S. (1977) *Fuzzy Variables*, Fuzzy Sets Syst. 1 (2), pp. 97–110.

Novák, V. (1989) *Fuzzy Sets and their Applications*, Techno House, Bristol.

Orlicky, J. (1975) *Material Requirements Planning*, McGraw-Hill Book Company, New York.

Peirce, C. S. (1885) *On the Algebra of Logic*, American Journal of Mathematics, **7**.

Peirce, C. S. (1965–1966) *Collected Papers of Charles Sauders Peirce*, eds. Charles Hartshorne, Paul Weiss, and Artur Burks, **8**, Hardvard University Press, Cambridge, Mass.

Poper, K. R. (1979) *Objective Knowledge*, Oxford University Press, Oxford.

Post, E. L. (1921) *Introduction to a General Theory of Elementary Propositions*, American Journal of Mathematics, **43**, pp. 163–185.

Russell, B. (1923) *Vagueness*, Australian Journal of Psychology and Phylosophy, **1**, pp. 84–92.

Schwartz, T. J. (1990, Feb.) *Fuzzy Systems Come to Life in Japan*, IEEE Expert, pp. 77–78.

Simon, H. A. (1960) *The New Science of Management Decision*, Harper & Row, New York.

Tahani, V. (1977) *A Conceptual Framework for Fuzzy Query Processing—A Step toward Intelligent Database Systems*, Information Processing & Management, **13**, pp. 289–303.

Terano, T., Asai, K., and Sugeno, M. (1992) *Fuzzy Systems Theory and its Applications*, Academic Press, Boston.

Tidd, C. (1996, Feb.) *The 20 Biggest Mutual Funds in Canada*, The Mutual Fund Advisory, **3** (1), Odlum Brown.

Trotsky, L. (1940) from *Fourth International*; in *The Age of Permanent Revolution: A Trotsky Anthology*, ed. I. Deutscher, Dell Publishing Co., New York (1964).

Whitehead, A. N. and Russell, B. (1927) *Principia Mathematica*, 2nd ed., Cambridge University Press, Cambridge.

Wittgenstein, L. (1922) *Tractatus Logico-Philosophicus*, Routledge and Kegan Paul Ltd., London.

Yager, R. R. and Filev, D. P. (1994) *Essentials of Fuzzy Modeling and Control*, John Wiley & Sons, Inc., New York.

Zadeh, L. A. (1965) *Fuzzy Sets*, Information and Control, **8**, pp. 338–353; also in *Fuzzy Sets and Applications: Selected Papers by L. A. Zadeh*, John Wiley & Sons, New York, pp. 28–44 (1987).

Zadeh, L. A. (1971) *Similarity Relations and Fuzzy Orderings*, Information Sciences, **3**, pp. 177–200; also in *Fuzzy Sets and Applications: Selected Papers by L. A. Zadeh*, John Wiley & Sons, New York, pp. 81–104 (1987).

Zadeh, L. A. (1973) *Outline of a New Approach to the Analysis of Complex Systems and Decision Process*, IEEE Trans. Systems, Man, and Cybernetics, **SMC-3**, pp. 28–44; also in *Fuzzy Sets and Applications: Selected Papers by L. A. Zadeh*, John Wiley & Sons, New York, pp. 105–146 (1987).

Zadeh, L. A. (1975) *The Concept of a Linguistic Variable and its Application to Approximate Reasoning*, Parts 1 and 2, Information Sciences, **8**, pp. 199–249, 301–357; also in *Fuzzy Sets and Applications: Selected Papers by L. A. Zadeh*, John Wiley & Sons, New York, pp. 219–327.

Zadeh, L. A. (1976) *The Concept of a Linguistic Variable and its Application to Approximate Reasoning*, Part 3, Information Sciences, **9**, pp. 43–80; also in *Fuzzy Sets and Applications: Selected Papers by L. A. Zadeh*, John Wiley & Sons, New York, pp. 329–366.

Zadeh, L. A. (1978) *Fuzzy Sets as a Basic for a Theory of Possibility*, Fuzzy Sets and Systems, **1**, pp. 3–28; also in *Fuzzy Sets and Applications: Selected Papers by L. A. Zadeh*, John Wiley & Sons, New York, pp. 193–218 (1987).

Zadeh, L. A. (1978) *PRUF—A Meaning Representation Language for Natural Languages*, Int. Journal Man–Manchine Studies, **10**, pp. 395–460; also in *Fuzzy Sets and Applications: Selected Papers by L. A. Zadeh*, John Wiley & Sons, New York, pp. 499–568 (1987).

Zadeh, L. A. (1983) *The Role of Fuzzy Logic in the Management of Uncertainty in Expert Systems*, Fuzzy Sets and Systems **11**, pp. 199–227; also in *Fuzzy Sets and Applications: Selected Papers by L. A. Zadeh*, John Wiley & Sons, New York, pp. 413–441 (1987).

Zimmermann, H. J. (1984) *Fuzzy Set Theory and its Applications*, Kluwer-Nijhoff Publishing, Boston.

Index